WRITING THE URBAN JUNGLE

WRITING THE URBAN JUNGLE

Reading Empire in London
from Doyle to Eliot

Joseph McLaughlin

UNIVERSITY PRESS OF VIRGINIA
Charlottesville and London

The University Press of Virginia
© 2000 by the Rector and Visitors of the University of Virginia
All rights reserved
Printed in the United States of America
First published in 2000

⊚ The paper used in this publication meets the minimum requirements
of the American National Standard for Information Sciences—Permanence of
Paper for Printed Library Materials, ANSI Z39.48-1984.

Library of Congress Cataloging-in-Publication Data

McLaughlin, Joseph, 1964–
    Writing the urban jungle : reading empire in London from Doyle to Eliot /
Joseph McLaughlin.
        p. cm.
    Includes bibliographical references (p.) and index.
    ISBN 0-8139-1924-X (alk. paper) — ISBN 0-8139-1972-X (pbk. : alk. paper)
    1. English literature—England—London—History and criticism. 2. Doyle,
Arthur Conan, Sir, 1859–1930—Political and social views. 3. Booth, William,
1829–1912. In darkest England, and the way out. 4. Eliot, T. S. (Thomas Stearns),
1888–1965. Waste land. 5. American literature—England—London—History
and criticism. 6. Literature and society—England—London—History. 7. London,
Jack, 1876–1916. People of the abyss. 8. Holmes, Sherlock (Fictitious character)
9. City and town life in literature. 10. London (England)—In literature.
11. Imperialism in literature. I. Title.

PR8472 .M37 2000
820.9'32421—dc21

                                                        99-043698

To Miriam

Under such circumstances I naturally gravitated to London, that great cesspool into which all the loungers and idlers of the Empire are irresistibly drained.

—ARTHUR CONAN DOYLE, *A Study in Scarlet*

How does newness come into the world? How is it born?
Of what fusions, translations, conjoinings is it made?
How does it survive, extreme and dangerous as it is? What compromises, what deals, what betrayals of its secret nature must it make to stave off the wrecking crew, the exterminating angel, the guillotine?
Is birth always a fall?
Do angels have wings? Can men fly?

—SALMAN RUSHDIE, *The Satanic Verses*

CONTENTS

Acknowledgments   xi

1   An Irritation to Metaphor:
    Late-Victorian London as Urban Jungle   1

2   Holmes and the Range:
    Frontiers Old and New in *A Study in Scarlet*   27

3   The Romance of Invasion:
    Cocaine and Cannibals in *The Sign of Four*   53

4   Colonizing the Urban Jungle:
    General Booth's *In Darkest England and the Way Out*   79

5   Writing London:
    East End Ethnography in Jack London's
    The People of the Abyss   104

6   Where Does the East End?:
    With Conrad in Darkest Soho   133

7   "What Are the Roots That Clutch?":
    Money, Migration, and *The Waste Land*   168

Notes   195

Bibliography   221

Index   229

ACKNOWLEDGMENTS

I pray that one of the strengths of a book so long in the making, such as the one before you, is that it has benefited from the advice and guidance of many people—far too many to name here. That being said, none of them has been more crucial than Marianna Torgovnick, who believed in it when it was simply an idea, attended to it in its dissertation phase with extraordinary diligence, and who enthusiastically improved every thought and its expression. My gratitude for her assistance with this project is exceeded only by my thanks for her continued professional and personal support.

Thanks are due also to others who kindly oversaw the manuscript's earliest versions, particularly Eve Kosofsky Sedgwick, Michael Valdez Moses, Ted Davidson, and Susan Thorne. Two very good friends, Barry Milligan and Naomi Wood, have read nearly all of this manuscript; they were invaluable readers and helped me to understand the wider aesthetic and cultural significance of the texts under consideration; they were also valuable and sympathetic sounding boards for many of the joys and frustrations that accompany a project of this magnitude. Many other friends from my years at Duke have provided careful readings of individual chapters; I particularly want to acknowledge Graham Hammill, Marty Hipsky, and Jed Esty. The anonymous reader at the University Press of Virginia provided me with insightful and detailed commentary; as I worked through my revisions, I found the reader's enthusiasm to be intoxicating. Cathie Brettschneider at Virginia was excited about my work from the very beginning. I do not know whether to be more thankful for the good humor that has characterized our relationship or the patience she has good-naturedly extended. Excellent copyediting by Dennis Marshall has helped me sharpen many points and made the book more readable than it would have been.

I cannot say enough about the friendship or the intellectual and moral support I received from Seth Koven, Eli Goldblatt, and Van Hillard during difficult times. For financial support, I am grateful to the Summer Seminar Program of the National Endowment for the Humanities. The 1995 seminar "The Culture of London, 1850–1925" was simply the most stimulating intellectual experience of my life. A great deal of the success of that endeavor was due to the creativity, energy, enthusiasm, and brilliance of its organizer, Michael Levenson; it would be a great honor to me if the other participants in that seminar saw something of themselves in this book. Ohio University has provided a fine environment in which to work and bring *Writing the Urban Jungle* to fruition. I am particularly grateful to my chair, Betty Pytlik, and also to my other colleagues in the English Department who provide me with intellectual and personal support on a daily basis. Lisa Cunningham, Rae Greiner, Corey Andrews, Elaine Andrews, and John Gallaher are the most recent, and therefore the most memorable, of the many fine students it has been my privilege to teach during the last ten years at Duke, Villanova, and Ohio. My students have always been my most kind and rigorous critics. I wish I had the space to list all of them here. Peter Donoghue has always been a great friend of this book, as he has always been for me.

A significant portion of chapter 2 first appeared in *Genre* 25, no. 2 (1992): 113–35, and is reprinted here by permission of its editor. Versions of other chapters benefited from the feedback of audiences at Virgnina Polytechnic University, the Northeast Victorian Studies Association, and a graduate colloquium at Duke University. In the final stages of preparing my manuscript, I received invaluable patient and calm technical assistance from Jan Harmon.

My deepest debts and acknowledgements—those most hard to define and, often, articulate, are surely due to my family: my sisters and brother —Kay, Liz, Sara, and Mike; my mother, who gave me a love of reading; and my father, who showed me, by his example, that language was a wonderfully funny instrument. My children Henry and Emma are constant sources of refreshment, exhaustion, and wonder; every day, they teach me how important it is "to care and not to care." Finally, and most importantly, this book owes its appearance to Miriam Shadis. She has, at many moments, believed in its worth more than I have. For that and many other things I owe her the deepest gratitude.

WRITING THE
URBAN JUNGLE

CHAPTER ONE

AN IRRITATION TO METAPHOR

Late-Victorian London as Urban Jungle

"One indication of the intense difficulty we experience when we try to perceive the city," writes Jonathan Raban, "is the way in which it irritates us into metaphor."[1] The pages that follow chronicle how a range of writers came to be "irritated" by a particular urban artifact—late-nineteenth- and early-twentieth-century London—and scratched that imaginative itch by deploying a particular metaphoric discourse—"the urban jungle"—in order to read the increasingly mysterious nature of their metropolitan world. In doing so, I combine the work of urban and postcolonial cultural analysis, showing how ways of describing peoples, places, and experiences on the periphery of empire became an effective rhetorical strategy for imagining the imperial center.

In the process of this transposition, these discursive activities destabilized any clear notion of centers and peripheries. As students of Joseph Conrad's *Heart of Darkness* have long understood, the narrative's title refers simultaneously to the Belgian Congo and modern, metropolitan London, two places that come to be imagined as one. Yet Conrad, in conflating the seemingly separate spaces of the urban and the imperial, the metropolitan and the peripheral, is not, as I will discuss later in this introductory chapter, doing anything new. As Raymond Williams documented in *The Country and the City*, a sharply dichotomized approach to the city—one is tempted to say schizophrenic—is a central literary trope dating back at least to the pastoralism of the Greeks; the city is, and has always been, a place of darkness and light, sin and salvation, barbarism and culture.[2] But despite this constancy in imaginative approaches to the city, something changes as well. One way to account for such change is by examining the material and social changes that give rise to the imaginative responses. In the present case, I see empire, the increasing "globalization" of culture, and contact with others as *the* social facts most important to the specificity of the urban fantasies that circulated around London at the turn of the century. Yet to use such cause-and-effect language obscures how these fantasies, whether literary or journalistic, were themselves important material causes that shaped the emerging modernist metropolis. Put simply, my premise is that writers in the late nineteenth century appropriated ways of thinking and talking about the colonies and discursively transformed the metropolis into a new borderland space: the urban jungle.

Two London fictions will provide a beginning orientation for a foray into the metaphorical urban jungles of the late-Victorian metropolis whose textualization is my focus—one from Arthur Conan Doyle and a second from Margaret Harkness. The first occurs on the opening pages of *A Study in Scarlet* (1887), Arthur Conan Doyle's initial Sherlock Holmes tale. Before the metropolitan icon, Holmes, is ever introduced, we hear Dr. Watson describing the London in which he suddenly finds himself as "that great cesspool into which all the loungers and idlers of the Empire are irresistibly drained."[3] Immediately, we can note the identification of London with "Empire." This "cesspool" imagery certainly does not speak well for London, and I present it as my first example of many metaphoric occasions in which the metropolis is conceived as an infernal space of darkness. Rather than presenting London as the life-sustaining heart or center of light from which emanates the good, the beautiful, and the true (or, as is more often the case, the reasonable), the discursive construction of London as an "urban jungle" will typically argue just the opposite: London is the collecting pool not simply for the dregs of the nation, but also for the empire over which it exercised control. These dregs sink to the bottom—London, as it were—with all the irresistible fatalism of gravity.[4]

While it is an important aim of mine to chronicle the representation of this urban jungle as an Africa-like place of darkness and playground for thrillseekers like Sherlock Holmes, it is not my primary task to identify it as either the best or worst of places, to adjudicate between competing visions of utopia and dystopia. Rather, I offer an account that demonstrates how, in this fin-de-siècle moment, we can note a crisis or confusion in what I call the spatial imagination of empire, a crisis that is marked not by an obviously new imaginative geography of the imperial metropolis but by an insistent reassertion of spatial metaphors—darkest England, the East End—that nostalgically seek to fix a metropolitan geography that no longer exists, if it ever did.[5] In the sanitary metaphor of Dr. Watson, what is crucial is not whether he accurately portrays London as the festering effect of Britain's imperial activities during the preceding centuries and, in the process, ignores London's role as empire's enlightening agent and first cause; instead, it is his evocation of an empire imagined as one vast plumbing network in which London is neither beginning nor end, but rather a location—a "pool"—into which things flow, and out of which things ooze and bubble. This difference in the spatial imagination is crucial. As absolute geographical difference (a world of us versus them) gives way to a world that is increasingly without boundaries (a world of us *as* them), personal identity becomes a matter of epistemological uncertainty and anxiety.[6] As kinship across national boundaries becomes ever more obvious, the denial of such relationship and the insistence of difference becomes even more widespread. But this collapse of boundaries also becomes a source of pleasure—specifically, the indulgently languid pleasure of "loungers and idlers," of being carried along with the imperial flow, of relinquishing the demands of the "white man's burden," even if, and in some instances because, that means being passively and "irresistibly drained" into the undifferentiated muck of the cesspools of empire. One manifestation of this pleasure is the decadent urban bohemianism that we see in late-Victorian texts like Robert Louis Stevenson's *New Arabian Nights,* Doyle's *The Sign of Four,* and Oscar Wilde's *The Picture of Dorian Gray.* The urban jungle is a space that calls forth a pleasurable acquiescence to something greater, more powerful, and, indeed, sublime.

But in its versatility, the literature of the "urban" cesspool or jungle, like the more traditional "literature of imperialism," does not just describe a locale of submission, but also an imaginative domain that calls forth heroic action: exploring, conquering, enlightening, purifying, taming, besting.[7] Alongside these texts, often in ones by the same writers, we see an increased popularity in narratives that foreground heroic masculine action. Elaine Showalter has referred to this assertion of virulent masculinity as a "revival of romance." Similarly, Sandra Gilbert and Susan Gubar have argued that late-Victorian adventure stories, like those of H. Rider Haggard, mark the beginnings of a modernist repudiation of a feminized Victorian literary culture, culminating in the works of writers such as Ezra Pound and Ernest Hemingway.[8] Over the course of the discussion here, I explore instances of both the will to submit and the will to master. But I think it more important to suggest that the two work together to comprise an identity that is active and passive, fascinating and terrible, one poised between a high-Victorian sense of power and postcolonial impotence. So to begin, one figure to note is Dr. Watson, the would-be imperial hero of the Afghan war who finds himself, brought low by enteric fever, back in London nursing his injuries. Here, he becomes sidekick to the action-hero of the 1890s; he becomes an authorial agent of empire who is dependent upon its star—one who creates by merely reflecting glory as a romance.

My other, more extensive, points of orientation are drawn from two scenes in *Captain Lobe* (1889), Margaret Harkness's novel about the Salvation Army. With this second example, one can see clearly how the spatial reconfiguration of my first example (Watson's description of London as imperial cesspool) coincides with a difficulty in placing, and consequently reading, understanding, and knowing, individual bodies. In the first instance, this difficulty is a result of the increasing permeability of national boundaries by people and things, a permeability that tends simultaneously to dissolve differences and yet, somehow, render them more significant or notable. Accompanying this dissolution of stable geographic location and identity are a range of other dissolutions of seemingly stable markers of identity along axes of class, gender, and sexuality.

In 1891, capitalizing on the notoriety of General William Booth's treatise *In Darkest England,* William Reeves published *In Darkest London: A New and Popular Edition of Captain Lobe, A Story of the Salvation Army.* This edition was a reissue of an 1889 novel written by John Law, the pseudonym of Margaret Harkness, who we learn opposite the title page was also the author of the successful slum novels *Out of Work* and *A City Girl.* Early in the novel, Harkness's narrator offers a vision of an East End street scene, a Saturday evening on the Whitechapel Road.

> That road is the most cosmopolitan place in London; and on a Saturday night its interest reaches a climax. There one sees all nationalities. A grinning Hottentot elbows his way through a crowd of long-eyed Jewesses. An Algerian merchant walks arm-in-arm with a native of Calcutta. A little Italian plays pitch-and-toss with a small Russian. A Polish Jew enjoys sauer-kraut with a German Gentile. And among the foreigners lounges the East End loafer, monarch of all he surveys, lord of the premises. It is amusing to see his British air of superiority. His hands are deep down in the pockets of his fustian trousers, round his neck is a bit of coloured rag or flannel, on his head is a tattered cap. He is looked upon as scum by his own nation, but he feels himself to be an Englishman, and able to kick the foreigner back to "his own dear native land" if

only the Government would believe in "England for the English," and give all foreigners "notice."[9]

This passage introduces a number of themes that contribute to the central argument of this book; namely, that metropolitan London and Londoners, far from being the antithesis of those colonial and imperial places and peoples that comprised the British Empire, were actually their curious doubles. London was just as much an imperial stage as India or Africa or any other number of exotic locales; it was an amalgam of multiple frontiers; it was that "vast cesspool" of Dr. Watson; it was the capital of General Booth's "darkest England"; it was an exotic market of pleasures and delights from the poor streets of Harkness's Whitechapel to the sumptuously oriental interiors of the West End described by Oscar Wilde in *The Picture of Dorian Gray* (also in 1891).[10]

In the above passage, the most notable aspect of the Whitechapel Road is its pleasurably lighthearted cosmopolitan quality. The Whitechapel Road offers a multicultural bazaar or menagerie of different types (their typicality is signaled by the indefinite articles that precede each: "an" Algerian, "a" Polish Jew). Within London, the passage claims, no other site is occupied by members of so many different nationalities. Here, one can see Algerians and Hottentots from Africa, "a native of Calcutta" from India, as well as Poles, Germans, and Italians from the other ends of Europe. All of these national types represent people who would have been in East London in the 1880s, whether there as permanent immigrants or as transient sailors who entered London via the docks of the East End waterfront.[11] The narrative voice also notes members of different religious traditions (a Gentile, a Jew). The Whitechapel of the late 1880s was filled with East European Jewish immigrants in flight from pogroms in Czarist Russia.[12]

The cosmopolitanism on display here is remarkable and different from the cosmopolitanism we might usually imagine. First, it is global and not merely foreign. The Whitechapel Road is not simply comprised of continental types—French, Italian, German, Spanish, Catholic—but is markedly intercontinental—European, Asian, African, and Jewish. Second, unlike the cosmopolitanism of decadent dandies and aristocrats who people the world of the Victorian novel such as Wilkie Collins's Count Fosco or the French-novel-reading Robert Audley of Mary Elizabeth Braddon, this cosmopolitanism has a decidedly working-class ambiance.

The menagerie of cultural types Harkness presents here might remind one of earlier Victorian sites of cosmopolitan celebration and anxiety such as the Great Exhibition of 1851, which induced a near hysteria among its opponents over the prospect of the foreign multitudes and huge working-class populations expected to attend. However, this Whitechapel Road "exhibition" is not actively staged or organized.[13] It is messy, vibrant, exuberant, and organic. It is not a collection, but an agglomeration. Harkness's Whitechapel Road spectacle differs from earlier panoramas of nations or urban populations because it seems more intent on connection, community, hybridity, and mixing. Like the cesspool metaphor of Doyle's Watson, the emphasis here is on blending rather than division. In the Great Exhibition, each nation's space had been cordoned off from the others in order to stress the separate and unique qualities of each people. This practice of separation, informed by scientific classification, continues to be the dominant mode of exhibition into the 1880s. Similarly, in the social journalism of Henry Mayhew, the laborers and poor of London had been intricately divided up into a catalogue of separate occupational types. While it is true that even in Mayhew's text the rich accumulation of particularities always is on the verge of overwhelming the classificatory scheme, one never quite loses hold of the order or category. But in Harkness's catalog, the intermingling of the types in the crowd reaches, as it were, a "climax" that threatens to transcend the very categories she still can employ. Her Whitechapel Road seems closer to the hotchpotch quality of Salman Rushdie's London than it does to Mayhew's fantastic vision of a Linnaean London. For we do not just simply see the members of different groups here. Instead, we see them in physical contact, a contact that may tamely bespeak a miscegenist sexuality: the "Hottentot elbows his way through a crowd of long-eyed Jewesses" and the "Algerian walks arm-in-arm with a native of Calcutta." An Italian plays "pitch-and-toss" with a Russian. A Polish Jew and a German Gentile share a meal of sauerkraut, a food that indicates an overlapping of traditions. Indeed, the narrative focus on mating rituals, games, and food reminds one of an ethnological description of a primitive culture. This scene presents a pleasing vision of community. It is not, as the novel's revamped title suggests, a presentation of "Darkest London." If anything, the novel presents a utopian London of multicultural harmony, or, at the very least, a more ambivalent London than the one invoked by the threatening title.

The narrator, however, does stress the distinct qualities of one character at greater length: the East End loafer. This type, who feels himself to be the "monarch" of the crowd on the street, puts on a "British air of superiority." Here, perhaps, one witnesses a version of narrative anti-nationalism. Not only is the British sense of superiority described as an airy charade, but further, it is precisely that quality of putting on airs of superiority that identifies him with the nation.

In fact, in this scene in the Whitechapel Road, there are actually three British onlookers. Although they are all, in a sense, part of the crowd, the narrative stresses their alienation from it. In addition to the East End loafer, there is also the novel's protagonist, Captain Lobe, who the narrator follows on his walk through the street scene. Lobe observes the scene ("Captain Lobe looked at more than one loafer as he hurried along the Whitechapel Road that evening") and is noticed by the people in the street (he "received many salutations as he passed between the booths and the public-houses"), but is never portrayed interacting with or speaking with those among whom he passes. Like Captain Lobe, the anonymous narrator of this scene is a distanced nonparticipant. As readers identify either with this voice or the novel's protagonist, they are encouraged to adopt and rehearse an attitude of spectatorship to the hybrid crowd of the Whitechapel Road. In its presentation of Lobe, the novel gives readers an experience of vicarious participation through being able to observe, close-up, yet separate, the urban specta-cle of the East End street. One can only imagine its reader behaving like Lobe and the narrator if and when they ventured out into the streets themselves; surely, the novel functioned to inscribe subjectivi-ties like those that it describes. At the same time, by turning the street scene into a spectacle subject to an anonymous gaze, it keeps the reader safely apart from it. Thus, late-Victorian readers are able to experience its exotic pleasures, while avoiding its fears. They don't have to go to Calcutta or walk "arm-in-arm with a native of Calcutta" or even share some sauerkraut with a Polish Jew, but they can vicariously indulge in that experience as fantasy and fiction. If they want more immediate contact, this locale is, after all, within walking distance of most places in London.

The passage introduces another important theme of the poetics of the urban jungle—the exoticizing and racializing of a group that we might call the "indigenous" urban poor. As mentioned above, Harkness's narrator stresses, above all, the separateness of the East End loafer. The narrative voice distances itself and its audience from this character by turning it into one (antisocial) type among many. In fact, the ethnographic voice spends more time describing and identifying the characteristics of the East End loafer than it does in detailing any of the other types. Besides his characteristic "British air of superiority," readers learn about his lounging posture and how he keeps "his hands deep down in [his] pockets." The narrator also attends carefully to his identifying clothing: "his fustian trousers, round his neck is a bit of coloured rag or flannel, on his head is a tattered cap." In this description, we not only hear the reemerging overtones of the Disraelian notion of "two nations" and, even more aptly, the discursive separation of London's East and West Ends during the 1880s, but we are also carefully positioned at a distance from the East End loafer type.

If the anthropological voice of Harkness's narrator can discriminate between the different types exhibited on the Whitechapel Road (as we shall see, in Holmes-like fashion), it is a voice that treats the East Ender no differently than the Hottentot or German Gentile. In fact, if anything, its anthropological interest in, and distance from, the East Ender is more pronounced than it is toward any other of the street types. Although we shall see below that the discourse of "two nations" is at least as old as the 1840s and 1850s and urban chroniclers such as Disraeli, Engels, Mayhew, and Gaskell, by the late 1880s it takes on more explicitly imperial overtones as the streets of East London become populated with a range of migrants and immigrants yet to be assimilated as national subjects. Though the East End loafer might want to articulate his own British uniqueness and superiority with xenophobic demands to "kick the foreigner back to his own dear native land," the narrator sees, and encourages the reader to see, the East Ender as one of the many foreign types on display in the cosmopolitan Whitechapel Road. In rendering the indigenous poor as members of a national type, the British become just one more species in the metropolitan jungle. Here, the gesture seems to result from an insistence on order. The narrator is willing to concede British superiority as long as it can still achieve a rationally readable text. But of greater significance here is the narrative act of rendering the East End loafer as a type. In doing so, the narrator estranges its own voice from Britain, from the poor of the streets, places itself outside of any identifiable "type" or national category or mappable site, and becomes a voice that can be, paradoxically, everywhere and nowhere. It lacks location in the scene, a gender, a national origin, an occupation; a scene made up of the identifiably alien produces the narrator's transcendental alienation. The relation of Harkness's narrator to its object differs from the romantic alienation of Wordsworth, who could achieve urban composure from the vantage point of Westminster Bridge in the early morning; Wordsworth's narrator, though distanced, is locatable and has a measurable perspective.[14]

The East End loafer is also equated with other migrants and immigrants in the scene by those members of his own nation who look upon him as "scum." Though the foreigners in this passage are not discussed as *scum*, this word is used to label migrants and immigrants by many characters throughout the novel; indeed, it is one of the most frequently used words in Harkness's novel. Elsewhere, it is used in discussions about the changing composition of the nation. For instance, one character comments on the practice of sending poor women of marriageable age to Australia in order to people and colonize it with Anglo-Saxon racial stock. She laments, "To send all these strong, healthy girls, and get in their place the scum of Europe, is a great mistake. . . . The country will have to suffer for it." Here, "scum" obviously refers to the immigrants, mostly Jews and Italians, moving into the East End in the moment when Harkness is writing her novel. Though I do not want to suggest that the voice of this particularly scum-obsessed character is identifiable with Margaret Harkness, the description of immigrants as scum was a common one at the time. Whether used to refer to European immigrant or East End loafer, the sanitary overtones of *scum* suggest other popular terms such as *residuum, dregs, filth, excess,* and *waste.* In both uses cited above, the reference introduces Victorian anxieties about sanitation, pollution, infection, decay, defilement, impurity, and contamination.[15] The reference to scum carries overtly negative and frightening overtones and is clearly part of a strategic distancing. However, these pejorative uses of *scum* about foreigners and the poor exist alongside connotations of fluidity, flow, and connection, as we have already seen with Dr. Watson's description of London as a "vast cesspool." For scum is a deposit; it was once and might still be in physical contact with the liquid flows. It is not separate from but part of the aggregate. To label a group, whether foreigners or the impoverished, as the scum of the nation or the scum of Europe is to render it inferior but also to articulate its kinship with, and citizenship within, the nation and Europe.

The final quality to highlight in Harkness's description of the Whitechapel Road is how the narrative presentation of the scene structures a range of responses, some contradictory, to the strange streets of London's East End. Although the scene comes at the beginning of a novel entitled *In Darkest London,* it may strike one as pleasurable and quaint. Though there are some references to separate types, those types get along, find common ground, and touch one another. Unlike those portrayed in other late-Victorian novels such as George Gissing's *The Nether World* or Arthur Morrison's *A Child of the Jago,* Harkness's streetscape does not dwell on poverty, filth, or a conflictual Darwinian struggle among species; it is a scene of community that vicariously draws us in. We stroll through it with Captain Lobe and the narrator. Yet, as I suggested above, there is a distancing pressure as well. Captain Lobe and the narrator, though part of the scene, create for themselves distanced relationships of observation and writing. Thus, we are both pulled in and kept apart. Finally, the Whitechapel Road is, simultaneously, British and foreign territory. It is British because of the presence of the East End loafer, Captain Lobe, the narrator, and, lest we forget, a number of immigrants who have left their homeland to become inhabitants of London. It is, on the other hand, foreign territory in the sense that those Britons present are alienated from the community of "foreigners," who seem to be getting along so well. Harkness's Whitechapel Road is a series of contradictory places: light and dark, attractive and distanced, delightful and dreadful, British and foreign, kindred and scum.

One other passage in the novel will illustrate how the East End and East Enders offer a range of often contradictory images and elicit ambivalent responses, such as feelings of kinship and moral and physical repulsion. In the passage, the hybridity that we have already seen in the social space of the Whitechapel Road is reconfigured as the identity of a single metropolitan subject, readable on the surface of his body. In the middle of the novel, two characters visit a penny gaff named the East London Palace of Royal Waxworks. The most interesting exhibit is not a waxwork at all but a tattooed "freak." Captain Dan Fisher, we learn, has been captured by Indians in the American West, tortured, covered with 570 tattoos, and, after escaping, parleyed the multiple signs of his captivity into a career as an urban spectacle in London's East End. Fisher's captivity narrative unfolds as follows:

> Leaving that place [Salt Lake City], we were surprised by Redskin Indians, disarmed and disrobed, and condemned to die at the stake. While we partook of sage-brush tea, jerked venison, and grasshopper bread, a

council of war was held. We were then tied to trees, with our hands upwards, the Indians howling and dancing round us, and gathering dry leaves to burn us. After the war-dance was concluded I was brought before the chief, who conversed about me with a half-breed. I was then tied to a tree, and the painful operation of tattooing commenced. For six and seven hours a day during six months the painful operation was continued, during which time five hundred and seventy designs were tattooed on my body. . . . After six months I made a most remarkable escape. (146–47)

Captain Dan Fisher's history recounts his captivity, forced conversion, escape, and return to civilization. Throughout, his passivity is stressed. Captured by a group of Indians defined by their "red" skin color, Fisher is "disrobed" of his Western or American clothing. His reconstitution as a physical Indian or half-breed begins when he partakes of their food: "sage-brush tea, jerked venison, and grasshopper bread." As the saying goes, one is what one eats.[16] Finally, his captors begin the laborious project of reclothing or recoloring him, by tattooing him from head to foot with the colorful and symbolic tattoos. In straightforward fashion, Dan Fisher, "condemned to die at the stake," is ritually stripped of his former self and is then resurrected as a Redskin Indian, before escaping and beginning his exhibitionary career. Fisher has not only gone native in the American West (like Jefferson Hope in Doyle's *A Study in Scarlet*), but the signifiers of his "savagery" have been inscribed upon his body. His hybridity is, first of all, a matter of his civilized interior covered by an imposed "savage" skin. But, perhaps more important than the contradiction between his civilized interior and savage exterior is the tale of the surface itself: the 570 tattoos that cover his body function as a symbolic collage that signify his hotchpotch identity.

Now he finds himself in London's East End on display as an exotic commodity, a remunerative object of popular entertainment. Why is Fisher able to be marketed (to market himself?), offering his tale and text in exchange for money? What draws the audience to the penny gaff and himself? One answer might be that Fisher mirrors, in extremely distorted form, the increasingly fragmented identities of those who come to see him on view. The sheer complexity of the writing on his body was a point of identification for both a collectivity and its individual members, who were increasingly divided by images of those selves they had become, were becoming, and all those selves they had been—in terms of citizenship, language, wealth, status, nationality, religion, gender, race, and occupation. Indeed, Dan Fisher's 570 signifiers lay waste to any sense of metropolitan identity formed around a simple binary opposition, such as East and West or rich and poor.

One character tries to debunk Fisher as an act of humbug and the audience of the penny gaff as ignorant dupes.[17] Although Fisher's body visibly testifies to his story's credibility, he fails to "answer the skeptical questions of the labour-mistress, who wanted to know how Redskins could have depicted on him St. George and the Dragon, a man of war, King Sol, and the Immaculate Conception."[17] For the skeptical Jane Hardy, these four European or nonindigenous representations nullify the authenticity of Dan Fisher's story and, thereby, the possibility of his hybridity. That is, her skepticism about the authenticity of the painted exterior renders Fisher's civilized interior as the "truth" or essence of his identity. Curiously, Harkness's narrator passes on without comment here; no credence is given to Fisher's reply about how he came to be tattooed with Saint George and the Dragon: "They learn these things from the half-breeds." The skeptical refuse to recognize or simply misrecognize the complex intermingling that has already taken place and marks the cultures of the American frontier. As Dan Fisher tries to explain, it is a place of half-breeds or those who have come into contact with and assimilated Europeans and their ideas, refashioning and disseminating them throughout their land. In doing so, the half-breeds have, to a degree, "Westernized" or "Christianized" peoples who have yet to come into immediate (person-to-person) contact with "authentic" Europeans or Christians.[19]

In the long passage cited above, we should note that there was a "half-breed" who translated and mediated the relationship between Fisher and his captors. The American West and those who inhabit it undo any stable notion of cultural purity, homogeneity, or essence. There is no American West that is not already an amalgam of savage and civilized, Christian and heathen, European and other. In this sense, the American West, those who inhabit or pass through it, and the texts produced there are what Mary Louise Pratt has called "contact zones." Pratt uses the term "contact zone" to describe "the space of colonial encounters, the space in which peoples geographically and historically separate come into contact with each other and establish ongoing relations, usually involving conditions of coercion, radical inequality, and intractable conflict."[20] We can use Pratt's notion of a "contact zone" in order to think about multiple textual spaces: the American West, the

East End penny gaff, or the surface of Dan Fisher's body. In the case of Dan Fisher, it is perfectly reasonable that characters such as Saint George or the Virgin Mary would have been integrated into a hybrid or half-breed cultural mythology, especially if we recall that the Spanish, French, and English have been active missionaries in the American West since the early sixteenth century. Thus, Fisher's body bears the complexity of not only his own self, but also the rich cultural matrix of those Native Americans who have transcribed the text of their own imperial encounters onto him. It is not any stranger that the "English" mythology of Saint George and the Dragon should be part of the American West, than it is that the tattooed body of the primitivized American (Dan Fisher) should have become a fascinating part of the culture of East London.

If, as the skeptical suggest, Captain Dan Fisher is a humbug, he is cheating the East Enders who expect to see a version of exotic otherness; he is an inauthentic fraud. The labor-mistress wants him to be doing a certain kind of cultural work—not posing as, but actually *being,* other—which he cannot perform if his hybridity is inauthentic. But what if, as I want to suggest, the East Enders who spend their scant resources on the penny gaff are not so naively ignorant as the debunking skeptical reading would have them be? What if the question of authenticity here is irrelevant?[21] If we begin to follow this line of interpretation, the hotchpotch Captain Dan Fisher does not sell tickets because he offers East Londoners a testament and touchstone of authentic otherness, but rather because he is, in an exaggerated yet manifest sense, a mirror of their own community, their own streets, their own selves. Fisher, then, functions as a visual analogue for the experiences of East Londoners and of East London itself. And, I would argue, we could say he also functions as a reflection of much of Harkness's readership, in West London and beyond the metropolis, for whom the multiplicity of the East London street is not an antithesis but an increasingly relevant mirror.

The surface of Fisher's body mimics that cosmopolitan crowd that Lobe sees on the Whitechapel Road. He is not simply emblematic of those strange or "queer" types that one sees there; he is also emblematic of those transformed Londoners who are doing the seeing—not a unified subject but a colorful collage of 570 texts—not unlike those famously plastic literary figures, such as Sherlock Holmes, Irene Adler, Dorian Gray, Henry Jekyll, and Count Dracula, who circulate in other cultural spaces during the last two decades of the nineteenth century.

Captain Dan Fisher intrigues not because he is so freakishly different, but precisely because he visibly embodies the heterogeneous experiences that increasingly mark the East End, the metropolis, and their inhabitants. He is their mirror, and he makes money because he has a story to tell them that is meaningfully and strangely about themselves.

In discussing Doyle and Harkness and their shared concern with transformations and confusions surrounding metropolitan space and personal identity, I surely do not wish to make the claim that what we see in their texts or even their historical moment is something radically new. Indeed, throughout the nineteenth century, from Blake and Wordsworth to DeQuincey and Engels, to Dickens and Greenwood, we are confronted with literary responses that depict the city as labyrinth, enigma, and mystery, and urban identity as pleasurably and frightfully fluid. The city, to use Raban's metaphysical language with which I began the chapter, always and everywhere incites to metaphor. If, though, we turn from metaphysics back to history, what is new can best be described as the ubiquity of a phenomenon—the conflation of imperial (exotic, oriental, colonial) and metropolitan discourses that I call the rhetoric of the urban jungle.

It is certainly this explicit imperial note that is lacking in Wordsworth's famous "Bartholomew Fair" section of *The Prelude* (book 7). Here, many of the themes and responses that I encounter at the end of the century are already present. Wordsworth's speaker, for instance, encounters the sublimity of the city as producing a sense of "mystery" and overstimulation:

> How often, in the overflowing streets,
> Have I gone forwards with the crowd, and said
> Unto myself, "The face of every one
> That passes by me is a mystery!" (lines 3–7)

Wordsworth's London is, like Conrad's a century later, "a hell / For eyes and ears!," "Barbarian and infernal," and "Monstrous in colour, motion, shape, sight, sound!" (lines 67–70). Indeed, much of the chaos described by Wordsworth has a foreign point of origin. His lengthy list of colors, sights, sounds, and motions that comprise his "Parliament of Monsters" (line 100) includes "chattering monkeys" (line 76), a "silver-collared Negro with his timbrel" (line 85), "Albinos, painted Indians, Dwarfs" (line 89), and "All out-o'-the-way, far fetched, perverted things" (lines 96–99).[22] And yet, despite listing many of the elements present in descriptions of the urban jungle, Wordsworth's speaker seems too overwhelmed by the chaotic multiplicity to notice its exotic qualities. Rather than being overwhelmed by the strange, he is overwhelmed by the simple fact that there are too many qualities here to reduce to an epistemologically comfortable pattern. The speaker is left numb and blasé, qualities we will see again in Doyle's description of Holmes, Conrad's assistant commissioner of police, and in Eliot's *The Waste Land*.

The dizzying array of sensory stimulation leaves Wordsworth in a state of "blank confusion" (line 104), one in which he loses the capacity to distinguish differences:

> Living amid the same perpetual flow
> Of trivial objects, melted and reduced
> To one identity, by differences
> That have no law, no meaning, and no end." (lines 110–14)

In search of "Composure" and "Harmony" (line 149), Wordsworth's speaker turns to a tranquil image of nature, to the "forms / Perennial of the ancient hills" (lines 134–35) that imbue him with a sense of "order and relation" (line 138).[23] In Wordsworth's poetry, the "elsewhere" is an unpopulated place of recovery to which one's thoughts can turn in order to escape the confusing mystery of the modern metropolis. His speaker turns to tranquil, generally picturesque, northern landscapes of cool mountains and forests to escape the teeming city. Wordsworth's other space is an antidote; in book 7 of *The Prelude*, we do not yet see a developed sense of invasion, a recognition that many of the "perverted things" that comprise his "blank confusion" have come from outside of the city, from places typically constructed as more natural. Nor do we yet see in Wordsworth any sense that another space, perhaps a jungle and not an alpine landscape, can serve as the psychic structure to solve the "mystery" and render the "anarchy and din" (line 68) of the London streets intelligible. Nor, finally, do we have any sense that the crowd of Bartholomew Fair is a potential source of pleasure, like the Whitechapel crowd through which Captain Lobe will move in Harkness's novel.

As we move forward into the nineteenth century, the connection between the urban and jungle, Londoners and Foreigners, becomes much more explicit. In *Bleak House*, Dickens satirizes those would-be philanthropists, such as Mrs. Jellyby, whose charitable gaze becomes fixated on Africa (the natives of "Borrioboola-Gha") at the expense of blinding herself to the suffering in the streets of her own city. In lampooning Mrs. Jellyby, Dickens draws a sharp parallel between the objects of "foreign" and "domestic" charity. Henry Mayhew makes a similar connection in *London Labour and the London Poor* when he divides "the population of the entire globe" into "two distinct and broadly marked races, viz., the wanderers and the settlers—the vagabond and the citizen—the nomadic and the civilized tribes."[24] Mayhew's anthropological division of the "races" of the globe is meant to be replicated in London. For him, it is not the case that London contains the civilized and that the nomadic dwell elsewhere. In fact, his multivolume endeavor testifies to what he sees as a rich and complex metropolitan nomadic society. Thus, his central division becomes one that collapses any sense of civilized center and periphery. For Mayhew, the nomadic tribes live in close proximity to the civilized, while, simultaneously, bearing striking qualities of kinship with the nomads of foreign lands.

Despite the continuity with Dickens's concern about "telescopic philanthropy" in *Bleak House* and Mayhew's voluminous cataloging and classifying of the very distinct culture or "race" of London poverty, we can talk about the texts and authors who are the focus of the chapters that follow as marking, if not something new, then at the very least a moment of transition or the intensification of a process. But a transition from what to what? The intensification of what sort of process? A constellation of answers comes to mind, all of which could be characterized as economic or historical materialist: the transition from entrepreneurial to monopoly capital; the transition from an economy based on production to one based on consumption and circulation; the transition from an age of national economies giving way to one that is global, one that V. I. Lenin famously named as "Imperialism, the Highest Stage of Capitalism" (not accidentally, Lenin's work was based largely on the texts of two Londoners, Karl Marx and J. A. Hobson). More recent historical-materialist criticism, in the domain of cultural studies, has sharpened the focus of more classically Marxist criticism onto commodity exchange. Consonant with the recent work of scholars such as Rachel Bowlby, Thomas Richards, and, most significantly, Anne McClintock, this book argues that one important reason, indeed the primary one, for the transformation of the metropolitan spatial imagination and the prevalence of the urban jungle trope is the intensification of an increasingly global commodity culture in late-Victorian London. Sensational plots, like those of a Doyle or Conrad, stage an exaggerated version of the foreign that was becoming a matter of everyday life for most metropolitan consumers.

In the latter stages of my own research, I have become especially influenced by McClintock's distinction between two dialectically related forms of consciousness that she describes as "scientific racism" and "commodity racism." The former is very close to Said's now famous Foucauldian paradigm of orientalism as a version of imperial/colonial "power-knowledge": to know them is to control them. According to McClintock, scientific racism is "embodied in anthropological, scientific and medical journals, travel writing and ethnographies." For the most part, it is elite, male, learned. At some point toward the end of the nineteenth century, McClintock argues, the prominence of this "scientific racism" loses sway to a more popular form of racism that she calls "commodity racism." This form occurs "in the specifically Victorian forms of advertising and photography, the imperial Expositions and the museum movement." This form of racism functions to convert "the narrative of imperial Progress into mass-produced consumer spectacle."[25] This element of mass production is crucial because it moves Victorian imperialist discourse out of the realm of the scientific societies and clubs and resituates it in the commercial and domestic spheres.

McClintock's discussion of this transformation is engagingly focused on the manufacture and marketing of a specific commodity—soap. Though she responsibly does not go so far as to offer dates for this transformation, I would like to suggest that the appropriate moment is perhaps the space between 1886 and 1896, the moment of Holmes, a decade that spans the years covered in my opening chapters, the soap ads presented by McClintock in her book, and, as we shall see more fully in chapter 3, two India exhibitions that show the "progress" from scientific education to commercial entertainment.[26] In citing significant instances of this moment of transition, I do not mean to suggest that Sherlock Holmes was its cause. Instead, my more modest claim is that Doyle's stories are particularly clear manifestations that allow us to see this moment as one of great change. Or, to put this perhaps more precisely, I will back up and claim that they are both cause and effect, as long as we recognize them as simply one cause and effect among many. This system of an increasingly global exchange was paradoxically dismissive of, and dependent upon, the nations and races that it fetishized, dislodging things and peoples from their traditional domains of authenticity with little respect for that relation between person or thing and place that Benjamin described as "aura" and, simultaneously, exploiting the exotic imagery of difference to market them to newer and larger groups of consumers.[27] Alongside this fluidity of things that commodity capitalism brings about is a related phenomenon: the increasing fluidity of labor-power that gave rise to unprecedented levels of immigration and emigration and a concurrent crisis in social geography or the lived experience of space and place.

Though the topic with which this book is ultimately concerned, the representation of late-Victorian London as an urban jungle, is infinitely vast, covering a range of intellectual and artistic practices of which a list including painting, theater, photography, cartography, spectacle, and ethnography can only begin to describe, I approach it largely from that angle most familiar to me—literary analysis. That choice not only reflects my training, but also indicates the trepidation with which one now confronts the dizzying sublimity of a historical and urban artifact that has been made available to us in an age of cultural studies. The reader will find deviations from the literary-analytical and literary-historical paths here, digressions that take one briefly into the worlds of exhibitions and cartography and cuisine, as well as urban history. Further, two of the chapters, those on General William Booth and Jack London, focus on texts that are difficult to classify and certainly fall outside the bounds of traditional literary genres. However, even in those cases my focus will be to argue for the "literariness" of works that might be better labeled political or scientific in readings that detail the writers' distinctly imaginative approach to their practices and objects. Despite these wanderings, that were among the most exciting to research, I have tried to resist the temptation to lose myself down paths that, for the time being, are better left to another day or specialists in other fields. While I could hide behind the mask of nonexpertise, I must confess that my focus on the literary is better understood as a desperate attempt to focus an act of description that has been continuously threatened by the fecundity of material. The "urban jungle," then, has become for me not simply an organizing trope to be described and understood, but a metaphor for the seemingly limitless quantity of texts, across a range of discursive practices, that inscribed that metaphor in London between 1885 and the early 1920s.

I have chosen, then, to proceed with close literary readings of particular texts for two diverging reasons. First, I strongly believe that the texts I have chosen as foci for my discussion are adequate to the task of introducing the outlines of a broad cultural argument I wish to make about late-Victorian London—a shared, if not universal vision, that transcends the individual particularities. At the same time, I have been captivated by a perhaps stronger recognition of the specificity of each of these texts and authors. Though they share certain broad outlines— for instance, all of the authors under consideration here are, in very real ways, outsiders—they also come to imagine London as exotically foreign for reasons that are distinct. I do not want to lose a sense of the urban jungle as a discourse that arose from multiple points of inscription and reinscription, from individual biographies that trace distinctive patterns of migration to and from London. Thus, it has seemed best, though not ideal, to proceed by close readings that respect the integrity of individual texts, rather than according to a schema that disentangles the narratives into a number of thematic chapters.

Hence, in the next chapter, I argue that *A Study in Scarlet*, Doyle's first Sherlock Holmes story, not only marks the genesis of Holmes and Watson, but more importantly presents a peculiar amalgam of crime story and Western—two plots that in the late nineteenth century had yet to be articulated as genres of their own. Literary critics have, in the past, overemphasized the importance of earlier detective fiction by Edgar Allan Poe and Emile Gaboriau in tracing Holmes's origins. While I do not want to deny the influence of these writers on the Holmes canon, I do believe that the tales make more sense in terms of another literary tradition, one associated with the frontier and historical plots focused on issues of cultural identity, a tradition that includes writers such as James Fenimore Cooper, Walter Scott, H. Rider Haggard, R. L. Stevenson, and the early Arthur Conan Doyle.

By recasting our attention on this other influence and side of Doyle's work, one that is typically treated separately if at all, my reading sees a greater consistency across the works of a very prolific fiction writer. Doyle's biography demonstrates how the Holmes stories arise from his own very confused sense of cultural identity, especially the conflict between his Irish Catholic ancestry and his role as an "enlightened" patriotic spokesman for England; that patriotism is most explicit in a series of texts he wrote to defend the involvement of Britain in the Boer War, but is no less present in the Holmes tales. Consequently, the first Holmes novella can be read as a historical novel (in that manner pioneered by Georg Lukács), with Holmes as an urban Natty Bumppo, who works outside the official police force to protect the modern national center from corrosively dangerous foreign influences. In the process,

Doyle reconfigures the romance plot in the modern metropolis and transforms London into a frontier space.

In chapter 3, I proceed to the second Holmes novella, *The Sign of Four* (1890), in order to show how Doyle continues to explore the presence of other peoples, things, and histories as formative and disruptive influences on the metropolis. This discussion, however, extends the argument of the other Holmes chapter by exploring more intimately the effects of carnivalesque chaos and the threats that occur with the invasion of "foreign substances" into individual and national bodies. As with Dan Fisher, imperialism is a bodily experience. In this second novella, one that uncannily bears a shared thematic interest and publication history with Wilde's *The Picture of Dorian Gray,* Doyle is more interested in the archaic and the exotic as forms of pleasure. While it is true that foreigners do show up in town wearing black hats (or, in this novel, as a returned convict with his cannibal sidekick), it is the arrival of the foreign as *commodity* and *work of art* to which Holmes is susceptible and about which he seeks to become knowledgeable. The novella's primary storyline is an imperial Gothic plot that has its roots in the colonial violence of the 1857 Mutiny. Once again, as in *A Study in Scarlet,* the plot merges two subgenres that were popular in late-nineteenth-century Britain: this time, the invasion narrative and the Mutiny narrative. This novella opens with a debate about Holmes's use of cocaine—an exaggerated example that, nevertheless, stands in for an increasingly global commodity culture, no less than that the plot's cannibal frighteningly symbolizes the immigrant populations of the metropolis. Holmes's drug use brings him pleasurable stimulation in a "commonplace" world (here the concerns shared with Wilde's Dorian Gray seem most obvious) and, as Dr. Watson reminds him, threatens constitutional deterioration or, to invoke another term germane to this moment, decadence. While Holmes's autoerotic drug use is, arguably, self-abuse, it is an exotic experience that provides him with an escape from his dissatisfactions with late-Victorian life. These dissatisfactions, especially his craving for meaningful work, were a point of identification with the largely middle-class, urban, professional audience who voraciously consumed the early Holmes stories. This autoerotic bodily invasion structures the entire plot, which is organized around a series of invasions that include the following: the invasion of romance into the "hopelessly prosaic" world of London; the invasion of colonial wealth (treasure) that disrupts the social order by introducing new possibilities for class mobility; the invasion of new things, commodities, that multiply the range of pleasures available to many metropolitan consumers; the invasion of new cultures and styles (orientalism and aestheticism); and the invasion of new peoples—for example, returned soldiers, convicts, Hindu servants, and, most significantly, cannibals.

While Doyle reimagines London as a frontier under threat of invasions from abroad, "General" William Booth, the founder of the Salvation Army, appropriates the popular rhetoric of African exploration in order to advance his seemingly domestic Christian crusade (chapter 4). Booth's extraordinarily popular book (written with the sensational journalist W. T. Stead) appears when Henry Stanley's account of his adventures, *In Darkest Africa,* was all the rage among London readers. Closely following Stanley's model, Booth reports on his own "explorations" and "adventures" among the impoverished working classes of London's East End. His report strengthens Victorian analogies between working-class and "primitive" peoples, analogies that had found their first full-blown articulation in Engels's *The Condition of the Working-Class in England in 1844* (the first English translation of Engels's book, revised by himself, was published in 1887). While analogies between savages and the urban poor are seemingly ubiquitous in nineteenth-century writing about the poor—the beginning of volume 1 of Henry Mayhew's *London Labour and the London Poor* and Dickens's satire of Mrs. Jellyby's "telescopic philanthropy" are among the best-known instances—Booth and Stead relentlessly embrace the connection as their guiding metaphor, the lens through which all must be viewed. In their language, London becomes the newest colonial venture. After making his comparison between conditions in the East End and darkest Africa, he asks the reader: "As there is a darkest Africa is there not also a darkest England?" His narrative and question encourage the audience to see themselves living in close proximity to a Lost Continent. In making this equation between Africa and the East End, Booth constructs the urban jungle as a place that is ripe for the colonizing, missionizing, and civilizing strategies that have formerly been carried out by the British in Africa. In fact, the name of his organization, Salvation Army, conjoins the twin arms of the colonialist venture: the Christian missionary and the conquering soldier.

In addition to writing a narrative of the East End as an urban jungle, Booth also constructs an implicit equation between himself and, the hero of the moment, Henry Stanley. The Booth constructed by Stead's racy prose sees himself as the Urban Stanley, the adventurer in the city who is missionary, explorer, soldier, and reporter all rolled into one.[28]

As missionary, he Christianizes; as explorer, he goes into the interminable heart of darkness; as soldier, he conquers the recalcitrant enemy; and as reporter, he tells us about his journey and exploits. His project articulates a forceful antipathy to modernity and sees so-called industrial progress as regression. Thus, Booth's description of "Darkness" is followed by a plan for "Deliverance" that promotes a romantic "back to the land" politics as a cure for social degeneracy. Booth, unlike Doyle and Holmes, then, never entertains the exciting possibilities of "going native," though he does write about the difficulty of preventing his "converts" from slipping back into urban savagery. As his biography will reveal, his puritanical steadfastness is that of a convert—one who will not even fantasize about the possibilities of becoming other because he is trying to forget (and mask?) his own impoverished origins on the streets of Nottingham in the 1830s and 1840s. Ultimately, Booth's plan for saving the urban natives also calls for harnessing the urban proletariat in the service of a worldwide Christian empire with himself at its head.

While Booth was interested in naming and colonizing the urban jungle in order to arouse support for his far-flung Christian empire, Jack London, the subject of chapter 5, ventured into the East End as an unemployed writer, an explorer, and a committed socialist interested in reform. Yet despite this more explicit public agenda, whose goal is knowledge and political justice, London's quest also has an urgent individual dimension. In *The People of the Abyss* (1902), London disguises himself as an urban "native" and applies ethnographic methods—an account of his trip to the field site, participant-observation, the use of a "safe house," and photography—to get firsthand, face-to-face knowledge about the inhabitants of an urban locale in the heart of empire. London's narrative is a supposedly realist portrait of a "savage" culture within the metropolitan center and of the urban ethnographer as adventurer; it is heavily indebted to the narratives of other American writers on slum conditions in New York, notably Jacob Riis and Stephen Crane.

As with General Booth's account, London's narrative demonstrates how a typically colonial strategy of description, when appropriated and applied to the city and its inhabitants, functions to constitute the city as the urban jungle and its inhabitants as "a new species, a breed of city savages." In adopting this strategy, he seeks support from those who live outside the jungle by raising the specter of an even more violent East End invasion of the West than those that occurred in the late 1880s. Despite his obvious and real sympathies with his poor subjects, the rhetoric of London's book is as much about working-class containment as it is about working-class empowerment. Thus, London's socialist plan for the redemption of the East Enders is motivated by a complex combination of sympathy and fear.

Again as with General Booth, social reform is linked to a romantic version of the self. *The People of the Abyss* indicates the deeper motivations of the (Western) self who writes about another culture. Jack London's ethnography forces us to examine the connection between the London who writes and the London that is written. It encourages us to ask questions about the relationship between man and city, subject and object, narrator and narrated, outsider and insider, writer and working class, West and East, civilization and savagery, self and other, in a book in which both terms have the same name. London's discovery and invention of "a new race of city savages" is motivated, then, not simply by his socialist politics, but also by his working-class origins and middle-class maturity, his ideas about Anglo-Saxon racial destiny, and his desire to construct himself as a type of virulently physical and active masculinity. Like Booth, he fears a return to poverty; but unlike the Salvationist Booth, Jack London is willing to be more nostalgic about those identities that form his past.

In chapter 6, I argue that Conrad constructs the modernist metropolis as a site of social anarchy, an urban heart of darkness. My focus is *The Secret Agent* (1907), the most explicitly London-based of Conrad's fictions.[29] The discussion attends specifically to a scene in which the assistant commissioner of police visits an Italian restaurant in Soho; these two sites, the ethnic restaurant and Soho, become terrains on which Conrad reconfigures the rhetoric of the urban jungle. It is no longer simply the East End or south of the river, but much more proximate to the homes of those urban adventurers of earlier decades. As in my chapter on *The Sign of Four,* the Conrad chapter brings together meditations on commodity culture and late-Victorian immigration as linked catalysts for a reinvention of social geography. The assistant commissioner is a former colonial administrator who, like Holmes, is acutely bored with his mundane London existence. Stuck behind a desk all day where he takes orders from superiors and delegates responsibilities to others, he nostalgically longs for an existence in which he was more independent, where the work had greater purpose and gave him greater pleasure, where he was allowed to move about freely. In order to combat these feelings of paralysis, he stages an urban version of "going native" that involves a descent, not unlike Jack London's, into the urban jungle.

In the Soho Italian restaurant, Conrad deromanticizes the metropolitan encounter with the exotic other that Doyle had presented in the Sherlock Holmes tales. Because of its inauthentic character, the Conradian ethnic restaurant offers neither a chance to re-create one's identity aesthetically by "going Italian," nor a chance to reconfirm one's identity through an encounter with that which is authentically different. Instead, the hollowness of both cuisine and setting serve to strip the restaurant's patrons "of all private and national characteristics." It becomes a site where identity is neither in flux nor reaffirmed, but rather a site where identity is lost by being rendered blank and meaningless. The Italian restaurant, which in my account stands as a microcosm for the increasingly multiethnic neighborhood, Soho, in which Conrad locates much of the novel's action, and London as a metropolitan whole, fails to make good on its exotic promise. The assistant commissioner discovers in cultural blankness the secret agent responsible for a social anarchy more pervasive than that which the novel's anarchists hope to achieve by blowing up the Greenwich Observatory. Conrad's novel presents yet another instance of the growing importance of commodity culture vis-à-vis science. Although Mr. Vladimir contends that "the fetish of the hour that all the bourgeoisie recognize" is science, the failure of the anarchists to blow up Greenwich does nothing to diminish the novel's dark overtones. That is, I contend, because the conservative Conrad can see social forces far more corrosive of traditional bourgeois pieties than those radical ideas advanced by Victorian intellectuals. While the bourgeoisie in its official rhetoric might still pay homage to science, it is the hedonistic promiscuity of a growing mass culture for the fruits of imperial prosperity that Conrad truly fears.

While Conrad deromanticizes the urban jungle as effectively as he does the colonial adventure in *Heart of Darkness* and *Lord Jim,* there is a twist that is Conrad's own saving illusion. Using Benjamin's famous essay "The Work of Art in the Age of Mechanical Reproduction," I discuss how Conrad's notion of fraudulent cookery and blank ethnicity depend upon a notion of "authentic cookery" and "Italianness" against which he can articulate his ideas of a fallen, degraded, and hollow modernity. Conrad's modernist angst about the monoculture of the metropolis is simultaneously, as Chris Bongie has argued elsewhere, the cry of a lingering, hollowed-out, romanticism.[30] Conrad's interest in issues of metropolitan ethnicity can be traced to his Polish background and his desire to become an assimilated Englishman. The force of biography, visible in Doyle and Jack London, also richly applies here. In writing his version of the urban jungle, Conrad meditates on and struggles with the extent to which personal identity is inextricably tied to one's place of origin or can be refashioned in the image of one's adopted city. A coda to this chapter briefly explores how Conrad's friend Galsworthy visits similar issues of cultural identity in Soho in the Forsyte saga.

I conclude with a chapter on Eliot's vision of the urban jungle, articulated across a range of texts but most powerfully in *The Waste Land*. I read Eliot's well-known cultural conservatism as a response to the London he depicts in *The Waste Land*—a linguistic Babel of cultural fragments—and the loathing he feels for a self that is a wanderer, geographically, professionally, intellectually. Indeed, as I argue late in the chapter, I believe that it is Eliot's own experience of migration that best, though not exhaustively, explains his famous and troubling anti-Semitism. Eliot experienced London not just as a poet, but also, in his most formative years, as a banker. The latter was a job he held by day while composing his epic during his off evenings: previous critics, most famously Pound, have been wrong to see the bank job as draining his energies as a poet; in the reading I offer here, that career actually fed the poetry. Following the work of others (most crucially, Marcus Klein), I see Eliot's cultural politics arising from his youthful experience in a rapidly industrializing and urbanizing United States and responding to his growing fears about immigrant challenges to male Anglo-American cultural hegemony. Because of these fears, Eliot leaves a turn-of-the-century America, that Upton Sinclair depicted as *The Jungle* in 1906, for an idealized London where he hoped to find a purer, more orderly cultural identity. As it was for Henry James before him, Eliot's London is idealized as an originary, ur-WASP culture, as yet untrammeled and untainted; it has, so he thinks, not yet been mongrelized by the forces of immigration that beset his own nation. But what he finds in London is not his Eden of noble English savages, but instead the urban jungle of industrialization and degenerate city savages. Against the backdrop of this cultural anarchy, Eliot seeks and discovers his Lost City, in the form of the literature and tradition he uses as a lever for the cultural renewal and purification of the urban jungle. Alongside the poetry that maps and orders this terrain, Eliot develops a poetic theory in which the keywords are *tradition* and *depersonalization*. By extension, these doctrines are his attempt to hew back the jungle and clear a space for the realization of his dream England.

The literature of the urban jungle advertised imaginative participation in new urban identities at the same time it posed dangerous threats. Through increasingly expanding networks of world trade, London was the center of circulation for a tangled jungle of styles, languages, immigrant laborers, and commodities. On the most massive of scales, it was modernity's intensified version of the ancient country fair, the Turkish bazaar, the Bakhtinian carnival. London encompassed an increasing diversity of people and goods that was experienced not only as a destructively chaotic Babel, but also as a teemingly exciting international culture or global village. Here, one could experience a wide variety of encounters with exotic others without traveling far from home; here, also, one could experience dangers heretofore imagined as safely distant. Indeed, in many instances, the expansion of commodity culture was daily deconstructing the distance between the imperial and domestic spheres. Shops, ethnic restaurants, anthropological museums, archaeological exhibits, and literary culture provided experiences of foreign travel. Escapist experiences and new encounters associated with travel became possible for the first time for the large numbers of the newly literate.

At the same time, it was increasingly clear that the foreign had come home. The prevalence of popular fiction peopled by criminals and monsters pointed, in exaggerated form, to a general anxiety about new metropolitan strangers. Like Jack London, Sherlock Holmes, or Conrad's assistant commissioner, one could live an urban version of "going native" simply by changing clothes and traveling to certain identifiable sites, inscribed with exotic significance, such as the opium den, the East End, or Soho. In London, one could purposefully lose oneself, find one's true self, and lead double lives like Dr. Jekyll, Neville St. Clair, and Dorian Gray. London was a utopia in which one could start over and refashion oneself; London was a dystopia in which the body politic was steadily undergoing change. In chronicling and enacting such refashionings, the texts analyzed in the following pages effectively rewrote London as an urban jungle rife with new pleasures and fears.

CHAPTER TWO

HOLMES AND THE RANGE

Frontiers Old and New in *A Study in Scarlet*

Recent adaptations of the Sherlock Holmes tales by Granada Television, shown in the United States on PBS's *Mystery!* series, demonstrate the lingering fascination of these stories for audiences on both sides of the Atlantic in the late twentieth century. Yet in academic discourse, the Holmes tales have been less popular, ignored because they lack the stylistic complexity, moral ambiguity, and intricate psychology that are the commonplaces of modernism.[1] We can contrast the relative silence about the Holmes stories with the attention and praise that is granted crime fiction with a modernist aesthetic. One notable example of this is F. R. Leavis's admiration for Conrad's *The Secret Agent:* "The tone is truly subtle—subtle with the subtlety of the theme; and the theme develops itself in a complex organic structure. The effect depends upon an interplay of contrasting moral perspectives, and the rich economy of the pattern they make relates *The Secret Agent* to *Nostromo:* the two works, for all the great differences between them, are triumphs of the same art."[2] Until the recent critical turn to more popular fiction, the critical focus has been on Verloc and not Sherlock.

But even among devoted readers of Doyle's fiction, the first Holmes adventure, *A Study in Scarlet* (1887), remains obscure, misunderstood, and ignored, largely because of its formal peculiarity. Despite its importance as a starting point, the novella has not been brought to the screen, most likely because of the expense that would be involved in spending equal time at two very distant locations. Today, interest in the novella survives solely because it marks the genesis of one of fiction's best-selling and longest running series.

Yet *A Study in Scarlet* deserves to be read not just because it marks a moment of genesis, but more importantly because it is an amalgam of two plots—crime story and Western—that in 1887 had not yet been articulated in genres of their own. While the Holmes plot introduces us to the crowded "cesspool" of late-Victorian London, the book's second half has a different hero and takes us around the world to the wide open spaces of the American West. While typically considered an artistic flaw, it is precisely this generic doubleness that provides the novella's source of interest. As a romance, it needs to be read as a product of the 1880s, a decade that saw a revival of the form in the masculinist fiction and criticism of Haggard, Lang, and Stevenson.[3] In relation to romance writing, *A Study in Scarlet* marks a moment of transition, after which plots will typically be situated in either urban or frontier spaces, each of which will gain its own individual generic identity. In order to understand the inextricable, yet largely invisible, significance of frontier narratives for the urban world of Holmes, it is important to linger on this novella in which the two stories—Holmes and the Range—still function as an admittedly uncomfortable unity.

At the beginning of the novella, we hear the history of the narrator and costar of the series, John H. Watson, M.D., "late of the Army Medical Department"(3).[4] His narrative reveals anxieties that reflect the changing status of empire in the national consciousness. The year is 1878, and Watson has just returned from a disastrous stint in the colonies. After taking his degree, he had shipped out to Bombay with the Fifth Northumberland Fusiliers. He served as an assistant surgeon in the second Afghan war, in which he was wounded at Maiwand and nearly captured by "murderous Ghazis." Rescued by his orderly, Watson is removed to convalesce at Peshawar. After nearly recovering from his wound, he is struck down again, this time by enteric fever, and nearly dies. He is pensioned back to England, where he nurses his damaged constitution in bachelor solitude. Imperial service has not brought Watson untainted glory, but rather has saddled him with "misfortune and disaster" (3). His adventure abroad has been good for neither body nor soul, and the empire is none the better for his effort. As narrator of the Holmes tales, Watson will eventually serve the empire better by creating a hero of mythic proportions.

Back in England, the aimless, out-of-work doctor tells us he "naturally gravitated to London, that great cesspool into which all the loungers and idlers of the Empire are irresistibly drained" (4). In Watson's account, the metropolitan capital is not described as the life-sustaining heart of the empire from which all good things emanate, but rather the "cesspool" into which the scum of the empire (including his battered self) are concentrated. Watson's metaphor unwittingly demonstrates the fluid, reversible character of imperial relations, rather than describing a unidirectional system of cause and effect. London sends forth

Christianity and Civilization; the colonies return exotic commodities and savage peoples. Holmes's London is this "cesspool" filled with colonial soldiers, returned convicts, Hindu servants, cannibals, beggars, cowboys, slums, drugs, ghettoes, and monotonous suburbia. Doyle's stories reveal urban problems—the "crisis of the inner city," sprawl, ethnic strife—that will become more prominent in British culture as the twentieth century unfolds. But in the twentieth century, a nostalgic popular consciousness has tended to ignore the messiness of Holmes's London. Most people now associate Holmes with fuzzy, warm, gaslit streets and the bourgeois comforts of late-Victorian and Edwardian England. Against this background, it is curious, but crucial, to read of London as a "cesspool."[5] For the Holmes tales are precisely about two phenomena in late nineteenth-century London: the recognition of urban blight; and its connection to an awareness of the colonies as an invasive source of new and even more menacing dangers.

Historians of detective fiction typically trace the lineage of the Holmes tale back to earlier-nineteenth-century tales of Edgar Allan Poe and Emile Gaboriau. As evidence, they cite a passage near the beginning of *A Study in Scarlet* in which Watson compares Holmes to characters in their stories. While Holmes arrogantly dismisses any comparison to his literary inferiors (Dupin and Lecoq), it is clear that Doyle had these two writers in mind.[6] Yet it is the argument of this chapter that the Holmes corpus, more importantly, arises as a response to a new imperialist frame of mind, one becoming less confident about the spread of English, European, or Western culture from the civilized center toward the savage periphery and more anxious about a decline accelerated by the incursive flows that travel back to the metropolis through these imperial channels. To a degree, these metropolitan and imperial anxieties were already present in Poe. In his "The Murders in the Rue Morgue," the protagonist interviews a number of witnesses who overheard the brutal assault, each of whom projects a different linguistic identity onto what turn out to be the grunts of an orangutan brought back to Paris by a sailor. The Poe tale delineates two features that will become central to the writing of London as an urban jungle by the writers studied in this book: (1) the metropolis as a dangerous jungle of ethnic confusion; and (2) the pressures exerted by this chaos on language itself.

Thus, *A Study in Scarlet,* Doyle's ur-story of the modern, urban detective, is generically descended not only from earlier detective fiction associated with Poe and Gaboriau, but also from another tradition associated with the frontier and plots that explore issues of cultural identity. This latter tradition would include writers such as James Fenimore Cooper, H. Rider Haggard, Robert Louis Stevenson, and the early Arthur Conan Doyle. Not yet a "classic" detective story, Doyle's first Holmes tale can be more interestingly read as a historical novel (in the sense defined by Georg Lukács)—one that juxtaposes a frontier crime, plot, and hero with their metropolitan counterparts. If read in this fashion, we can then see how Doyle modeled the urban detective on the tracker figure he admired in his boyhood reading of Cooper and others.[7] From his first appearance, Holmes is portrayed as an urban Natty Bumppo. On the one hand, he is powerfully attracted to, and, in Cooperesque fashion, identifies with, the criminals, foreigners, and socially marginal types he loves to dress up as and impersonate. His marginality is further cultivated by his distance from the official metropolitan police; he is only an amateur, a consultant. On the other hand, his work protects the national center from corrosively dangerous foreign influences. The socially marginal Holmes is the protector of the "home"-land. Watson testifies to the need for a hero like Holmes who fulfills the fantasies of frustrated imperialists. As Doyle and Watson construct him, Holmes becomes popular as a new masculine model— a champion of justice who is part hot-blooded savage warrior of the urban jungle and part cold-blooded civilized intellectual of an emerging modernity.

Part 1 of *A Study in Scarlet* takes place in London and introduces us to Watson and Sherlock Holmes, his mysterious new fellow lodger. Watson meets Holmes in a chemical laboratory after being warned about Holmes's obsessive passion for weird science concerning the introduction of foreign substances into the body. A mutual friend tells him, "I could imagine his giving a friend a little pinch of the latest vegetable alkaloid, not out of malevolence . . . but simply out of a spirit of inquiry in order to have an accurate idea of the effects. To do him justice, I think that he would take it himself with the same readiness. He appears to have a passion for definite and exact knowledge" (6). In the 1880s, the lab is on the verge of becoming a typical site of modern adventure, with the advent of science fiction in the work of writers like H. G. Wells. Holmes is a contemporary of Dr. Jekyll and a precursor of Dr. Moreau. The laboratory is a place where Holmes can take risks, make discoveries, pursue his passion for "exact knowledge," and put his life on the line. Although Holmes's well-known use of cocaine does not emerge until the second novella, *The Sign of Four* (1890), here and elsewhere Doyle's narratives will continuously stage invasions of personal and national bodies.[8]

As Part 1 proceeds, Watson gradually discovers the vocation of the enigmatic Holmes. At first, he cannot place the theatrical dilettante who dabbles in chemistry and receives visitors from all social classes. Eventually, after displaying his powers of observation and deduction to a mesmerized Watson, Holmes reveals that he is the world's only "consulting detective" (15). He is someone to whom both the official police and private investigators turn when they have reached a dead end. He is an adjunct to whom the incompetent police can turn in order to save public face and a trained investigator to whom private citizens can turn in order to keep their affairs out of the public gaze. Like a Western hero, he represents civilized law and order despite lacking any professional ties to an official state bureaucracy. He is an inventor, an entrepreneur.

Through Watson's fascinated narration, we watch Holmes investigate the murders of two mysterious Americans. The mystery is seemingly unsolvable because there are neither suspects nor motives—just two corpses. Watson is fascinated by Holmes's dazzling ability to elaborate hypotheses from the slightest of clues: footprints, cab treads, cigar ash, a wedding ring, and bloodstains. As the novella nears its midway point, Holmes lures his suspect, a cabdriver, to his and Watson's Baker Street apartment and, with a dramatic flourish, handcuffs him before anyone knows what is happening. The murderer, the police, Watson, and the reader are left hanging with this sudden arrest. Nobody has any idea how Holmes tracked down the murderer or what this stranger's motive might have been. Modern readers of detective fiction, trained by stories in which they are given the necessary clues, are especially disappointed.

At this point, much to the dismay of the confused reader, Doyle takes us into a seemingly different plot. The overall disorientation involves shifts of narration, plot, genre, place, and time. Doyle shifts from Watson's first-person narrative of London to an omniscient narrator who follows the Mormon migration across the arid plains of the American West and into the promised land of Utah. This second section is titled "The Country of the Saints." Generically, Doyle moves from the urban murder mystery to a proto-Western.[9] We also travel back in history from 1878 to 4 May 1847.

"The Country of the Saints" presents, in contrast to the modern empire whose heart has become a stagnant cesspool, the story of a people at an earlier moment of imperialist expansion, during its exodus across a desert that is dazzlingly empty and clean.[10] As the setting for a Victorian genesis or origin myth, Utah is a place in which things can begin anew. For the Mormons, Utah is a blank space, a land without history in which they can start from scratch. Likewise, for Doyle, it is a place where the narrative can start over. Here, he can tell a new story that transports his audience outside of the corrupt, violent space of modern London. Utah provides a temporal and a geographic escape from the present, from the modern, from civilization. It is the romantic realm of exotic possibility, a realm in which conservative or premodern values and ways of life can be reestablished. But as Doyle's narrative unfolds, the past and the frontier will become less the site of an imaginative escape from civilized modernity and increasingly the foul source of present social conflicts. That is, the literary escape into a past located on the frontier will eventually lead the reader back home (to Holmes) by following the trajectory of a violent colonial past into the modern urban present.

In Doyle's Mormon community, triumph and prosperity are tempered only by the lingering unease and detachment of John Ferrier and his adopted daughter Lucy, Gentiles (that is, non-Mormons) rescued by Brigham Young and the Mormons and forced to convert in the opening chapter of part 2. Doyle's narrative reflects the split in his culture's highly stereotyped attitudes toward the Latter Day Saints.[11] On the one hand, there is admiration for them as empire builders, as the vanguard of Western advancement into supposedly savage lands. On the other hand, there is disgust and horror for polygamy, theocracy, and Mormon secret societies. At first, Doyle applauds the Mormon ability to build an economically prosperous civilization on the most inhospitable terrain. He praises them as embodiments of "Anglo-Saxon tenacity." He writes:

> From the shores of the Mississippi to the western slopes of the Rocky Mountains they had struggled on with a constancy almost unparalleled in history. The savage man, and the savage beast, hunger, thirst, fatigue, and disease—every impediment that nature could place in their way— had all been overcome with Anglo-Saxon tenacity. Yet the long journey and the accumulated terrors had shaken the hearts of the stoutest among them. There was not one who did not sink upon his knees in

heartfelt prayer when they saw the broad valley of Utah bathed in sunlight beneath them, and learned from the lips of their leader that this
was the promised land, and that these virgin acres were to be theirs for
evermore. (63–64)

This is a pioneer story of "constancy," "struggle," and perseverance,
one that closely resembles the later frontier thesis of Frederick Jackson
Turner. Doyle's Mormons overcome religious persecution, the "terrors"
of the transcontinental trek, and the "impediment" of "savage man,"
"savage beast," and other forces of nature. The land they confront is
"virgin" and "promised"; there is no suggestion that it may have a prior
history or that they may be displacing the "savages," human and beast.
This is exodus without conquest—a divinely ordained Manifest Destiny.
We hear that "in the [Mormon] town streets and squares sprang up as if
by magic" (64). And when Doyle attributes the successes of Mormon
primitive accumulation to "Anglo-Saxon tenacity," certainly he displays
a boastful hint of pride in acknowledging his racial kinship to these
brave pioneers.

Yet despite Doyle's respect for Mormon economic successes, *A Study
in Scarlet* functions as a forceful attack on what Doyle and most of his
contemporaries saw as an overzealous religion based on polygamy.[12]
From the 1850s onward, Mormons came under attack in Anglo-American society for three reasons: (1) their attempt to establish a modern
theocracy on the fringes of the United States, "the great democratic
experiment"; (2) their missionary activity among the Native Americans
that was viewed by outsiders as a strategy to provoke attacks on non-
Mormon immigrants headed further west of Utah;[13] and (3) their pro-
motion of polygamy. The Mormons justified polygamy on economic
and social grounds; it responded to the need for an increased population; it was a moralistic means to absorb all women into marriage and
thereby prevent prostitution; it was a means to provide children with
larger families and make them more socially and community minded.[14]

Despite these justifications, Doyle shared dominant views of Mormon society as one structured around a licentious, lustful, greedy sexuality that lacked any notion of restraint. In his fictional Mormon
community, Doyle sensationally focuses on the elders, who reportedly
had many wives. But according to Gustave Larson, the "much-married"
elders "were the exception in a system where the average polygamist
was content with two, or at the most, three wives."[15] Like many writers
about exotic cultures, Doyle emphasizes the extreme, the unusual, the

excessive in Mormon culture. The convert Ferrier embodies Doyle's amalgam of praise for, and critique of, Mormon culture. He is an example of hard work and prosperity, yet he refuses to accumulate wives. In his bachelorhood, Ferrier remains unorthodox, aloof, and marginal, doubly heroic as an example of pioneer economic success and a champion of respectable, civilized celibacy.

The Mormon plot progresses with the introduction of a generically unoriginal love story of the type sure to displease readers who place a value on novelty or surprise. Lucy Ferrier grows up to become the stereotypical heroine of romance. The "flower of Utah" is described as being "as fair a specimen of American girlhood as could be found in the whole Pacific slope" (65). Although the Mormon elders covet Lucy for her beauty and the Ferrier lands she stands to inherit, she falls in love with an outsider—a "tall, savage-looking" silver prospector who is traveling through Utah, named Jefferson Hope (67). In turn, Hope is smitten by Lucy—"the sight of this fair young girl, as frank and wholesome as the Sierra breezes, had stirred his volcanic, untamed heart to its very depths" (68). For Doyle, a marriage between the feminine nature-child, a flower rooted in the Utah soil, and the chthonically "untamed" masculine entrepreneur who signifies the "hope" of a "Jeffersonian" America, is a simple allegorical matter of Manifest Destiny. Like all of Doyle's characters, Lucy and Jefferson are important for the types they represent in systems of classification involving gender, class, race, age, nationality, sexuality, and occupation. The love plot that brings them together is not part of a literary economy that values originality, but one in which unoriginality functions like a religious ritual, a repetitive invocation of national or racial ideals.[16]

The plot comes to a predictable crisis when it is revealed that the Mormon elders have designs on Lucy that threaten to turn Doyle's tale of the American Dream into a nightmare. They refuse to let her betray them by marrying outside their community, a refusal that the narrative depicts not as sound economic policy but as motivated by greed, lechery, and the base logic of frontier economics: "The supply of women was running short, and polygamy without a female population on which to draw was a barren doctrine indeed. Strange rumours began to be dandied about—rumours of murdered immigrants and rifled camps in regions where Indians had never been seen. Fresh women appeared in the harems of the Elders—women who pined and wept, and bore upon their faces the traces of an unextinguishable horror" (70).

The narrative closely links Mormon polygamy to both the savagery of "Indians" and the "harems" of oriental potentates, fully activating negative views of Mormons. Like many of his contemporaries, Doyle sees the Mormon flight to Utah as a flight from a modern civilization organized on the basis of monogamy back to a more barbarically masculine form of communal organization in which women are accumulated as breeders. In going out to the desert, they are also going back to ways of life—the Indian and the oriental—that supposedly have been transcended.[17]

While Doyle sees this regression as morally repugnant, some Victorian readers may have been attracted to the Mormon plot for the same exotic reasons that Sir Richard Francis Burton transported himself to Salt Lake City in 1860. Burton, the premier orientalist of his day, was the most sympathetic Victorian writer on the Mormons. The liberal Burton traveled to Utah and published a voluminous account of his experiences: *The City of the Saints and Across the Rocky Mountains to California*. In his preface, Burton relates that he will "avoid the capital error, especially in treating of things American, of looking at them from the fancied vantage-ground of an English point of view"; he will assume a point of view he calls the "cosmopolitan character." He sees his trip to Salt Lake City as completing his tour of the world's great holy cities. It will be the latest addition to an impressive list: "Memphis, Benares, Jerusalem, Rome, Meccah." Based on his experiences of the Orient and Africa, he suspects "that the Mormons might turn out somewhat less black then they were painted." And his suspicions are confirmed by his later observations: "The Mormon household has been described by its enemies as a hell of envy, hatred, and malice—a den of murder and suicide. The same has been said of the Moslem harem. Both, I believe, suffer from the assertions of prejudice or ignorance. The temper of the new is so far superiour to that of the old country, that, incredible as the statement may appear, rival wives do dwell together in amity; and quote the proverb 'the more the merrier.'"[18] Burton's sympathetic, utopian orientalism is the reverse fantasy of Doyle's disdain for the regression to barbarism. Of course, even this generalization is too neat. It would be fairer to say that Doyle's attitudes toward the Mormons, like those of many late-Victorians, were a complicated amalgam of admiration and disgust. Both attitudes are voiced in *A Study in Scarlet*.

In response to the crisis, Lucy and her father make the obvious choice—they decide to flee the home that never fully felt like home.

Ferrier exclaims, "I'm a freeborn American" and tells his daughter he would rather see her in her grave than the wife of a Mormon. Dutiful Lucy agrees and hopes that Jefferson Hope will come to their rescue. He does indeed arrive and leads the father and daughter in flight from the vigilante group of "Avenging Angels." After the heroic family thinks itself beyond the Mormons' reach, they pause to build camp and Hope goes off in search of food. Returning to the campsite, he finds his bride-to-be missing and his prospective father-in-law murdered. Like a detective of the American West, Hope tracks Lucy and her captors back to "the country of the saints" where he hears she has been forced to marry.

As we might expect in this romance plot, Lucy dies less than a month after her marriage. Hope barges in on the funeral, steals Lucy's wedding ring, and vows to dedicate his life to the revenge of his lover's captors, violators, and murderers. In the following years, he lurks in the wilderness, moving from job to job and place to place, as he keeps on the trail of two Mormons who had fought over Lucy. Due to a schism with their elders, this pair break with the Mormon community and head back to civilization. Hope also leaves the range and follows the two back East to Cleveland and, eventually, to Europe. Finally, disguised as a cabdriver in London, he seizes his chance for revenge and murders the Mormons. Thus, the narrative arrives back in London in the apartment of Holmes after a journey of many miles, years, and chapters.

The length of the novella's Western plot makes it hard to label it a mere "digression" or an inessential frontier romance that interrupts the murder mystery. Yet this is just how twentieth-century readers of *A Study in Scarlet* have tended to undervalue and misunderstand the work. Critics and commentators repeatedly label its disruptive formal structure a problem, a symptom of Doyle's yet imperfect art, a flaw that will be overcome in later work. Their attention, which is scant, concentrates on apology. Their reaction to the "problem" is aesthetic. Or, to be more precise, they read the novella in terms of an aesthetic particular only to the unfolding genre of mystery or detective fiction, one that divorces the work's symptomatic split from considerations of generic hybridity, politics, and history.

In the introduction to the most recent edition of Holmes, detective writer Loren Estleman voices the practitioner's aesthetic complaint about the novella's structure in a typical fashion: "For those who prefer their Sherlock Holmes served up pure and without digression (and I am one), it is possible to skip over the long omniscient passage entitled 'The Country of the Saints' without losing 'the scarlet thread of murder.' Indeed, rare is the reader who can resist the temptation to leapfrog the Great Alkali Plain and learn the fate of the person responsible for the singular expression of horror and hatred on the dead man's face at No. 3 Lauriston Gardens and the incarnadine 'RACHE' scratched on the wall."[19] Here, we can hear the connoisseur's aesthetic disdain for impurity and "digression," and an implicit desire for slick, fast-paced action and narrative momentum. For Estleman, a writer and consumer of detective fiction, the readers who submit to the "temptation to leapfrog," to "simply skip over" the boring parts that constitute a substantial section of the novella, will find themselves in the majority. This temptation is a desire for erasure that he sanctions and encourages others to repeat. But to submit to such a temptation is to ignore procedures of good detection. Coming from a creator of detectives, this advice to ignore evidence should strike one as odd.

Understandably, academic critics have felt a greater responsibility to talk about the work as a whole; unlike popular writers and readers, their hermeneutic consciences have not allowed them to ignore half the novella. Scholarship is serious business and scholars are not supposed to play "leapfrog." So they adopt a voice of critical apology. For them, Doyle just hasn't got it right yet. Doyle's "failure" is a matter of undeveloped technique, necessary failure, and a youthful inability to maintain the "detective interest." According to critical biographer Jacqueline Jaffe, "Doyle did not yet know how to do that, therefore the interest in the detective in this story *is* broken. The two parts of *A Study in Scarlet* are completely different from one another. The American adventure story, set in the arid, sunbaked plains of Utah, is juxtaposed to the English detective story, set in gaslit, foggy London, without any viable transition. By using two different locations, Doyle had to write two separate stories, a position that left him with a badly split narrative."[20] I do not suspect that Doyle, or his first readers, ever saw this plot as "broken" or "badly split," nor imagined that the two sections were "completely different" or "separate stories." In fact, one early reader actually praised the plot as "exceptionally ingenious," "daringly constructed," and bearing "no trace of vulgarity or slovenliness."[21]

While it is true that the narrative has no "transition," it is because he is more interested in the *juxtaposition* of two stories and two locations, a juxtaposition that reveals their inseparability. In this discussion of the pure or well-wrought tale, we hear a voice for whom the historical and geographic excursion is an ugly interruption instead of a vital and necessary condition of possibility.[22] As modern readers, we are asked to excuse Doyle's early embarrassment and read the novel through the haze of a condescending sympathy. "The modern reader, however, is usually willing to overlook the flawed structure of this story and affectionately remember Holmes's part of the novel not only because it contains all the excitement and charm of the world of 221B Baker Street but also because it is the story that first introduced us to Sherlock Holmes."[23] Coming back to this first novel with expectations produced by later tales, the apologetic critic is understanding but disappointed. Critics have diverted attention away from the fruitful analysis of a complex generic issue, engaging in a doomed-from-the-start evaluation of Doyle's ability to write a flawless detective story or spellbinder.

Instead, we need to read the novel's mixed generic quality as a clue to the novelist's desire to tell a story for which there does not yet exist a seamless form. I propose a historical reading that sees the split structure as symptomatic of a particular moment in imperialist expansion. As the idea of the American West as a frontier begins to fade in the late nineteenth century, there is a need for a new site of adventure on which the writer can stage epic dramas of cultural definition. In writing *A Study in Scarlet,* Doyle would discover that this new frontier was to be found in London.

In order to understand *A Study in Scarlet,* we have to imagine what it would be like to read this text in its historical moment, without the weight of the other Holmes material and without the expectation that there will be a sequel or a series. Today, Sherlock Holmes stories are always published in collections that encourage a specific, and very fruitful, intertextual reading. While it is certainly enjoyable to discover how the tales speak to each other, the intertextual reading can tend to remove the tales to their own separate world, a fantastic literary space that easily becomes divorced from the social and historical world. Yet each one of the tales was published separately over a period of thirty-five years.[24] If we remember this fact, it becomes possible to see each story not as simple entertainment, but as interventions in a rapidly changing social world.

In the first place, this means suspending our expectation that Holmes will occupy center stage throughout the work. Perhaps Hope, not Holmes, was intended as the initial text's hero. It also means we have to question our notion of "center stage." Is center stage London or the American West? Certainly, there is much more to be learned from juxtaposing the two heroes and locales, rather than relegating one set to literary obscurity.

One initially helpful critical move is to reverse the priority of the two plots. Critic Pierre Nordon proposes that the Holmes plot is supplementary, subordinate, a lengthy prelude to the Mormon material. In his reading,

> Only the first part follows the plan of the later Sherlock Holmes stories. . . . As the scope of the Adventures widens, these pages gain in significance. But this effort of perspective could not of course have been apparent to the first readers of *A Study in Scarlet* in 1887. . . . The first part serves simply as prelude to the long adventure story contained in the second. Later on, in the short stories of the Sherlock Holmes cycle, such a narrative as this would have been subordinated to detection. But we cannot merely take this long second part as the explanation or justification of Jefferson Hope's behaviour.[25]

Modern readers insist upon the priority of the Holmes plot, but such a reading would have been unavailable to a reader in 1887, and may have been far from the design of Doyle, who did not decide to write another Holmes tale until late in 1889 (and this at the prompting of an editor). Nordon cites Doyle's interest in historical novels as further evidence that the Mormon plot would have been more important for Doyle. He also argues that the American story would have been more interesting to a late-Victorian reader, backing up this claim by citing an unpublished stage adaptation of the novel, *Angels of Darkness*. This stage version of the story concentrates on the book's Western part, erases Holmes from the narrative, and reconstructs Watson as a San Francisco physician. Finally, Nordon indicates that the book was initially more successful among American audiences and that it was an American publisher who approached Doyle to write another story starring Holmes and Watson. For Nordon, all of this suggests that modern readers of the novel assign opposite values to the two narratives in *A Study in Scarlet* to those of Doyle's contemporaries.

Unlike Nordon, I do not want to read *A Study in Scarlet* as it might have been read in its historical moment. I understand that readers turn to it today in order to witness the literary birth of Holmes and Watson.

One cannot help but read this text in terms of a return to origins, as a tale that will give us some deeper understanding of the later tales. However, and this is the significance for us of Nordon's reading, we cannot let our interest in the Holmes material allow us to discard the weight of the historical detail, to leapfrog over that which fails to be immediately intelligible or fit harmoniously. Instead, we have to understand that the importance of Doyle's plot is its juxtaposition of two locales (Utah and London), two historical moments (1847 and 1878), and two heroes (Hope and Holmes). In reading this split narrative, we must articulate the meanings of these juxtapositions.

In doing so, Georg Lukács's work on *The Historical Novel* is especially helpful. For Lukács, "different problems of form are but artistic reflections of . . . social-historical transformations."[26] In Lukács's narrative theory, formal problems are not read as signs of artistic immaturity, but rather as symptoms of nonliterary transformations. Lukács borrows from Hegel the idea of the "world-historical individual" who "is a representative of one of the many contending classes and strata."[27] This focus on representative individuals is especially germane to a discussion of Doyle's fiction, in which character depends on easily recognizable types. Lukács fuses Hegel with Marx, linking characters ("world-historical individuals") with moments of capitalist development.

In reading *A Study in Scarlet* in Lukács's terms, we can see three overlapping phases of imperialist development. First, Brigham Young and the Mormon elders represent an initial phase of imperialist expansion into the virgin wilderness; in economic terms, this is the phase of primitive accumulation. Second, Hope enters the plot representing a phase of frontier individualism; forbidden to compete for Lucy, Hope's continued commitment to individualistic frontier justice embodies the spirit of entrepreneurship. The conflict between these two types or moments is the plot of "The Country of the Saints." Finally, the metropolitan Holmes represents a more specialized, compartmentalized system of civilized law and order; he appears during a later phase of imperialist development, when the distance between city and frontier, civilization and savagery, has all but disappeared. For Doyle, the first two types are both heroic and villainous: the original Mormons are courageously industrious yet tyrannically oppressive; Hope is an admirable individual yet also a vigilante or loose cannon. All three types collide on Doyle's London streets. The Mormons are killed by Hope, who in turn is apprehended by Holmes. In the narrative chain—Mormons,

Hope, Holmes—hero-type succeeds hero-type as we move through history and from the periphery of civilization to its center.[28]

For Lukács, the form of the historical novel is symptomatic of history's dialectical character. Although dialectical studies of form tend to emphasize revolution over evolution, break over continuity, the novel over the traditional, the emergent over the residual, and divergence over convergence, for Lukács, as for Marx and Hegel, "dialectic" involves the synthesis of these pairs or moments. Precisely this form of synthesis governs *A Study in Scarlet*. The juxtaposition of Doyle's two plots and two heroes—Hope and Holmes—stresses their kinship as well as their difference. In later Holmes tales set entirely within London, it will become much more difficult to trace this seminal kinship between the detective and the frontiersman, between Holmes and the Range.

Like James Fenimore Cooper's Natty Bumppo and the Native American "savages" from whom Hawkeye learns the skills of his woodcraft, the erudite Sherlock Holmes is a tracker—the Leatherstocking of London. He never seems so engrossed in his work as when he examines the dirt and dust, reading a text invisible to most eyes, written in a language that is incomprehensible to others. In *A Study in Scarlet*, Watson describes the first of what will become a typical Holmes scene:

> [H]e proceeded slowly down the path, or rather down the fringe of grass which flanked the path, keeping his eyes riveted upon the ground. Twice he stopped, and once I saw him smile and heard him utter an exclamation of satisfaction. There were many marks of footsteps upon the wet clayey soil; but since the police had been coming and going over it, I was unable to see how my companion could hope to learn anything from it. Still I had had such extraordinary evidence of the quickness of his perceptive faculties, that I had no doubt that he could see a great deal which was hidden from me. (21)

Holmes's specialized ability to read the ground enables him to produce seemingly impossible yet accurate hypotheses. In this respect, his rationality often has the effect of convincing Watson and others that his powers are supernatural. As a master rationalist, he is both scientist and shaman. In attending to the story on the ground, Holmes employs a knowledge that civilized, urban man has forgotten. His technique, though seemingly ultranew and modern, has its roots in an earlier time, a time when—to shift to Doyle's other locale—Native Americans had a theoretically different, more intimate connection to their physical surroundings. In the detective genre as exemplified by Holmes, modern science and Native American folklore become one.[29]

Outside the metropolitan capital, Jefferson Hope is also an Indian-like tracker. He is the Holmes of the American West, just as Holmes is the Hope of London. When Hope returns to the mountain campsite and finds the Ferriers missing, he comes upon the Western plot's crime scene. His reading of this scene repeats Holmes's reading of the crime scene in part 1. While narratively, Hope's reading repeats Holmes's, it is important for purposes of historical clarity to remember that Hope's reading precedes Holmes's by several years, important because Holmes is Hope's historical descendant. Hope is also confronted by a set of confusing tracks—a ground "all stamped down by the feet of horses" (84)—out of which he must construct a narrative of what happened in his absence.

Hope, the frontier type, is adept at this kind of work. Because of this, as we watch through the eyes of the omniscient narrator, we are neither amazed nor impressed as we are when Watson describes Holmes's brilliance. In some sense, our greater admiration for Holmes is structured by Watson's fascination and incredulity. Holmes's scene is more fascinating because he withholds his conclusion, while the narrator of Hope's scene lets us inside his head and gives us an immediate reading. Yet our relative lack of amazement for Hope's reading is not simply a matter of greater narrative clarity or apathy. It also depends on our expectations as we read the scene. Hope's attentiveness and skill seem natural to the plot in which he is embedded. His talent is what we expect from a frontier hero like Natty Bumppo (or Jefferson Hope) and, as such, is a commonplace and unremarkable feature of this literary landscape. Only when defamiliarized in Holmes's London does "reading tracks" become remarkable and magical.

Holmes and Hope are also connected through narrative references to their savage and bestial qualities. In watching Holmes, Watson is "irresistibly reminded of a pure-blooded, well-trained foxhound, as it dashes backward and forward through the covert" (26). The image of the "well-trained foxhound" brings together civilized discipline and the primitive instinctiveness of the hunt. When "hot upon such a scent," Sherlock Holmes is "transformed" in a fashion worthy of Jekyll and Hyde.

> Men who had only known the quiet thinker and logician of Baker Street would have failed to recognize him. His brows were drawn into two

hard black lines, while his eyes shone out from beneath them with a steely glitter. His face was bent downward, his shoulders bowed, his lips compressed, and the veins stood out like whipcord in his long sinewy neck. His nostrils seemed to dilate with a purely animal lust for the chase, and his mind was so absolutely concentrated upon the matter before him that a question or remark fell unheeded upon his ears, or, at the most, only provoked a quick, impatient, snarl in reply.[30]

Holmes is both exotic tiger and domesticated foxhound. It is apt to recall Doyle's recollection of his adolescent literary attempts: "There was a man in it and there was a tiger who amalgamated after they met."[31] Holmes assists the forces of civilization in hunting down those who act outside its laws. Like the foxhunt, in which humans ritually reassert their dominance over the most wily of animals, the formulaic Holmes tales will continuously reenact the same basic plot in which Holmes displays his mastery over those who live outside civilized boundaries. And, once again to posit the important formative influence of Cooper, as a foxhound Holmes takes on the part of Cooper's Leatherstocking, whose antagonist in *The Last of the Mohicans* is Magua, also known as the fox—"Le Renard Subtil."

To an even greater degree than Holmes, Hope is repeatedly linked to the savage and the bestial. The "savage-looking" Hope, whom Lucy first encounters, is a character without a past, without antecedents, whose physical description and name hint at a racial background that is not white. Furthermore, Doyle links Hope's obsessively passionate devotion to revenge and the stereotypical "Oriental" patience of the Native Americans among whom Hope had spent a great deal of time during his days as a nomadic, entrepreneurial prospector. As the years pass quickly in the narrative, we learn that "with indomitable patience and perseverance, Jefferson Hope possessed also a power of sustained vindictiveness, which he may have learned from the Indians amongst whom he had lived" (85). Thus, even if we ignore the textual suggestion of Hope's non-Anglo origins, we are invited to believe that his time among the "savages" has contaminated him with a racial "vindictiveness." Because he has lived on the margins of society, he has "gone native." Hope's aloofness from civilization has not only turned him into a savage, but also a beast. When he hears about Lucy's marriage, he stalked "off into the hearts of the mountains to the haunts of the wild beasts. Among them all there was none so fierce as himself" (86). In nurturing his revenge, Hope becomes a Holmes-like hound with a dogged commitment to his task: "he traveled from town to town throughout the United States in quest of his enemies. Year passed into year, his black hair turned grizzled, but still he wandered on, a human bloodhound, with his mind wholly set upon the one object to which he devoted his life" (88).[32] In his obsession to track down his object, Hope is like the detective Holmes who devotes himself to work without sleeping or eating. Both heroes, in pursuing their work with the relentlessness of hounds on the scent, disregard their physical constitutions and appearances. This fierce devotion produces the appearance, if not the reality, of savagery.

But despite these similarities, the dialectical relationship between Holmes and Hope is clearest when we look at how their plots intersect. Hope avenges the deaths of the Ferriers; Holmes discovers the murderer of two visitors to England. Both characters are representatives of justice who track the perpetrators of a crime. If their plots remained separate, they would both remain heroes within their separate moments and realms. But for Doyle, the two are not separate. Hope's plot and world, his struggle to revenge the barbaric evils of polygamy and murder, flow into the "cesspool" world of London, where his frontier heroism is refigured as criminal tragedy. On the center stage of civilization, Doyle sets a struggle between detective and tracker, between Hope, the representative of an older code of frontier justice and primitive revenge, and Holmes, the representative of a more modern, rational, civilized law. Discussing his victims, Hope tells Holmes, "I knew of their guilt . . . and I determined that I should be judge, jury, and executioner all rolled into one" (91). This John Wayne justice is, in Hope's terms, less civilized, but more masculine and natural.[33] "You'd have done the same, if you have any manhood in you, if you had been in my place." Hope's justice is continuous with a "natural" masculinity and is consistent with his "place." But Hope is no longer in that "place," nor is Holmes its representative.[34]

Holmes is the representative of a more civilized law and a more restrained type of "manhood." He represents a more "advanced" type because his work involves the intellectual purity of detection without his becoming involved in the bloodthirsty task of punishment. The progression from Hope's justice to Holmes's parallels the one traced by Michel Foucault from the public execution to penitentiary discipline, from the public spectacle of torture to the hidden practice of power. In Foucault's narrative, the sovereign and his descendant, the state, developed technologies of punishment that disassociated them from "tyranny, excess, the thirst for revenge, and the 'cruel pleasure taken in punishing.'"[35] The modern Holmes derives his pleasure from pursuit and capture, never from the "barbarous" practices of punishment or revenge. Holmes displays a higher intellect in outsmarting the resourceful Hope, a character who has tracked his prey around the world and ingeniously arranged an almost unsolvable pair of murders. Both men track and capture their prey, but Holmes turns his quarry over to other officials, rather than making the kill. His function is more specialized and less physical. While Sherlock Holmes plots are action-packed, it is a more cerebral action than in Westerns. In this sense, Holmes is the perfect hero for the urban bureaucrats who comprised Doyle's early readership.[36] While Holmes is a "new" hero who represents a "new," urban, civilized masculinity, his newness is dialectical—he is a hero who contains traces of heroes like Hope, whom he has supplanted.

The same dialectical relationship pertains as we move from Doyle's frontier to Doyle's metropolis: *A Study in Scarlet* and the subsequent adventures of Holmes and Watson produce an image of metropolitan London as a stage rich with romantic adventure—often adventures whose criminal roots come from the colonies or peripheries of civilization. When Holmes wins out over Hope, we witness not just the victory of the new over the old, but also the outcome of a clash between city and frontier. Yet in Doyle's novel, as in the historical novel in general, it is not right to conceive conflict in terms of victory and loss. Although Holmes is the survivor, he is not to be seen as more heroic. Hope is not inferior, but the tragic embodiment of historical change. To return once more to Cooper, Hope is like a late-Victorian Chingachgook, the "noble savage" of the Leatherstocking novels, the "Last" of the Mohicans, the representative of a glamorous past. Even his creator finds it difficult to punish Hope for his frontier heroism and manliness; he refuses to pass judgment. Rather than subject him (and British law) to the indignities of a trial and sentence, Doyle has Hope die of an aneurysm after only one night in jail. Hope cannot be tried and hanged.[37] In this conflict, Holmes is not victor but survivor, not Hope's executioner but his double and descendant. Holmes, like Hope and Ferrier in the Mormon plot, masters the new frontier, London, but never becomes a routine, assimilated denizen of the city.

Read as a historical novel, *A Study in Scarlet* is valuable to literary historians because it is written just prior to a moment of schism in romance writing between modern urban plots and nostalgic colonial plots. In 1893, six years after the publication of *A Study in Scarlet*, Frederick Jackson Turner cited a bulletin of the superintendent of the census for 1890 and declared that the American frontier was "closed" and that the first phase of U.S. history had ended.[38] Written at a moment when one kind of frontier was ending and a new imperialism and a new urban frontier were taking shape, the form of *A Study in Scarlet* is symptomatic of an unraveling that will become a generic split. Subsequently, imaginative writers will set their epic conflicts either in a nostalgic space (like the American West) or in the equally imaginative modern space of the Big City. That is, after Holmes *and* the Range, the reading public of male romances is offered either Holmes *or* the Range. Yet, this either/or is not really a matter of choice. For in the later Holmes fiction, it will be obvious that Doyle did not abandon the frontier in opting for the urban. Rather, it would be more accurate to say that, discursively, the Home (London) becomes the Range. And Holmes is simply the new sheriff in town.[39]

In Doyle's own life, the issues of cultural identity so important to the Mormon plot and the historical novel precipitate his career as a writer. Prior to crafting the first Holmes novella in 1886, Doyle published several short stories in order to support his developing medical career. He had first turned to writing out of financial necessity after a break with the Irish Catholicism of his wealthy relatives. Doyle was descended from an old Irish Roman Catholic family who traced their roots to a Norman comrade of Richard Lionheart. They were given property in County Wexford, Ireland, in 1333 by Edward III. Subsequently, their history is not marked by fame and glory, but rather punctuated by persecution and dispossession. They were dispossessed of nearly all their Irish land in 1668 and the rest in 1762.[40] During the early nineteenth century, the family settled in London, where Doyle's grandfather gained fame as H. B.—the most popular political caricaturist of his day. One of his uncles, Dicky Doyle, was the principal artist at the satirical magazine *Punch* in the late 1840s and was a friend of Dickens and Thackeray. However, Roman Catholic persecution continued to strike the family, and Dicky Doyle left *Punch* in the 1850s when it took an aggressively pro-Protestant stance against what it saw as an act of "papal aggression."[41] His resignation demonstrates the strength of his commitment to carrying on the legacy of his persecuted Irish ancestors.

Doyle's father, Charles, settled in Edinburgh, where he married into another Irish-Catholic family. Young Arthur Conan Doyle attended Jesuit schools in Edinburgh and Austria before taking a degree as a physician in 1881 from the University of Edinburgh. Doyle's father was an unsuccessful artist, generally depressed, and institutionalized from 1879 onwards. This left Doyle financially dependent upon his uncles. He turned to them in order to secure the letters of recommendation needed by a young doctor seeking to develop his practice. However, at this point, a rift developed. Doyle's scientific training had given him a thoroughly positivistic belief in the methods of empirical observation. For him, the commitment to rationality precluded him from any longer making the "leap of faith" necessary for Roman Catholic belief. When he announced his rejection of Catholicism to his family, they were scandalized and refused to do anything to assist their apostate nephew. Doyle's uncles saw his rejection of the family religion as an insult to their martyred ancestors, the survivors of centuries of persecution of Catholics. The family rift was never overcome. Instead, it drove him to develop his talents as a storyteller in order to support his medical practice.

Doyle's early stories are adventures or romances set in exotic locales. According to Jacqueline Jaffe, they demonstrate the "emergence of what were to be characteristic themes in Doyle's work: the heroic code of behavior with its attendant costs and benefits, a love of physical action, and emphasis on male camaraderie and friendship, and a delight in adventure and excitement."[42] These early tales were shaped not only by his boyhood reading of adventure narratives by Cooper and the historical novels of his grandfather's friend Walter Scott, but also by his own brief stints at sea as a ship's doctor. In 1880, Doyle had sailed as a doctor on a seven-month whaling expedition to the Arctic, and in 1882 he served as ship's physician aboard a cargo boat to West Africa. For Doyle, the latter voyage was particularly troublesome since he fell ill. He returned to England in a physical and spiritual state akin to that of his own creation, Dr. Watson, and Conrad's later creation, Marlow.

The best of these early tales, "J. Habakkuk Jephson's Statement," expresses Doyle's early concern with what we might now call the "Fear of a Black Planet." The main character is a half-caste and former slave from the southern United States who commandeers an Atlantic steamer by murdering its captain and several passengers. He then takes the narrator captive to the jungles of coastal Africa. On a previous trip to Africa, the half-civilized Septimus Goring had enslaved a primitive African tribe through his ostensibly "white" force of character. He returns to Africa to use this tribe as his tool for wreaking vengeance upon the entire white race. Slave-owning whites had separated him from his mother and psychically scarred him for life. Like Heathcliff in *Wuthering Heights,* Goring attains the wealth and refinements of white civilization with the obsessive hope of one day getting his revenge. The narrator, Jephson, escapes to tell his tale to an unbelieving white world. Goring's army is left behind in Africa to prepare for its day. Ten years later, on his deathbed, Jephson writes his "statement" as a final warning to civilization: "I feel the responsibility of holding my peace no longer. I make no vague statement. Turn to your map of Africa. There above Cape Blanco, where the land trends away from north and south from the westernmost point of the continent, there it is that Septimus Goring still reigns over his dark subjects, unless retribution has overtaken him."[43]

"Jephson's Statement" plays on white anxieties about the possible vengeance of former American slaves and African tribes against the perpetrators of European imperialism and the slave trade. The story brought Doyle his first literary success and kept his medical practice afloat. Doyle was especially flattered that some critics attributed the anonymous publication to Stevenson. Many readers, including members of the government, inquired in the papers about whether the tale were fiction or a factual state secret, indicating the public's predisposition to accept its truth.[44] For the West and, more specifically Doyle's British audience, the world "out there" had become a dangerous place and was, increasingly, less "out there."

The family plot and conflict that launched Doyle as a writer is important for understanding Doyle's staunch patriotism—at times, the fanaticism of the convert—and creation of Holmes. Holmes is not only an icon of Englishness, but also functions as an analogue for his creator and as a means to a home within English culture. In the upbringing I have described above, one can sense the competing claims of Irish, Scotch, and English cultural identities. The explicit rejection of his ancestral Roman Catholicism, his subsequent rejection by his family, and the resulting confusion of identity—of not knowing where and to whom he belonged—combine to strengthen Doyle's desire to become

English. And, at the same time, we can see in Holmes's cultivated marginality and attraction to outsiders a lingering fascination for that seemingly mystical Irish Catholicism that Doyle has consciously repudiated. His writing can be seen in the light of a need to create a place for himself at the heart of English culture and, at the same time, on its margins. In writing the Holmes stories, Doyle writes his way "home," or at least to a more plural sense of "homes."

A Freudian might be tempted to read the significance of Doyle's repudiation of Irishness as loudly announced in the Holmes tales by its conspicuous absence. The only Irish characters who explicitly appear are Chicago gangsters.[45] This absence is remarkable given the obvious attention of the tales to political and social issues of the day and to nationality as a fundamental category of metropolitan identity. Although the Irish question and Fenian terrorism were among the most prominent political issues throughout the period in which Doyle wrote Holmes stories, they are never taken up in any of the sixty-four plots. The Holmes canon contains plots that treat, among others, German socialists, the Ku Klux Klan, the Sicilian Mafia, Russian anarchists, and exiled Latin American dictators. Violence associated with foreign conspirators is a fundamental fact of life in Holmes's London. But there are no Irish Nationalists. Doyle avoids, even in the world of his fiction, his painfully strained relationship with his Irish Catholic heritage. Politically, Doyle was opposed to Irish independence. The idea conflicted with his dream of a future unity of English-speaking peoples that would bring together Britain, the United States, Canada, and Australia under one government. In his fiction, Doyle explores Anglo-American relations, but he hesitates to comment on the more immediate vexed relationship between Protestant England and Catholic Ireland.

Yet while he may not have been comfortable engaging with these issues directly, Doyle does discuss issues of religious persecution and cultural definition through the mediation of his tales. We have seen how *A Study in Scarlet* examines the conflict between modern Britain and older religious and moral codes: Mormonism, theocracy, polygamy, revenge, and frontier justice. Indeed, it is not too bold to imagine that Doyle's Mormon plot is a working out of his own relationship to Roman Catholicism, which like Mormonism is a highly structured, hierarchical religion that emphasizes adherence to the group in opposition to dictates of individual conscience. Doyle's "historical novels" display a concern for moments of tension between religious groups—

Catholic and Protestant claimants to the throne in *Micah Clarke,* the Huguenots and the Catholic king of France in *The Refugees.* His writing is always attempting to explore and define the evolving constitution of cultures and, I would argue, his evolving self.

Politically, Doyle was a staunch conservative and close friend of imperialists, including Kipling, Haggard, Lang, and Baden-Powell. His literary fame as the creator of Britain's most famous rationalist earned him a platform from which to espouse his politics. Twice, in 1900 and 1906, he attempted to get into Parliament on a jingoist platform, but was defeated. During the Boer War, Doyle organized militia or "Rifle Clubs" in order to defend England from invasions in the absence of the regular army.[46] His writing should be seen in the context of this political and patriotic commitment. With the outbreak of the Boer War in late 1898, Doyle was unable to get into the army. Frustrated, he went to South Africa anyway and served as a physician in a field hospital. Returning home, he found his country under attack in the European press for atrocities being committed in South Africa. Based on his own experience in the war, Doyle wrote a lengthy propagandistic defense of British conduct titled *The War in South Africa: Its Cause and Conduct* (1902). The work turned the tide of public opinion back in favor of the British. For writing this work (and curiously not for his contributions to popular fiction), Doyle was knighted during the coronation of Edward in August 1902. With this knighthood, Doyle was symbolically baptized as an Englishman.

In 1893, Doyle had killed off Holmes in "The Final Problem" and vowed never to write another tale about him. Despite the financial rewards of the series, Doyle was upset that the reading public was not paying attention to what he considered his more important work: the historical novels. But to the great relief of an enraged public, he broke his vow after returning from South Africa with *The Hound of the Baskervilles,* which began appearing in late 1901.[47] I find it significant that Doyle brought Holmes back to life during a moment of national crisis and doubt. I suspect that he resurrects his hero because he felt England needed a good jolt of patriotism and that a successful Holmes case was the best way to supply it. The plot of *The Hound of the Baskervilles* supplies further evidence: it is a struggle over an estate in which the wealth derives from South African mining.

From the outset of the Holmes stories, Doyle awakens his reading public to the encroachment of a dangerous and exciting world, whether it take the form of new peoples (like Hope) or wealth (like the South African gold of *Hound*). The writer of "J. Habakkuk Jephson's Statement" arouses similar fears in *A Study in Scarlet*. Both narratives indicate the importance of writing as an intervention in a specific moment of cultural definition. The stories are neither simple entertainment, nor manifestations of some transhistorical, metaphysical struggle between good and evil. This point leaps off the page at the conclusion of *A Study in Scarlet*. Watson reads Holmes a newspaper account of their case that argues that "if the case has had no other effect, it, at least, brings out in the most striking manner the efficiency of our detective police force, and will serve as a lesson to all foreigners that they will do wisely to settle their feuds at home, and not to carry them on to British soil" (103). Like the newspaper account, Doyle's novella functions as a warning and deterrent.⁴⁸ *A Study in Scarlet* also invites one to extract a moral: Holmes's London must be kept free of conflict and remnants of "barbarity," and, most importantly, must be kept as wholesomely pure as Hope's Lucy. London reflects and nurtures anxieties of the British about the encroachment of the foreign. Yet, the novella also invites the extraction of another moral, perhaps a countermoral: London is a place of conflict, savagery, and pollution. As such, it is a place teeming with adventure. Home is where the action is.

The Holmes saga continues to follow the basic structure of the frontier narrative come home to roost. First, the tales arouse fear and pleasure that the foreign has invaded and threatens to contaminate and exoticize the homeland; then, they introduce the hero Holmes to protect England and regulate the incursion of insidious and welcome interlopers. In this national story, London functions as an entrepôt of peoples, commodities, and stories. Because Britain's empire was so large and diverse, "foreignness" in the metropolis could take many forms— hence, the proliferation of plots and villains that can follow this same basic structure. It was a politically useful formula that, for Doyle, worked to produce and reproduce definitions of Britain and its others. The London of Sherlock Holmes is the most dynamic frontier in the Empire; in fact, it is a place of multiple, simultaneous, and overlapping frontiers. Within London, cultural boundaries, not to mention boundaries of class, religion, sexuality, gender, and genre are continuously crossed and recrossed, drawn and reinscribed. The metropolis is no mere background or setting, but rather, as it was for Dickens, a condition of possibility for the form and content of the tales.

In his next appearance in *The Sign of Four,* Holmes will be called upon to protect himself from the penetrating dangers associated with invasions of the nation, the home, his own body, and the modern world. Yet while he guards against these invasions, Holmes is powerfully drawn to those exotic people and things that show up in London. His task will be not so much to keep the foreign out—although he will do that—as it will be to regulate its incursion by assigning new things to their "proper" places.

CHAPTER THREE

THE ROMANCE OF INVASION

Cocaine and Cannibals in *The Sign of Four*

Arthur Conan Doyle's second Sherlock Holmes tale—the novella *The Sign of Four* (1890)—is framed by two instances of a domestic scene. At both beginning and end, the detective is seated in a comfortable chair next to a fireplace, the hearth that is the central symbolic locale of Victorian domesticity. Watson's lingering narrative opening is worth our close attention.

> Sherlock Holmes took his bottle from the corner of the mantel-piece, and his hypodermic syringe from its neat morocco case. With his long, white, nervous fingers he adjusted the delicate needle and rolled back his left shirtcuff. For some little time his eyes rested thoughtfully upon the sinewy forearm and wrist, all dotted and scarred with innumerable puncture-marks. Finally, he thrust the sharp point home, pressed down the tiny piston, and sank back into the velvet-lined armchair with a long sigh of satisfaction.[1]

Holmes's forearm is scarred by the "innumerable" signs of his cocaine habit, "signs of [his] fore [arm]" that playfully and immediately invoke the novella's title.[2] We are reminded of Holmes's passion for chemical research and science, a spirit of inquiry that discounts his own personal safety. In *A Study in Scarlet* (1887), we first met Holmes in a chemistry lab; he enters literary history in the guise of a theoretician exceedingly interested in the reactions that occur when different substances mix, especially when one of the sites of reaction is himself. In this passage, that passion for bodily experimentation takes on clearly erotic overtones. There is foreplay and striptease: "with his long, white, nervous fingers he adjusted the delicate needle and rolled back his left shirtcuff." There is a naked object and a lingering gaze: "for some time his eyes rested thoughtfully upon the sinewy forearm and wrist." And there is climax and luxuriant relaxation: "finally, he thrust the sharp point home, pressed down the tiny piston, and sank back into the velvet-lined armchair with a long sigh of satisfaction." The sexuality described here is

neither simply passive nor aggressive. It is both. Holmes, English literature's ultimate "control freak," is in control of both moments of pleasure—the "thrust" of the needle and the acceptance of the carefully
regulated 7 percent solution into his system.

Despite the clear masturbatory imagery in the scene, it is important
to note that Holmes is not alone. Watson's recollection of his doubled
presence at this ritual, as doctor and chronicler, reflects an intense confusion about the erotics surrounding the growing intercourse between
Britain and its colonial others, commodities and peoples, here represented by South American cocaine.[3] Watson's fascinated narration indicates that the ritual of consumption occurs often, and, as a physician,
he ultimately protests. When Holmes invites him to partake of the
cocaine, he declines and cites his debilitating imperial legacy: "My constitution has not got over the Afghan campaign yet" (107). Eventually,
the doctor chastises Holmes, citing the dangers of "increased tissue-
change," "permanent weakness," and the possibility of Holmes's own
"constitutional" crisis. He asks Holmes: "Why should you, for a mere
passing pleasure, risk the loss of those great powers with which you
have been endowed?" In the coming together of Holmes and the
cocaine, the medical voice charges that that pleasure is purchased at
too dear a price; Holmes's body will be damaged and his "great powers"
will decline.

But despite the explicit protest of Watson's medical self, he is also
clearly fascinated. Although he knows Holmes is injecting himself
from the scene's outset, Watson-the-chronicler waits for the conclusion of the ritual before raising his objection. As he watches Holmes, it
is both men's eyes that linger "thoughtfully," and, at the moment of
writing, it is Watson who re-presents and vicariously re-experiences the
scene in careful, lingering detail. His writing registers not only an articulated disgust but also an unarticulated identification. There is fear for
Holmes; but there is also pleasure in the spectacle. This is the novella's
first sign of a contradictory response to colonial invasion, one that
functions as the model for the seemingly "innumerable" invasions that
the novella subsequently enacts. Yet while it is the narrative's beginning,
it is not the story's origin. For Holmes's forearm is, like this novella, a
historical text. The signs it bears point back into history; they are signs
of (be)fore.[4]

As I hope the discussion has indicated thus far, I propose that we read
Doyle's The Sign of Four allegorically. In the above scene, the language

reveals that the personal frontiers of Holmes's body have become charged with the same anxieties and pleasures as the frontiers of Britain's political body.[5] Watson's admonishment of Holmes, couched in language about "mere passing pleasures," "permanent weakness," and a crisis of the "constitution," simultaneously invokes popular arguments against the sins of masturbation and in favor of political and commercial isolation. In early drafts of this chapter, I wanted to privilege the overtly political plot in this novella, one concerning the invasion of an Andaman Island cannibal. I argued that the "cocaine plot" was a coded way of introducing the more significant discussion of imperial politics that was Doyle's main concern. However, as I have thought more about the relative significance of the "levels" in this allegory, I have come to think that perhaps the opposite emphasis is more appropriate. For while the invasion of cannibals and returned convicts that I discuss below is clearly a haunting story of the return of the colonial and imperial repressed, its fantastic qualities (Andaman Island cannibals and one-legged convicts running amok on the streets of London) surely remove it from the day-to-day experience of Doyle's largely metropolitan readership. However, what these readers were doing every day was participating in an expanding global marketplace, one that was constantly being "invaded" by new commodities and cultural styles whose origins, conditions of production, and uses were, to a large extent, still a mystery.

As I move through the unfolding of Doyle's romance of invasion, it now seems that, at its most significant level, this is a story about romancing the exotic commodity or living in the romantic midst of a rapidly changing imperial/material culture. It is possible to argue that the importance of the novella was that it could imagine only a world in which immigrants were represented and perceived as grotesque "invaders"—that is, the figure of the cannibal. I do not want to downplay that argument. However, my emphasis is, instead, to stress that colonial encounters happened much more frequently, in mediated fashion, in the act of commodity consumption. Furthermore, it is these encounters that activated anxieties and hopes about the changing constitution of national and individual subjectivities and bodies. Positioned structurally at the beginning and end, *The Sign*'s cocaine plot sits on the boundary and functions as a threshold between text and world; the way in and out of the novella proceeds through a domestic ritual of commodity consumption.

Like Holmes's forearm, the novella bears/bares signs that mark the introduction or invasion of foreign substances into the body politic. Decades before Forster imagines *A Passage to India,* Doyle is already obsessed by passages *from* India—as well as South America (cocaine) and the Andaman Islands (the home of the tale's primary killer). Alongside cocaine and cannibals, there is also the threat of a cultural invasion. The story's most grotesque character is a decadent aesthete. As the beneficiary of "new colonial" money, Thaddeus Sholto uses his unearned wealth to create an "oasis" of eclectic oriental art behind the nondescript facade of his suburban dwelling. Like the wealth on which it depends, the importation of foreign art, products, and styles are accompanied by pleasure and corruption, bodily satisfaction, and the decline of British masculinity. Finally, *The Sign of Four* stages the invasion of colonial peoples, both the colonizers and colonized. Both are figured in terms of their most menacing representatives: the convict and the cannibal. The returned convict in this novella, a character similar to Dickens's Magwich, had been imprisoned for disloyal conduct during the violence of the Indian Mutiny of 1857.[6] The cannibal is from the geographically and, in Doyle's formulation, evolutionary remote Andaman Islands. As we saw in the previous chapter, the sudden return and presence of these strangers in metropolitan London make it the most up-to-date setting for the kinds of imperial romances formerly set in distant lands.

For Holmes, intercourse with cocaine is a ticket to romance; it provides an escape from routine boredom and access to exotic pleasure. Holmes risks his physical self in order to stimulate his mental self. He craves excitement and departures from the "commonplace" (the word *commonplace* seems to appear more frequently than any other in the Holmes stories). The opposite of the "commonplace" is the "unique," and it is this quality that he constantly seeks as an escape from his mundane London existence. Hence his drug habit. "Hence the cocaine. I cannot live without brainwork. What else is there to live for? Stand at the window here. Was ever such a dreary, dismal, unprofitable world? See how the yellow fog swirls across the dun-coloured houses. What could be more hopelessly prosaic and material? What is the use of having powers, Doctor, when one has no field upon which to exert them? Crime is commonplace, existence is commonplace, and no qualities save those which are commonplace have any function upon the earth" (113).

Holmes uses cocaine because he lacks meaningful work, work that is his urban salvation. In the monotonous urban jungle where Holmes has lengthy bouts of lassitude, he resembles Kayerts and Carlier who go to seed in the African jungle of Conrad's "An Outpost of Progress." Most of the time, he is a hero without a plot, a displaced person. "That is why," he tells Watson, "I have chosen my own particular profession, or rather created it, for I am the only one in the world" (108). In inventing the profession of amateur consulting detective, Holmes merges work and art, utility and play.[7] Holmes's work almost always involves encounters with dangerous foreigners: a cannibal in this text, the Mafia in "The Adventure of the Six Napoleons," an African ritual poison in "The Adventure of the Devil's Foot," a deadly Sumatran microbe in "The Adventure of the Dying Detective," and so on. Thus, the cocaine serves not only as a substitute for those many drugs and poisons with which Holmes willingly experiments when he is involved with a case, but also for those uniquely foreign criminals who arouse his passion when he is hot at work. In both encounters, Holmes risks danger to his physical self in order to prove his mastery and experience pleasure.

Holmes's lament about the commonplace and the discussion about his drug habit is instantly dropped when interesting work invades his apartment. It does not return again until the novella's final paragraph, when the mystery has been tidily explained. When Watson announces that he will marry Mary Morstan, the initial victim in a chain of crimes that Holmes unravels, the doctor's anxiety for Holmes returns. Watson argues that "the division seems rather unfair. . . . You have done all the work in this business. I get a wife out of it, . . . pray what remains for you?" "For me," Holmes replies, "there remains the cocaine bottle" (205). After he reaches the solution to the murder case, Holmes will reach once again for another "case," the "neat morocco case" that contains his syringe. Although the mystery case is the novella's focus, it is the "morocco case" that contains business as usual; for Holmes, it is one kind of "case" or the other. The mystery introduced by Mary Morstan, the romantic hunt for treasure and cannibal killers, is an interruption, a substitution that disrupts the series of experiments Holmes conducts on his body. With Holmes once more out of work, he, Watson (his chronicler), and his readers must await the next invasion of the exotic into commonplace London. He returns from "the sign of the four" to the signs on his forearm.

The mystery "case" in *The Sign of Four* brings us into contact with other signs indicating the presence of imperial culture in metropolitan London. These signs extend the analogy between drugs and culture and the complex conjunction of pleasure and danger I have already described. When Holmes and Watson accompany Mary Morstan to a mysterious appointment in the London suburbs, they are introduced to the subtly seductive world of the Orient, one that Doyle suggests has penetrated or insinuated itself into a metropolitan world that is spreading into the English countryside. Upon pulling up to a nondescript English residence, to Watson's amazement "the door was instantly thrown open by a Hindoo servant, clad in a yellow turban, white loose-fitting clothes, and yellow sash. There was something strangely incongruous in this Oriental figure framed in the commonplace doorway of a third-rate suburban dwelling house" (122). As in the cocaine plot, here the "commonplace" is sharply contrasted with the unique. The juxtaposition of subject ("Oriental figure") and frame (suburban doorway) is an increasingly common event in the London world of 1890 and is a crucial component of what attracted readers to the Holmes tales. This particular juxtaposition raises a number of questions or mysteries for Holmes and Watson: How can the presence of this "Oriental figure" be explained? To what larger presence does this sign point? What strange things lurk behind other common facades? What will develop out of these novel arrangements? The concurrence of the oriental figure and the "commonplace" frame is a puzzle, a tangled thread of the social fabric, that requires a scientist like Holmes, who can unravel and restitch it.

Indeed, this image might serve as a visual analogue for the entire Holmes canon in which the exotic is repeatedly framed or contained by the familiar and homely.[8] Just as the puncture marks on the forearm signify a crossing of the boundary between the interior of the English Holmes and the external, non-English cocaine, this orientalized suburban image unravels oppositions and dissolves boundaries between the English and the Orient, the known and the unknown, the home and the exotic. The Hindu servant is thus very carefully framed, not only by something English, but on a threshold between exterior and interior. Such images estrange English readers from their own home, offering them simultaneously a sense of escape from the commonplace and a sense of not-belonging, of being outsiders in what they thought was their own home. Such confusing juxtapositions typify an experience that is modern and metropolitan. Indeed, as we shall see in my concluding chapter on Eliot, the metropolitan experience of incongruous juxtaposition will become a chief characteristic of modernist poetics. In the late nineteenth century, London is an urban jungle for Holmes to explore, map, conquer, and decipher. It is not a mere setting for the Holmes tales, but the textual mystery that underwrites all other puzzles.

Holmes and Watson follow the Hindu servant down a long passage and discover a sight even stranger than the out-of-place Hindu in the "commonplace" door frame—a grotesque Englishman in an aesthetic room of eclectic Eastern decor: "There stood a small man with a very high head, a bristle of red hair all around the fringe of it. . . . He writhed his hands together as he stood, and his features were in a perpetual jerk—now smiling, now scowling, but never for an instant in repose" (123). Like Holmes, Thaddeus Sholto is a drug user. As the scene progresses, we see him constantly puffing on a hookah. But in sharp contrast to the machine-like control-freak Holmes, Sholto is an out-of-control physical freak. He has been subjected by the drug that contorts his bodily expression. Like some "writhing" fish, he has taken the bait and is hooked on the hookah. He is an extreme example of what Holmes could become if his "trips" were not carefully regulated. When Holmes carefully measures his 7 percent solution, he subordinates the substance to his will and pleasure. Sholto's unregulated inhalation of smoke separates Sholto's dependence from Holmes's mastery. Sholto is a sign of Watson's typical late-Victorian fears—"permanent weakness" and degeneration—and, like Holmes, brings together the body and the imperial economy, especially conservative fears about the lack of trade "regulation."

The grotesque Sholto is a product of Britain's imperial mission, not simply as a drug user but, as we shall see, also as the beneficiary of tainted, ill-gotten colonial wealth. His upper-middle-class aesthetic lifestyle is supported by the great financial wealth that his father-soldier brought home from service in India. This inherited capital allows the son to pursue his own whims free from the discipline of capitalism and the purposiveness of work. His aimlessness is signified by his "perpetual jerk." Undoubtedly, there is some degree of ironic contrast intended between the disciplined lifestyle of the soldier-father and his decadent heir. Sholto's body and his apartment can be read as texts that indicate the benefits and costs of the colonial mission; his framing is just as "strangely incongruous" as that of his Hindu servant.

By linking the dangers of drugs and aesthetic opulence, Doyle conflates decadence and the decline of rugged British masculinity with the fruits of Britain's imperial and colonial ventures. Indeed, the effeminate Sholto is an echo of the decadent eighteenth-century aristocrat against whom middle-class Victorian heroes are structured. Holmes, the unemployed amateur, is nevertheless an embodiment of the values of work, discipline, temperance, and, thus, the middle class. In the "commonplace" London suburbs, Sholto, a self-styled creature of colonialism, has surrounded himself with a generalized Eastern luxury that he describes as "an oasis of art in the howling desert of South London" (123). Like the drug, Sholto's "oasis" is a bulwark against the "rough materialism" of modern London (125). While his apartment is full of imported commodities, Watson's description of it could have been imported straight out of an Arabian Nights tale.[9] "The richest and glossiest of curtains and tapestries draped the walls, looped back here and there to expose some richly mounted painting or Oriental vase. The carpet was of amber and black, so soft and thick that the foot sank pleasantly into it, as into a bed of moss. Two great tiger-skins thrown athwart it increased the suggestion of Eastern luxury, as did a huge hookah which stood upon a mat in the corner. A lamp in the fashion of a silver dove was hung from an almost invisible golden wire in the centre of the room. As it burned it filled the air with a subtle and aromatic odour" (123). In Sholto's "sanctum," the East is conflated with the sensual. It is a place of luxuriant visions, textures, and smells. It is rich—a style of excess. Here, the Orient is not simply encountered from a safe, aesthetic distance, but actually invades the bodies of the spectators in the form of smoke: "the balsamic odour of the eastern tobacco" (124). In physically mixing with the oriental smoke, Holmes and Watson participate intimately with the East. Watson's description pays special attention to textures—"rich" and "glossy" fabrics, "soft" and "thick" carpets, and "tiger-skins." While the smoke invades the body, Sholto's surroundings signify the erotic caress of the exotic commodity in an encounter that is skin-to-skin.

Watson's fascinated narrative structurally echoes his reaction to Holmes in the opening drug scene. Again, at the moment of writing, his narrative lingers. Yet this seductive intimacy and intercourse is not to be fully embraced since its potential dangers are signified by the "writhing" body of Sholto, the sign of a dangerous subordination to colonial smoke. Again, we can read this allegorically as a meditation on imperial pleasures and anxieties associated with invasion—like Holmes's earlier drug use. As an effeminate character "partial to the modern French school" (125) of painting and decorative arts, Sholto signifies the seductively attractive aesthetic life that is entertained, only to be ridiculed, by Doyle as a possible escape from the "hopelessly prosaic" drudge of modern work and urban life. Such an escape, as this novella strikingly demonstrates, was largely enabled by the colonial wealth that afforded freedom from work, especially manual labor, and the importation of cultural styles, artifacts, and commodities that contrasted with the cold, realist middle-class culture of industrial and utilitarian Britain. But in losing control over his aesthetic cravings and consumption, Sholto has been subjected by an Eastern beauty and opulence that threatens, like Circe, to turn him into a slave-like beast. In retreating from the "rough" materialism of the crowd into a "sanctum" of pleasurable consumption, Sholto has been engulfed by a feminized Eastern luxury.

Holmes, unusually silent in this scene, is not so far remote from Sholto. We should remember that, besides cocaine and pipe smoking, his other signature pastime is the distracted, autoerotic playing of the violin. Like Sholto's predilection for modern French painting, Holmes's musical taste and practice is decidedly protomodernist. What Watson hears as screeching, we might hear as the decadent dissonance that Schoenberg will develop in his modernist musical compositions. The ascetic Holmes is also prone to Sholto-like bouts of aesthetic decadence. When trying to solve a mystery, Holmes will often arrange a divan of pillows on the floor and, seated like a Buddha, spend the night puffing away on his pipe, lost in meditation. Like Sholto, Holmes is drawn to drugs, aesthetics, and the East as a bulwark against "commonplace" modern London. In looking at these two figures, we can see domestic space as not simply a retreat from the harsh realities of public life, but as an escape into a carefully composed orientalized fantasy. That is, when Holmes reaches for the cocaine, he is reaching for his ticket to an exotic imperial adventure—one that can be experienced, through the mediation of the commodity, without ever leaving his comfortable chair on the hearth. Like Sholto, Holmes welcomes and, actually, creates these encounters with alien invaders. But unlike Sholto, whom the alien invaders colonize and subject, Holmes is portrayed as one who controls them and subjects them to his will and pleasure. He emerges from the encounter with the commodity not as a "writhing" degenerate but as rigidly machine-like and masterfully heroic.

Holmes's confrontations with cocaine and orientalist culture are pre-texts for *The Sign of Four*'s most threatening, yet most fantastically remote, version of colonial invasion, the figure of a savage cannibal loose on the streets of London. Like the drug's influence on the body, the savage cannibal is potentially dangerous to the bodies of individual Londoners. His threat signifies an extreme version of subordination, passivity, and dependence—the transformation of the English into raw food for cultural invaders. Yet like the cocaine that Holmes discreetly administers to himself, the cannibal ultimately functions as a social stimulant, a romantic relief from a mundane urban existence, and, as I will discuss below, a crucial imaginative element in the dialectic of self-control, self-mastery, and self-definition. Like the "passing pleasure" of the drug, Holmes transforms this cannibalistic threat to his "great powers" into a field for the exercise and further development of his detective powers. Thus, in representing the greatest threat to civilization and individual English bodies, not necessarily in everyday life but certainly in the ideological sphere of fantasy and romance literature, the cannibal is also necessary for the self-assertion of those persons and cultures that it threatens to abolish. The ideology of the text is, it should go without saying, deeply paranoid.

As the narrative continues, more threatening dimensions of the colonial experience—namely, violence and murder—invade Holmes's quiet, boring London world of domesticity. On his deathbed, Sholto's father reveals to his sons that he had swindled Mary Morstan's father, a fellow officer, out of a treasure they had deceitfully acquired in India. Unfortunately, the major dies before indicating the whereabouts of the full treasure. Troubled by guilt over the sins of his father, Thaddeus Sholto had annually sent Mary pearls of great worth. But now, he informs his visitors that his twin brother has discovered the bulk of the treasure in a hidden attic, and that he, Thaddeus, wants to set things straight with Mary. Thus, the letter calling the detectives to the appointment described above.

Sholto then invites Holmes, Watson, and Mary to accompany him to Pondicherry Lodge (the family's suburban villa), where Mary can receive her due. The naming of the estate built with Major Sholto's illicit colonial gains is another sign of the colonial presence in South London; indeed, the act of naming it after an Indian city reverses the typical imperial practice of naming conquered cities after places in Britain. Although Doyle disappointingly fails to give us a detailed portrait of its architectural exterior, we do learn that it "was girt round with a very high stone wall topped with broken glass. A single narrow iron-clamped door formed the only means of entrance" (131). In a very direct manner, we can see how the siege mentality of the colonial officer has served as a model for the fort-like construction of this piece of London suburbia. The allusion to Pondicherry, curiously, signifies more than simply India.[10] It is a city (on the southeast coast of India, near Madras) that has a strong French influence and background. Doyle's choice of this particular city—Indian, French, with some Anglo—signifies a cosmopolitan or transnational quality to the Sholto estate. It is, above all, a site of ambiguity.

The Sholtos' Pondicherry Lodge is located in Upper Norwood, a suburb south of the Thames. Unlike Thaddeus Sholto's invisible oasis, Pondicherry Lodge displays its orientalist character both inside and out. As I argue above, the significance of the allusion to Pondicherry lies in its transnational character—Indian, French, and English—and the manner in which it juxtaposes the colonial and the suburban, the exotic and the domestic. In addition to the allusion, Doyle's choice of his London site, Upper Norwood, was also far from casual. A quick scan of G. W. Bacon's *New Large-Scale Ordnance Atlas of London and Suburbs* (1888) reveals a number of suburban villas or lodges, like that of the Sholtos, in the vicinity: Castlehill Lodge, Hazelwood, and Norbury Lodge.[11] If one's glance moves northeast of Upper Norwood, not even a half-mile in distance, it runs smack up against the Crystal Palace at Sydenham.

It is in the shadows of the Crystal Palace, moved here in 1854, that Doyle chose to locate his Anglo-Indian suburban villa. In so doing, he brings the controversies surrounding the Great Exhibition of 1851 into a suburban context, just as we have already seen him resurrecting the 1857 Mutiny in Surrey and Kent. According to Thomas Richards, the exhibition of 1851 in Hyde Park "brought together the representatives of thirty-two nations from Europe, America, Africa, and the Far East. The delegations were housed in a single structure built expressly for them. The building occupied fourteen acres on the north edge of the park, and it contained, not an army of diplomats and attachés, but an assembly of manufactured articles, the largest display of commodities that had ever been brought together under one roof."[12] At midcentury,

the Great Exhibition crystalized the debate between liberals and con-
servatives. Led by the prince consort, the promoters of the exhibition
optimistically saw it as a symbol for the increasing coming-together
of one modern world family of nations.[13] But the Tories, stung by the
repeal of the Corn Laws in the 1840s, saw it as further evidence of the
erosion of rural interests at home, British hegemony abroad, and national integrity on both fronts.[14] For Richards, the exhibition at the
Crystal Palace signaled the beginning and victory of commodity culture. The planners of the exhibition had, after all, gained the highly
symbolic field of Hyde Park as a site for their spectacle of nations. Forty years later, Doyle restages this earlier contest between expansion
and isolation when he sets his own version of the pleasures and anxieties of foreign invasion—*The Sign of Four*—in the suburban shadows
of the reconstructed Crystal Palace at Sydenham.

Upon arriving at Pondicherry Lodge, a place where the crime
against Mary is supposed to be righted, the detective discovers a new
crime. Holmes finds the corpse of Sholto's brother; he has been murdered in a locked upstairs room. And of course, the treasure has been
stolen. Bartholomew Sholto is the victim of a deadly penetration;
Holmes and Watson discover a poisoned "long dark thorn stuck in the
skin just above the ear" (136). Watson comments that the instrument
of death is not "an English thorn" (141). The scene of the murder reen-
acts, once again, the drug scene at the novella's opening. Here, at the
center of the novella, the foreign thorn serves as a deadly double for
the needle used by Holmes in the opening paragraph, while the poison
recalls the potential dangers of cocaine or the smoke inhaled in Thaddeus's oasis.

But in this scene, Watson's grimmest fears have come true. For if
Holmes's body is endangered by the cocaine and if Thaddeus's "writhing" body signifies an Englishman's potential enslavement by a commodity culture that is imagined as "Oriental," then Bartholomew's
stiff, inert corpse informs us that the foreign also brings death. As one
who has experience reading puncture marks, Holmes shudders at the
thought of the poison and tells Watson that the darts are "hellish
things" and that he would "sooner face a Martini bullet" (149). The intensity of his repulsion is indicated by his discourse: the coldly rational
Holmes does not usually ascribe metaphysical explanations such as
"hellish" to the sensory data he encounters.

The anxiety in this scene also depends on its violation of English masculinity and the victim's home. Sensitive to all its horror, Watson feels compelled at this point to take Mary Morstan away from this site of domestic violation, back to her own, safe home. While he wants to shelter her from the vision of violence (in a manner that resembles Marlow's encounter with Kurtz's Intended), he also must reassure himself and the reader with a vision of a tranquil English home. The site of violence, Pondicherry Lodge, is a strange home: from the outside it looks like a fortress; on the inside it is a grander version of Thaddeus's orientalized apartment. In contrast, Watson finds it "soothing to catch even that passing glimpse of a tranquil English home in the midst of the wild, dark business which had absorbed us" (146). The English home is a beacon of light and a symbol of civilization—an outpost of progress in the midst of the urban jungle.

At the crime scene, Holmes discovers two sets of footprints in the dust, a primitive stone hammer, and an ominous message scrawled on a piece of paper: "The Sign of Four." Earlier, Holmes had discovered a similar message scrawled on a treasure map among Captain Morstan's papers. The message had been followed by four names: Jonathan Small, Mahomet Singh, Abdullah Khan, and Dost Akbar. One set of the footprints clearly belongs to a wooden-legged man, whom Holmes quickly identifies as Jonathan Small. But for Holmes, it is the other assailant who arouses his curiosity—lifting this case "from the regions of the commonplace" and into the realm of the exotic: "I fancy that this ally breaks fresh ground in the annals of crime in this country— though parallel cases suggest themselves from India, and, if my memory serves me, from Senegambia" (138–39). Holmes's ability to solve crimes depends upon his extensive knowledge of criminal history, a knowledge that knows no geographic or cultural boundaries. For if all imperial roads lead to London, then one important thing that travels these roads is information. There is nothing new under the sun for Holmes. As this and subsequent Holmes tales develop, Holmes, the armchair criminologist, demonstrates a knowledge no less global in reach than James Frazer's encyclopedic compendium of primitive myths and customs. Holmes's abilities depend then, in part, on his specific location within an imperial network of knowledge and information. That which he does not personally consume, he has, at least, within his reach in the great archives, libraries, and museums that comprise the material culture of the imperial metropolis. Holmes quickly dismisses Watson's interpretation of the other set of barefoot prints as belonging to a woman or child. Instead, Holmes quickly attributes them to a non-Englishman.

When Watson's suspicions next turn to Small's Indian coconspirators, Holmes surveys the evidence and rejects this theory, too. "When I first saw strange weapons I was inclined to think so, but the remarkable character of the footmarks caused me to reconsider my views. Some of the inhabitants of the Indian Peninsula are small men, but none could have left such marks as that. The Hindoo proper has long thin feet. The sandal-wearing Mohammedan has the long toe well separated from the others because the thong is commonly passed between them" (161). The solution to this case, like the one in *A Study in Scarlet,* also depends upon Holmes's ability to read the ground and its data against a detailed, comparative anthropological framework. It appears that if one wants to become a modern metropolitan detective, one must first possess an inordinate knowledge of anthropology. Classically anthropological, Holmes's interpretation depends upon his deployment of a set of generalizable racial and cultural characteristics such as "the Hindoo proper" and "the sandal-wearing Mohammedan." With this knowledge, he can determine that the killer is not of the "Indian variety." His knowledge must be global in reach because his metropolitan community has become global in its composition.

Or, to put this slightly differently, Holmes's knowledge is global in reach because the globe, dislocated and relocated, is now within arm's length. His anthropological reading, like his cocaine habit, is an exotic escape from the commonplace and routine. In Holmes's world, anthropology is linked to the cocaine not only as mental stimulation, but also in the physical arrangement of his domestic space. Like the cocaine on the mantel in the opening scene, the book sits on a shelf only an arm's length from his chair. And just as he reached for the cocaine in the earlier scene, here, "he stretch[es] his hand up and [takes] down a bulky volume from the shelf" and begins, once again, to entrance Watson.

> The aborigines of the Andaman Islands may perhaps claim the distinction of being the smallest race upon this earth, though some anthropologists prefer the Bushmen of Africa, the Digger Indians of America, and the Terra del Fuegians. The average height is rather below four feet, although many full-grown adults may be found who are very much smaller than this. They are a fierce, morose and intractable people, though capable of forming the most devoted friendships when their confidence has once been gained. . . . They are naturally hideous, having

large misshaped heads, small fierce eyes, and distorted features. Their feet and hands, however, are remarkably small. So intractable and fierce are they, that all the efforts of the British officials have failed to win them over in any significant degree. They have always been a terror to shipwrecked crews, braining the survivors with their stone-headed clubs or shooting them with their poisoned arrows. These massacres are invariably concluded by a cannibal feast. (162)

The problem here is that this exotic curiosity is no longer at a safe, textual, anthropological distance, but is now loose in London—the armchair anthropologist is no longer safe in his armchair.[15] Holmes must capture and contain him, if not drive him away, in order to preserve the safety, purity, and integrity of both individual Londoners and the national body.

With Holmes's discovery of this naked footprint in the Norwood attic, Doyle echoes and rewrites perhaps the most famous moment in the literature of British imperialism—Robinson Crusoe's discovery of "the print of a man's naked foot" on the beach. Holmes and Crusoe have many similarities as resourcefully heroic middle-class figures. They have kindred reactions to their respective savage footprints. Like Holmes's uncharacteristic remark that something "hellish" is afoot, Crusoe also assumes that he has been visited by the devil. After dismissing this idea, his thoughts turn to cannibals, whom he fears will invade his island "in greater numbers, and devour [him]," or, at the very least, steal his goods. Crusoe's thoughts travel from devil to cannibal to thief.[16] Like the Crusoe scene, Holmes's discovery of the footprint in the attic is an important allegorical moment for the British imagination. Through Holmes, Britons discover that they are not alone on their island. However, in this case, the island is not a mythically remote one but their own home. What differs in these two literary cases, separated by 170 years, is the distance between a nation engaged in imperial conquest and one in which there is a dawning awareness of the possibility of a reconquest, not *by* the nation, but *of* it. At one level, *The Sign of Four* is a prophetic nightmare of decolonization imagined as reverse colonization and savage vengeance by the vanquished.[17]

Like the drug plot, the cannibal plot presents an allegorically violent threat to individual and national integrity. As in the case of the degenerate Thaddeus Sholto, the drug masters its slave from within. It is an insidious element representing medicine and poison, pleasure and pain, life and death. Through it, the body becomes a site of struggle and discord, rather than the instrument of an independent, harmonious, and unified individual will. It arouses, excites, and nurtures a greedy craving for more. It is a dependent parasite that threatens to reverse the relationship between parasite and host. Typically, the cannibal presents a different threat than insidious invasion and dependence; the cannibal threatens to destroy the object from without by bodily engulfment and incorporation. In this tale, the cannibal poses these external threats, but also functions like the internally savage drug such as cocaine or poison. Read as a figure in an imperial allegory, the cannibal represents the threat of being eaten from within, the consumption of the consumer by the consumed. The cannibal plot and drug plots introduce Holmes to a pleasurable struggle that he cannot resist and whose attractiveness depends on an uncertainty over several outcomes—to control or be controlled, to kill or be killed, to subject or be subjected, to assimilate or be assimilated, to feast or be feasted upon, and, finally, if we think about the cannibal and cocaine as allegorical figures for the commodity, to consume or be consumed by.

Holmes eventually locates Jonathan Small and his cannibal companion Tonga and learns of their plan to escape London with the treasure. In the ensuing chase on the Thames, we can see how Holmes functions as an imperialist regulator; that is, he is not an antiimperial isolationist (like Watson) interested in maintaining British purity and separation, but rather one who wants to ensure a smooth (nonviolent) exchange between Britain and its colonies. If Holmes were an isolationist, he would probably be more than happy to let them go. Although this metropolitan cultural encounter is potentially life-threatening, Holmes goes out of his way to ensure that the colonial is properly studied and assimilated. In the case of the treasure, he must ensure that the wealth stays in England and does not return to its point of origin. And in regard to the cannibal, he is also more interested in capturing, controlling, and, perhaps, studying him than sending him back to the Andaman Islands. For he is a real-life curiosity unlike the textual ones from whom Holmes must normally get his kicks.

The encounter between Holmes and the cannibal repeats, of course with a far more satisfactory outcome (at least for Englishmen), the previous encounter in which the savage dart penetrated the flesh of Bartholomew and killed him. In this scene, Holmes "straightens out" the colonial relations of English mastery and colonial subjection. When the two boats close upon each other, the heroes get their first glimpse of the savage. At first, he appears as "a dark mass, which looked like a Newfoundland dog." Then, he moves and straightens himself erect "into a little black man" (177). As the narrative brings us closer, the creature moves easily up the evolutionary scale from incomprehensible "mass" to animal (dog), then from animal to human. Such a quick transcendence of one's origins is clearly, for Doyle, a destabilizing threat. In a game of evolutionary and cultural King-of-the-Hill, he must be metaphorically put back in his place.

As they approach the fleeing aborigine, he fires one of his poison darts; it misses its mark, and in retaliation Holmes and Watson accurately fire off pistol shots. The "little black man" collapses into the stream and disappears unrepentant amid the swirling waters. Watson catches what he describes as a final "glimpse of his venomous, menacing eyes" (178), as if even the gaze of the dead savage can infect its beholder with a poisonous or contaminating venom. In the Granada Television version of *The Sign,* the camera lingers on the face of the savage in the water—lingering as Watson does in the novella's opening scene. On the one hand, the camera fixes the gaze of the audience on the cannibal, where he can be empirically observed; yet on the other, this is a scene in which the gaze is reversed and we become, frighteningly, the object of this man suddenly revealed as a subject.

Small and the chest of treasure are recaptured and (British) harmony is seemingly restored. Yet as the narrative leaves the scene of this violence, the unsatisfied eyes of the heroes scan the river banks for one last glimpse of the departed Andaman Islander. Like the cocaine, he is not only a danger that must be brought under control, but also a sight of lingering fascination—a feast for the eyes of Watson and, by extension, Doyle's readers. Here, we again see Watson-the-physician, who knows of the cannibal's threat to national and bodily health, at odds with Watson-the-chronicler, for whom the cannibal is an attractively exotic spectacle. But unfortunately for Watson, the intractable cannibal's last act of resistance is to sink out of sight before the Englishmen can satisfy their hungry eyes. Watson narrates that "somewhere in the dark ooze at the bottom of the Thames lie the bones of that strange visitor to our shores" (179). With this twist of the plot, Doyle symbolically restores the unassimilated primitive visitor to his "true home" amidst the undifferentiated primal muck and evolutionary ooze. Yet this muck is a quintessentially English muck; it is the foundation of the Thames, that most symbolically English of rivers. Paradoxically, it is a fundamentally

English site that also provides the conduit to and from the rest of the world. Just as the Andaman savage is paradoxically both distant (a member of another race) and close (related to the English through evolutionary kinship), Thames mud is ambiguously here and there. According to this ideologically charged narrative, there are good savages, like Sholto's Hindu servant, who can be controlled and domesticated, and bad ones, like the aborigine, who refuse to submit, and who in his particular case can be relegated to the excretory sediment at the bottom of the stream flowing out of and into the heart of civilization.

The cannibal's end is followed by the tale of the convict, Jonathan Small, who explains his involvement with the cannibal and the treasure (which, in his final act of resistance, has been thrown into the river to join the cannibal Tonga). As the narrative moves forward beyond the solution of the crime, Small takes us back into history; his explanation connects the criminal violence of the recent past with another scene of colonial violence and guilt—the Mutiny of 1857. Like the returned convict Magwich in Dickens's *Great Expectations,* Small raises another threat of invasion—the return of colonial convicts or the criminally repressed.

As a young man, Small had left his provincial English town in order to serve in India. While swimming in the sacred Ganges, his leg is bitten off by a crocodile in what can be seen as cosmic justice for his desecration. Unfit for military service, Small becomes an overseer on an indigo plantation owned by an Englishman named Abel White, whose very name should put to rest any doubts that we are in the presence of a thinly disguised allegory. While Small served White, the Great Mutiny of 1857 breaks out. As Patrick Brantlinger has written, this event was the most significant and terrifying act of armed resistance by a colonized people in the nineteenth century. The Mutiny took such a hold on the British public imagination that, more than thirty years later, Doyle can still evoke its memory to play upon public fears. Small describes it as follows: "One month India lay as still and peaceful, to all appearance, as Surrey or Kent; the next day there were two hundred thousand black devils let loose, and the country was a perfect hell" (187). By juxtaposing a frightful vision of "hell" and "black devils" with the "peaceful" English countryside, Small imaginatively brings the Mutiny home.[18] That is, his description of the Mutiny explicitly invokes the ultimate horror hinted at by *The Sign of Four:* a whole nation of devil-like Tongas let loose in rural England. By raising the explicit specter of the Mutiny,

Small articulates the fear that has underwritten the cannibal plot. This fear is what necessitates a hero like Holmes to regulate the frontier town of London, the metropolitan point of entry. In trying to discover Tonga and Small, an incognito Holmes had spent days slinking about the docks of the Thames.[19]

Finding refuge from the Mutiny in the fort at Agra, Small is assigned the task of guarding a gate with the help of three loyal Sikhs. He recalls a frightful siege in which a small group of English are surrounded by the "tomtoms" and "yells and howls" of restless natives, "drunk with opium and bang" (189). Once again, Doyle's narrative associates ideas of rebellion and foreignness with narcotics. One night, Small is forced by his companions into a conspiracy to kill the representative of a base rajah who wants to hide and protect his treasure in the fort. With his life threatened, Small enters into the compact—the sign of four—that gives the novella its title. Small's loyalty, formerly pledged to Abel White, is now given over to the nonwhite Sikhs. The four carry out their plot but, because the corpse of their victim is discovered, they are sent to the Andaman prison colony for treasonous activity in a time of crisis. Here, Small suffers the ultimate indignity for an Englishman when he is placed under the whip of native guards. Seeing a chance for escape, he offers to disclose the treasure's whereabouts to the English officers (Sholto and Morstan) in return for his own freedom and that of his coconspirators. Sholto double-crosses everyone involved and escapes back to England with the treasure and builds his Pondicherry Lodge.

As the only white prisoner on the island, Small is eventually assigned a job in the infirmary dispensing drugs. And where there are drugs in Doyle's world, there will be cannibals not too far away. At the infirmary, Small nurses the cannibal Tonga, a native, back to health. Like a devoted dog, Tonga takes a fancy to Small, never leaves his side, and helps him escape the island. Eventually, the two find their way to England, where Small makes his living by displaying Tonga as a circus freak, meanwhile actively seeking out Sholto to get his due. He haunts Sholto, peering in at the window while he is on his deathbed and, eventually, kills Bartholomew and seizes the treasure that he feels is rightfully his.

Doyle resurrects fears of the Mutiny in order to show his audience that the event is not so far removed from their daily lives; a chain of events seen as originating in the colonial sphere can and does continue to play itself out on the streets of London, and even, as we see in the instance of Bartholomew's murder, is capable of invading the strongly

fortified domestic space of suburbia. As visitors from afar—both geographically and historically—Small and Tonga represent the return of
colonialism's repressed; they are twin representatives of a "New Mutiny." While the convict acts out of an injured sense of justice, Tonga
acts out of innate savagery and barbarism. Ideologically, he is the colonial subject who, because of his nature, will never be subjected. Far
from a curiosity piece, he is an always-present danger that must constantly be oppressed. But as such, he affords the heroes of English fiction, such as Holmes, ongoing opportunities for adventurous heroism
and displays of mastery. Tonga is a necessary evil. Just as the colonies
have formerly functioned as an imaginative field for the reproduction
of Britain, Doyle now constructs London as a site for the reproduction
of national identity.

   Like the cannibal and cocaine plots, the Mutiny tale and the treasure
plot explore Britain's colonial mission and its repercussions. In juxtaposing these different kinds of invasions and linking concerns about
bodily health and national security, as well as the integrity of the domestic sphere and the repercussions of colonial violence, *The Sign of Four*
raises several disturbing questions about Britain's increasing involvement with and dependence upon other cultures: Is colonialism worth
all the bother? Does it bring more harm than good? Has the attempt to
enrich the home opened the door to uninvited and unwelcome guests?
Is "their" retribution reasonable and just? And perhaps, most provocatively disturbing, are these life- and nation-threatening invasions what
the British really desire?

   While *The Sign of Four* is the uneasy sign of a future that includes a
more widespread colonial presence, in the final analysis, the Holmes
plots are not meant to scare but to reassure. The presence of the foreign in London and individual Londoners, whether as cannibal, cocaine,
or cultural style, may be a potential danger in some dystopian future,
but the foreign has yet to gain the upper hand. In fact, Holmes needs
the foreign to continuously reproduce and display his mastery; the constitutional crisis he brings on actually structures his desire to order and
put things aright. In the midst of the disruption caused by colonial
wealth, exotic new commodities, and even peoples, Doyle offers a hero
who will (and needs to) do the culture's dirty work. By so doing, his
narrative places a formulaic or "commonplace" frame around that
which threatens to rupture domestic security and stability.

   As I argued earlier, Doyle's Holmes tales are of course fantasies and, at least at the level of the cannibal plot, deal with the most extreme and exotic examples of foreign invasions. But since even these can be demonstrably contained (albeit imaginatively), the implication is that Britain can assimilate strange new peoples and commodities, sort out those who by their nature cannot be assimilated, and pursue "passing pleasures" with a degree of moderation that does not threaten "permanent weakness" to its "great powers." As such, the Sherlock Holmes tales rechannel paranoid protectionary fears about invasion into stimulating optimism about new kinds of expansionist consumer consumption and reassurances about Britain's continuing imperial mastery.

As my use of the term *paranoid* suggests, these are also stories that use the thematics of invasion to assuage a sense of imperial guilt and project the practice of violence and aggression as the desire of their colonial others. Finally, at all levels of this allegorical argument, from the commodity to the cannibal, we can read the popularity of the Holmes tales as a sign that a great many of Doyle's readers (and Britons in general) were neither cut-and-dry expansionists nor isolationists. Like Watson, they were concerned about threats to bodily integrity and national character (constitution), while at the same time they were voyeuristically drawn to the Holmesian experience of cultural mixing, whether in the face-to-face encounters or the highly mediated, yet eroticized, encounter of commodity consumption. As lived experience, politics and ideology are often a lot messier than social criticism would have one believe; and fiction—even, and perhaps especially, the genres of fantasy and romance—is often better suited as a vehicle to express that complexity. It is such a complicated ambivalence about Britain's colonial mission and the day-to-day experience of consuming new kinds of products whose histories were illegible that Doyle lends narrative form and the reassurance of ritual containment and mastery.

And yet, Holmes is only a fiction. So perhaps, after all, it is not strictly reassurance that readers were after, but, in addition, the exciting possibility that any reassuring containment of the other is only a fiction, too.

As we have seen in this reading of *The Sign of Four*, Holmes has two things within arm's reach that bring him great pleasure: cocaine and his bulky volume of anthropological knowledge. As I have argued, the two are interchangeable: they both stimulate his brain and alleviate his boredom with the commonplace. In the following section, I will place this narrative of cocaine and cannibals within a broader cultural framework—one that attends both to an important evolution in the mode of consuming empire in late-Victorian London and, at greater length, to one important metropolitan site of its consumption: Imre Kiralfy's Empire of India Exhibition at Earl's Court in 1895.

In her recent book *Imperial Leather*, Anne McClintock describes "an epochal shift . . . in the culture of imperialism" at the end of the nineteenth century. "This was the shift from *scientific racism*—embodied in anthropological, scientific and medical journals, travel writing and ethnographies—to what I call *commodity racism*. Commodity racism—in the specifically Victorian forms of advertising and photography, the imperial Expositions and the museum movement—converted the narrative of imperial Progress into mass-produced *consumer spectacles*" (McClintock's emphases).[20]

McClintock's distinction between two different forms of racism, distinguished by their forms of discursive representation, offer a number of insights on Doyle's novella. For one, the distinction is helpful for helping us to note the shift between the imperial text Holmes reads, a "bulky volume" full of thick, ethnographic description, and the one Watson supposedly writes, a romance novella called *The Sign of Four*. In Doyle's novella, we can note how imperial matters gravitate from the sphere of experts (whether professionals or gentleman amateurs) to the sphere of an emerging and increasingly commodified popular culture. Or, to put this another way, we can use the novella to see how empire was no longer being consumed in the study, but was now being bought up avidly by the middle classes and read on the trains that took them to and from suburbia.[21] In addition to reading the transition from empire as arcane science to a much more widespread form of popular entertainment, McClintock's definition also helps us to see the increasing significance of empire as an expanding market of consumables. For Holmes, imperial pleasure is to be found in the cocaine as well as the scholarly tome. In this respect, we can see Holmes as a transitional imperialist, with one foot firmly ensconced in an older, more respectable science, and the other in a proliferating world of imperial commodities.

In seeing Holmes and *The Sign of Four* as historically situated at a moment of shift between regimes of imperial consumption, I want to conclude this chapter by describing changes in another important form of imperial representation, that of the metropolitan spectacle. This form undergoes an important change between 1886 and 1895, the respective dates of the Colonial and Indian Exhibition at South Kensington and

Imre Kiralfy's Empire of India Exhibition at Earl's Court. Published between these two events, Doyle's novella is a cultural artifact closer to Kiralfy's spectacle, and it is his exhibition that will be my focus.

At the heart of Kiralfy's exhibition was "The Indian City," a presentation of the subcontinent as a happy, traditional, and self-contained village, that today would rate as Disneyesque. In it, the multiple regions, economies, and traditions of India were condensed into a series of urban locales, inhabited by specially imported craftsmen, entertainers, wooden buildings, cattle, and elephants. At Earl's Court, one strolled through the Maidan and Shakra Gates, down Bombay Street, Hyderabad Street, Lucknow Street, and Delhi Street, into Lahore Square, and, at the very core of this "Indian City," through a taxidermic exhibit called the Jungle. The Indian City provided a spatial analogue that Londoners could visit in conjunction with Kiralfy's lavish spectacle play *India*. The play offered a historical condensation of subcontinental history that ideologically glorified Britain's imperial interventions. Unlike earlier colonial and imperial exhibitions, the Earl's Court venture was primarily commercial and concerned with entertainment, not education or a government-sponsored ideological message.[22] As one contemporary noted, "It will perhaps be asked if any one learns much, or even a little, from these exhibitions. It does not answer the question, but there is very small doubt that not one in a thousand goes to Earl's Court to get knowledge or information . . . they go to Earl's Court to be amused, to see the Show, to talk, to hear the music, to flirt, to 'pick something up' (not necessarily information)."[23]

Kiralfy's urban landscape, not unlike Doyle's novella, held out the promise of an imperialism of pleasure. It was a knowable, walkable, sanitized version of India, free of visible exploitation, poverty, filth, and conflict. It also offered a vision of the "city" that was markedly unlike London, the city inhabited by Kiralfy's audience; in fact, Kiralfy's city was more un-London than it was authentically Indian. Imre Kiralfy was a disciple of P. T. Barnum.[24] He evolved out of the tradition of entertainment, theater, and spectacle. In the early 1890s, he staged a lavish spectacle at the Olympia Theatre, *Venice, the Bride of the Sea,* with a concurrent Venice exhibition. In 1893, he produced the spectacle *America* at the Columbian Exhibition in Chicago. Unlike earlier organizers of exhibitions at the Crystal Palace or South Kensington, Kiralfy sought not to educate or ideologically demonstrate Britain's industrial prowess and the subordinate role of his colonies. His goal, simply, was to make money. His relationships with governments in London and India were strained, though his exhibition tried to maintain a veneer of official sanction and cooperation.

In 1894, Kiralfy bought the exhibition grounds at Earl's Court, comprised of three parcels of land sandwiched among the confluence of the Midland Railway, the West London Railway, and the District Railway. He demolished temporary buildings built in 1887, replacing them "with permanent buildings in such a manner as to render them amenable to transformation from year to year."[25] Kiralfy's goal was Exhibition for Exhibition's sake. The formal structure would remain, but the content would change from year to year. While Kiralfy's architectural choices were Indian and vaguely oriental, the more important model for his exhibition grounds was the exhibition grounds at Chicago. Thus, while one might be tempted to see Kiralfy as engaged as reconfiguring India in London, he was, to an even greater extent, reproducing Chicago in London—much as the various Chinatowns around the world today are as much reproductions of a San Francisco neighborhood as they are simulacra of any Chinese locale.

India seemed the obvious choice to lead off the parade of an endless succession of exhibitions: "In looking about for the subject of the first Exhibition, none seemed to me to be more fitting than that of THE VAST EMPIRE OF INDIA which forms so important a part of the English Possessions. The beauty of its Oriental architecture, the warmth of its colouring, the picturesque costuming of its peoples, the skill of its artisans, and the interest with which its history is regarded by Englishmen were reasons for my selection of India for my initial effort."[26] Kiralfy's marketing decision reveals why it would be wrong or, at the very least, too limited to see his exhibition as doing clear-cut, uncomplicated, jingoist cultural work. His Indian City is not simply about inculcating an opposition between Western civilization and Eastern underdevelopment. Rather, his representation of India is about the aesthetic pleasures of imperialism that we saw in Sholto's suburban apartment—"beauty," "colouring," "picturesque costuming," and "skilled" artisans—and not the sadistic pleasure of military domination or the egoistic pleasure of cultural domination. If there was a contrast at Earl's Court, it was surely not one that favored England.[27]

As Britain turned its attention toward India, it was confronted by an agglomeration of cultures, peoples, religions, climates, languages, and traditions. We can see the complex diversity that India presented to outsiders in the catalogue for the scientifically oriented 1886 Colonial and Indian Exhibition. There, the organization of the Ethnology Court included separate exhibits for Burma, Assam, Bengal, Chutia Nagpur, Orissa, Hill Tribes (North), Hill Tribes (East), Bombay, Madras, Rajputna, Central India, Central Provinces, Mysore, Coorg, Hyderabad, North-West Provinces, Nepal, and Punjab.[28] This emphasis on regional division and discrete compartmentalization (in 1886) contrasts markedly with Kiralfy's Indian City (in 1895). With the latter, the spatial emphasis was on flow; one seamlessly moved from Bombay Street into Lucknow Street or into Delhi Street and Lahore Square. The experience of the visitor at Kiralfy's exhibition is of India as a pleasurably homogenized unity. This contrasts with the earlier exhibition which, in good classificatory form, had stressed the discreteness of each particular region. At the same exhibition, the Art Ware Courts were divided into an even larger number of sections. Imagined in terms of regional and economic taxonomies, India was simply too complicated for all but the committed specialist.

In order to lend his Indian City verisimilitude, Kiralfy had imported people from India, including eighty-five craftsmen and more than one hundred entertainers (there were also cattle, elephants, and camels to walk the streets).[29] Despite this attempt to present authenticity, this was, by any stretch of the imagination, a strange sight. To begin, more than one-half of the imported Indians were entertainers—an array of jugglers, snake charmers, street performers, magicians, and animal trainers—who produced nothing, other than a show. If taken as representative, the image of India communicated here was a carefree one whose primary business was quaint entertainment. While the remaining imported laborers produced things, they were not very representative of the forms of labor or modes of production that were increasingly occupying India and Indians. The following craftsmen are noted in the exhibition catalog: a brassfounder, glassworkers, potters, gold- and silversmiths, iron workers, a puggree (or turban) maker, potter painters, a tailor, a brass moulder, a shoemaker, and carpet weavers.[30] Here, the emphasis is not on agriculture, raw materials, or manufacturing but on crafts. The objects are not mass-produced, nor are the laborers specialists. We seem to be as much in the presence of the arts and crafts medieval village of William Morris as we are in India.

This depiction of India contrasts with the presentation of the Economic Courts at the 1886 Exhibition. These had emphasized India's imperial importance as a source of raw materials such as cotton, jute, foodstuffs, indigo, dyes, and timbers.[31] Kiralfy's India is a place of nostalgia for lost ways of life and modes of production. It is in no way representative of a place fully integrated into a large-scale imperial and industrial economy. It is seen as the antidote to civilization rather than British industry's source of cheap raw materials, exploited labor, and captive market. In this sense, it is worth remarking on the Indian City's sharp boundedness. Kiralfy does not offer the vision of a city connected to a world market, but rather the fantasy of a city or community that is self-sufficient and other.

Placed alongside each other, Doyle's novella and Kiralfy's spectacle point to new pleasurable possibilities for the consumption of empire within metropolitan London. Like Thaddeus Sholto's inner sanctum or Pondicherry Lodge itself, Kiralfy's Indian City attempts to introduce the foreign as an antidote to the sterility of modern London. And, just as Holmes, Watson, and Doyle's readers are able to enter and view the Sholtos' spectacles, Londoners found their passage to India at Earl's Court. In 1890, there were still crime, danger, decadence, and death associated with this incursion of India into suburban London. But, five short years later at the Indian City at Earl's Court, empire was a less-dangerous place "to be amused, to see the Show, to talk, to hear the music, to flirt, to 'pick something up.'" The empire in London was becoming a venue open to new and increasingly large audiences. Not everyone could be Sherlock Holmes or go off to India for an exotically dangerous adventure. But just about anyone in the metropolis could consume them.

CHAPTER FOUR

COLONIZING THE URBAN JUNGLE

General Booth's *In Darkest England and the Way Out*

For Doyle, London had come to be imagined as a new frontier, threatened, energized, and eroticized by both real and fantastic penetrations of the national borders. Sherlock Holmes sent the cannibal invader Tonga back to the primal ooze in the spring of 1890, making London and, by extension, England safe from foreign invaders. Later in that same year, metropolitan readers were again confronted by a claim that the metropolis had become a site for imperial work. In October, General William Booth, the founder and charismatic leader of the Salvation Army, published his tale of the urban jungle, *In Darkest England and the Way Out*. Booth warned that the presence of savages in London was much more pervasive than the dilettantish aesthete, the cocaine user, or the random Gothic cannibal. In contrast to the xenophobic scaremongering and romantic exoticism of Doyle's plots, Booth imagined London's East End as an urban jungle that signified physical and spiritual decay, deterioration, and degeneration—a once-lovely garden that had gone to seed.

In late-Victorian London, the East End has a special relationship to the middle- and upper-class West Enders and suburbanites who were Booth's primary audience. While it is very close to home geographically —as Booth reminds, it is "a very short walk from their own dwellings"[1]—it is extremely different and remote experientially. According to Gareth Stedman Jones,

> In the course of the nineteenth century, the social distance between rich and poor expressed itself in an ever sharper geographical segregation of the city. Merchants and employers no longer lived above their places of work. The old methods of social control based on the model of the squire, the parson, face to face relations, deference, and paternalism, found less and less reflection in the urban reality. Vast tracts of working-class housing were left to themselves, virtually bereft of any contact with authority except in the form of the policeman or the bailiff. The poor districts became an immense terra incognita periodically mapped

out by intrepid missionaries and explorers who catered to an insatiable demand for travellers' tales.[2]

Such urban travelers' tales had been "an insatiable demand" since at least the late-1860s and the narratives of James Greenwood;[3] 1870 was also the date of the "terra incognita" passage discussed in chapter 1.[4] While it is certainly true that these tales reflected the experiential gap between the classes described by Jones, I would emphasize that the use of this narrative form greatly contributed to *reproducing* and *widening* the imaginative distance between the classes. Certainly, by 1890 no Londoner needed to be informed of danger and poverty in the East End. This chapter will argue that Booth's narrative extends an imaginative distance already in place, and in so doing materially contributes to the real distance between rich and poor. Earlier writers—Engels, Dickens, Mayhew, Greenwood, Sims—prefigure Booth's figuration of the East End as an imperial space.[5] But none of them use an imperial metaphorics as their guiding trope. In calling attention to "Darkest London," Booth is assured of a large audience comprised of those concerned with the barbarians already within the gates. Yet because the daily lives of West Enders provided little or no contact with the urban poor, they could understand these people and their world only through the mediation of something familiar. General Booth discovered the key metaphor that allowed him to translate the East End—Africa.[6]

In calling for a modern, metropolitan "mission," Booth reimagines the urban poor as African natives and the East End as a jungle. In his mind's eye, the primitively dark environment has transformed the London working- and nonworking classes into a collection of savagely primitive tribes in need of Christian salvation. Thus, while "primitives" like Doyle's Tonga were relatively scarce in London of the 1890s, the city and its inhabitants were discursively Africanized by the very movement (General Booth's Salvation Army) that was working so hard and, largely, with the best intentions to alleviate their suffering and to integrate them fully into modern civilization. Although Booth cringes at the brutalization of the East Enders, his descriptions actually function to further instantiate their status as brutes. When Africans and other postcolonial peoples arrive in London in the twentieth century, a jungle of the imagination, one partially authored by General Booth, was waiting to receive them.

In 1890, London readers were infatuated with Henry Stanley's recently published *In Darkest Africa, or the Quest, Rescue, and Retreat of Emin Pasha, Governor of Equatoria.* This adventure narrative recounts Stanley's last African expedition of 1886–89 to rescue the governor of Equatoria Province in southern Sudan. Emin Pasha was beleaguered and under attack by the same Mahdists who had defeated General Gordon at Khartoum; suddenly, the unknown Emin and his domain became charged with highly patriotic significance—to save him from defeat would mollify the shame and embarrassment Britons felt for their recent failure to aid General Gordon. When approached, the famous explorer Henry Stanley eagerly grabbed at the job. It took him more than two years to lead an expedition through the heart of "Darkest Africa." When his account appeared in 1890, it was an immediate best-seller.[7]

One could see Booth's allusion to Stanley as a matter of exploiting or capitalizing on Stanley's already popular title. But, as Herman Ausubel has argued, Booth had "little need to exploit a catchy title" because he was already a "prominent and controversial figure" in late-Victorian London. Ausubel adds that "any volume that bore his name was likely to have a wide sale."[8] While Booth's reputation and his culture's interest in issues of social reform are indisputable and, thus, he may have had "little need" to exploit Stanley's title, he did in fact exploit Stanley's rhetoric and this appropriation did much more than sell a few extra books. Booth's appropriation of Stanley goes much deeper than marketing concerns. Rather, as Robert Sandall points out in his *History of the Salvation Army,* "[f]rom the day General William Booth's famous book appeared its title and contents enriched the English language giving new significance to familiar words."[9] When Booth published the results of his explorations among the urban poor and his plans for their conversion and salvation, he chose a title that also invoked Stanley's key themes of "darkness," "quest," and "rescue." While Booth was undoubtedly a master fund-raiser and popularizer of his religious crusade, it would be wrong to see the "Darkest England" metaphor as a mere matter of marketing. As we shall see, its importance runs much deeper.

To Booth's mind, Stanley presented a "terrible picture, and one that has engraved itself deep on the heart of civilization" (18). Visions of Africa like Stanley's aroused pity and indignation in the hearts of civilized Britons, who throughout the nineteenth century funded explorers and missionaries who ventured into the "Lost Continent." In telling us that these visions have been deeply "engraved" on civilized hearts, Booth tells his reader not to expect anything new. He is invoking an already familiar picture. Yet, Booth's comment also unwittingly suggests that, with the publication of *In Darkest England,* this "terrible picture" of Stanley will become indelibly "engraved" on London, the symbolic "heart of civilization." After Booth, to imagine or look at certain sections of London will be to see that "terrible" portrait of Africa that Booth engraves and labels Darkest England.

Although General Booth seems naive about his role in inventing Darkest England, he is not naive about the congruence he sees between the African and urban jungles. His vision is detailed and carefully studied. Stanley's narrative is a catalyst that inspires and shapes his vision of London. Booth recalls that "while brooding over the awful presentation of life as it exists in the vast African forest, it seemed only too vivid a picture of many parts of our own land. As there is a darkest Africa is there not also a darkest England? Civilization, which can breed its own barbarians, does it not also breed its own pygmies? May we not find a parallel at our own doors, and discover within a stone's throw of our cathedrals and palaces similar horrors to those that Stanley has found existing in the great Equatorial forest?" (18) Booth must discover and articulate "parallel" and "similar horrors" before he can convince his readers to join his new crusade or holy war. In constructing his new urban imperialism, Booth is extremely adept with metaphors. In addition to the Africanization of the East End and its inhabitants, the name that Booth gives his organization—the Salvation Army—conjoins the twin arms of previous European imperial adventures: the Christian missionary and the conquering soldier. Booth found a twin in Darkest England for everything that Stanley found in Darkest Africa. He writes that "the more the mind dwells upon the subject, the closer the analogy appears" (18); his narrative encourages London eyes to dwell upon the subject, until the two jungles, African and metropolitan, dissolve into a single vision.

The would-be missionary hero must first convince his audience that his "natives" live in physical and spiritual darkness ("Darkness" is the title of part 1 of Booth's book, a darkness that he paradoxically illuminates and produces simultaneously) and that they cannot escape if left alone. Only then can he put forward his plan for rescue or deliverance ("Deliverance" is the title of part 2). Part 1 details the persons who inhabit the East End and their living conditions. Booth builds his case by interweaving long passages from Stanley, statistics, reports published by the government and philanthropic organizations, reports by his "soldiers" and "officers," and, most importantly, his own personal anecdotes and observations. The chapter titles provide a rich sense of both the groups he documents and his representations of them: "The Submerged Tenth," "The Homeless," "The Out-of-Works," "On the Verge of the Abyss," "The Vicious," "The Criminals," "The Children of the Lost," and "Is There No Help?"

While all of these chapters powerfully convey Booth's vision of East End life, the most memorable chapter is his discussion of Stanley that frames his project and articulates his guiding metaphor. Booth's selective reading of *In Darkest Africa* in chapter 1 ("Why Darkest England?"), depends upon five key analogies that imaginatively fuse Stanley's Africa and Booth's East End into a single landscape. These include the following four explicit analogies: (1) the interminability, immensity, and inevitability experienced by dwellers (Booth obsessively refers to them as "denizens") in both the jungle and the slum; (2) African savages and the London poor; (3) Stanley's native assistants and Booth's reformed Christian soldiers; and (4) Arab slave traders and those businessmen—particularly publicans—who prey upon the urban poor.

Underlying these explicit analogies, there is an implicit one that links General Booth to Stanley himself. For in invoking Stanley's story to frame his "heroic" urban Christian crusade, Booth speaks as Stanley and becomes, as it were, the "Urban Stanley." He is the heroic adventurer in the city who is explorer, missionary, soldier, and reporter all rolled into one. As explorer, he goes into the interminable heart of darkness; as missionary, he converts and Christianizes the natives; as soldier, he battles and conquers the enemy; and as reporter, he tells about his journey and exploits and seeks money for future ventures. With Booth's publication of *In Darkest England,* the imperial plot of salvation, for both heathen savages and Christian heroes, comes home to a London rendered fertile for the colonizing missionary and the conquering hero.

First, Booth focuses on Stanley's evocation of the natural environment as a force and foe worthy to test the courage and patience of the European explorer.

> In all that spirited narrative of heroic endeavor, nothing has so much
> impressed the imagination as his description of the immense forest,

which offered an almost impenetrable barrier to his advance. The intrepid explorer, in his own phrase, "marched, tore, ploughed, and cut his way for one hundred and sixty days through this inner womb of the true tropical forest." The mind of man with difficulty endeavors to realize the immensity of wooded wilderness, covering a territory half as large again as the whole of France, where the rays of the sun never penetrate, where in the dark, dank air, filled with the steam of the heated morass, human beings dwarfed into pygmies and brutalized into cannibals lurk and live and die. Mr. Stanley vainly endeavors to bring home to us the full horror of that awful gloom. (15)

Stanley's jungle is barely penetrable by humans, either physically or epistemologically. It defies representation both for the reader who "with difficulty endeavors to realize" its size and for Stanley who "vainly endeavors to bring home to us the full horror of that awful gloom." It is a hot, damp, sunless, feminine place (an "inner womb") of masculine "heroic endeavor." Stanley's depiction of the jungle as the incarnation of a feminine, malevolent Nature prefigures Conrad's vision of the jungle as an evil, feminine "heart of darkness" in which conquering European imperialists can test themselves.[10] As a site of male "heroic endeavor," the darker and more sinister the jungle is made to appear, the more exalted is the "intrepid explorer" who survives the experience.

Although Booth reminds us that he is only pursuing an analogy (that "becomes wearisome when it is pressed too far"), he cannot seem to let it go. For Darkest England is not simply Booth's translator's key that mediates between him and his audience. It is also an Africanist vision of the world that defines his purpose and affords him pleasure by structuring a vision of East London as the terrain for his own "heroic endeavor." Thus, for Booth, the East End is not a community built by people or the outcome of economic exploitation as a Marxist reading would have it. Instead, it is a primitively natural place of rampant vegetation—hot, steamy, dark, and infested with disease. He imagines it as a dystopian state of nature that requires human intervention to either cultivate it or clear it to the ground and start over.

> The Equatorial Forest traversed by Stanley resembles that Darkest England of which I have to speak, alike in its vast extent—both stretch, in Stanley's phrase, "as far as from Plymouth to Peterhead"; its monotonous darkness, its malaria and its gloom, its dwarfish de-humanized inhabitants, the slavery to which they are subjected, their privations and their misery. That which sickens the stoutest heart, and causes many of our

bravest and best to fold their hands in despair, is the apparent impossibility of doing more than merely to peck at the outside of the endless tangle of monotonous undergrowth; to let light into it, to make a road clear through it, that shall not be immediately choked up by the ooze of the morass and the luxuriant parasitical growth of the forest—who dare hope for that? At present, alas, it would seem as though no one dares even to hope! It is the great Slough of Despond of our time. (19)

As this passage proceeds, Booth elides any sense of difference between Darkest England and the Equatorial Forest: "both stretch" a great distance; but, after the passage's first semicolon, *both* becomes a singular *it* that refers to both Africa and the East End. While either place could be the referent of the luxuriant *it,* the exact referent of *it* does not really matter any more for Booth. Instead, what is crucial here is not pinning down exactly which locale Booth is describing, but the fact that he is describing both with a singular pronoun and a singular vision. In his mind's eye, the two visions are one.

Significantly, Booth's ideas about what one might want to do in his Africanized East End include a plan "to make a road clear through it." It is precisely this solution or "Way Out" that urban historians point to as creating the horrific overcrowding of the East End in the first place. That is, Booth's solution to Darkest England is its very condition of possibility. The building of new roads and railways was, in Victorian London as in Paris, the primary justification for, and method of, slum clearance. According to Stedman Jones, "in its arbitrary and unplanned way demolition and commercial transformation of nineteenth century London must have involved a greater displacement of population than the rebuilding of Paris under Haussmann."[11] Stedman Jones cites the following specific projects: "Between 1836 and 1856, New Oxford Street was cut through St. Giles," Victoria Street through the rookeries of Westminster, Commercial Street through Whitechapel, and Farringdon Street, New Cannon Street, and New Victoria Street through the poorest and most densely populated parts of the city. It was intended that the new streets should remove as much slum housing as possible. The buildings of New Oxford Street displaced over 5,000 persons: it was estimated that the Farringdon Street clearances involved the displacement of up to 40,000."[12] More immediate to General Booth's moment are Charing Cross Road and Shaftesbury Avenue, built in 1877 and 1886, respectively. All of these projects contributed to increased overcrowding in London's East End.

Booth continues, "As in Africa, it is all trees, trees, trees with no other world conceivable; so is it here—it is all vice and poverty and crime" (18). For Booth, "vice and poverty and crime" are the natural growths of the urban jungle. He asks, "Who can battle against the ten thousand million trees?" The slum, like the jungle, is too immense a foe. The would-be adventurer and gardener can do no more than "peck at the outside of the endless tangle of monotonous undergrowth."[13] In the face of this natural adversary, human action is inconsequential. If one were to make any headway, it would be "immediately choked up again." The ever-expanding forest cannibalistically threatens to choke or engulf all who enter. Here, personal boundaries dissolve as one gets tangled up with everything else and loses individuality in the monotony. As "ooze" or "morass," it functions as a fearfully feminine opposite to more utopian visions of identity-loss like Virginia Woolf's sense of the "oceanic."[14] The urban jungle threatens not only to suck in those who venture into it, like Booth, but also as its endlessness suggests, it threatens to spread, engulf, and colonize those who remain outside it, like West End Londoners or, even, those who are fleeing to the new world of the suburbs. The "morass" and "ooze" are more shapeless versions of the London described by Doyle in *The Sign of Four* as "the monster tentacles which the great city was throwing out into the country."[15]

For most, the natural forest elicits despair and despondency. Booth's characterization of Darkest England also reveals how, in his mind, the two visions of jungle and slum overlap with a third—hell.[16] This infernal vision is also conjured by two of his chapter titles: "The Submerged Tenth" and "On the Verge of the Abyss." While Booth imagines himself as an African explorer and missionary who heroically tests himself against the "monotonous darkness" of dense vegetation, he is first and foremost a Christian colonizer, one who has visited Dante's dark wood and Bunyan's "Slough of Despond" and returned to tell of his adventures.[17] Many know the way in, but only he has a program for "the way out."

> And what a slough it is no man can gauge who has not waded therein, as some of us have done, up to the very neck for long years. Talk about Dante's hell, and all the horrors and cruelties of the torture-chamber of the lost: The man who walks with open eyes and with bleeding heart through the shambles of our civilisation needs no such fantastic images of the poet to teach him horror. Often and often, when I have seen the young and the poor and the helpless go down before my eyes into the

morass, trampled underfoot by beasts of prey in human shape that haunt these regions, it seemed as if God were no longer in His world, but that in His stead reigned a fiend, merciless as Hell, ruthless as the grave. (19)

The city, which had become Nature in the metaphorical link with Stanley, now undergoes another metaphorical change and becomes a malevolent hell. Before, Booth told us there was no light. Now, there is no God in the world. In battling Nature, the urban adventurer must wrestle not with social evils but metaphysical ones—the devil himself.[18]

In addition to Africanizing, naturalizing, and demonizing the physical environment of the East End, Booth of course also turns his Christian gaze on its natives. Booth's most important analogy is between the primitive African savages and poor Londoners. Again, it is important to insist that this linkage is not a new one; it is at least as old as Mayhew's work in the 1850s. However, Booth, by deploying Stanley's rhetoric to the full, extends the metaphor to a degree far in excess of Mayhew. In linking these two groups, he fuses two Victorian master narratives—natural selection and socialism[19]—and further instantiates the discourse of hybridized urban primitives. Booth focuses our attention on Stanley's African natives as Nature's passive victims; they are "human beings dwarfed into pygmies and brutalized into cannibals" by the wilderness itself. They are the victims and the creations of the morass in which they live and die.

Like a naturalist, Booth divides the "denizens" of Stanley's jungle into two "kinds." The first is "a very degraded specimen with ferret-like eyes, close-set nose, more nearly approaching the baboon than was supposed to be possible, but very human" (17). Members of the second "tribe" are practically the opposite of the first. They are "very handsome, with frank open innocent features, very prepossessing. They are quick and intelligent, capable of deep affection and gratitude, showing remarkable industry and patience." These two categories mimic conventional divisions of African natives and other primitive peoples into extreme species of beast-like brutes or noble savages. Booth's two types recall the different personality traits of Doyle's Tonga, a fierce, morose cannibal who, dog-like, was also capable of great loyalty and affection for his master. They also resemble the late-Victorian philanthropic distinction between the "deserving" and "undeserving" poor. In Darkest England, Booth discovers the twins of these African savage-types. "The two tribes of savages, the human baboon and the handsome dwarf, who will not speak lest it impede him in his task, may be accepted as the two varieties who are continually present with us—the vicious lazy lout, and the toiling slave" (18). Booth's analogy works all the more effectively because of its subtlety; not only does he find resemblances between Africans and East Enders, but also a mirror image of the differentiated subspecies articulated by Stanley.

These two types allow Booth to tell different stories about the urban jungle dwellers and to play two different roles: the brave warrior and the compassionate savior. The "degraded specimen" functions as a sign of the urban jungle's malevolence. Its qualities—"ferret-like" and "approaching the baboon"—render it an animal and in need of civilization's humanizing work. Though Booth is careful to point out that this type is "very human," one senses from the description that it is the more bestial and requires a great deal more humanization. Booth's depiction is intended, one can guess, to arouse fear in Booth's affluent audience. Like Tonga, the urban "vicious lazy lout" is a wild animal on the loose; something must be done to contain it.

The second type allows Booth to tell a story more clearly concerned with victimization. Whereas the first animalistic type seems appropriate to the jungle, this second type seems pathetically out of place. For Booth, their "features" indicate intelligence, industry, affection, and patience. This type needs to be rescued from its degrading environment and the baboon-like slum dwellers. One can imagine Booth sees this as a category of those who have slipped into the "slough" or gotten lost in the jungle rather than as creatures who have arisen from the depths of the morass. This division allows Booth to sidestep debates about whether poverty is metaphysical—divinely ordained or natural—or social. In giving us some specimens who seem to be at home and some who seem to be captive, Booth leaves room for both sides of the argument.

In addition to reading the primitivized bodies of the poor as clues to generalizable character traits, Booth reminds us that Stanley's natives are also the jungle's moral and spiritual victims. For them, the whole world is jungle darkness. "The denizens of this region are filled with a conviction that the forest is endless—interminable. In vain did Mr. Stanley and his companions endeavor to convince them that outside the dreary wood were to be found sunlight, pasturage and peaceful meadows" (15). The endlessness plants in the minds of its inhabitants a sense that their world is the only world; they can imagine no alternative, especially the English countryside that Stanley proposes. The Africans view Stanley's attempts to convince them of an alternative world as strangely quaint: "They replied in a manner that seemed to imply that we must be strange creatures to suppose that it would be possible for any world to exist save their illimitable forest" (16). In addition to this imaginative impoverishment, the jungle dwellers suffer from spiritual impoverishment, and this distresses Booth most of all. Knowing no alternative, they can neither despair nor hope for a better life. Spiritually, they are even worse off than Stanley's native bearers, who lose faith that they will ever find their way out of the jungle again. For the Christian Booth, at least the bearers know that there is a better life in the next world.

Likewise, the urban natives are mentally and spiritually impoverished: "They, too, have lost all faith of life being other than it is and has been. As in Africa, it is all vice and poverty and crime. To many, the world is all a slum, with the Workhouse as an intermediate purgatory before the grave" (18). Like Stanley's Africans, Booth believes that his natives can imagine no alternatives. His characterization of them as a people without history belies the fact that many residents of the East End, especially those chronically homeless or unemployed, were recent immigrants from either the countryside or abroad. Although he wants us to believe they can imagine no alternative, many of them can remember the rural impoverishment that drove them to the city. Even though the horrors of their present in the urban jungle may exceed those they knew before, clearly the countryside is not, for them, the romantic utopia envisioned by Booth in his plan for their "Deliverance."

In addition to adopting the Stanleyesque mission of clearing roads through the wilderness and pathways out of it, Booth must compel his natives to travel those roads. He believes that the inhabitants of the urban jungle "are in many cases so degraded, so hopeless, [and] so utterly desperate" that they will be unwilling to deliver themselves. Like the Stanley who framed his mission in terms of "rescue," Booth must rescue his natives and drag them into the light; one of his corps of soldiers was known as the London Rescue Brigade. This group walked the city streets at night on "raids" during which they "captured" lost souls and brought them into Salvation Army shelters. There, they provided nourishment and shelter while, at the same time, trying to convert them. "It is necessary," Booth writes, "to organize rescue expeditions to free the miserable wanderers from their captivity, and bring them out into the larger liberty and the fuller life" (164).

While the goal was "liberty" and a "fuller life," the rhetoric of "raids" and "capturing" lost souls suggests Booth's kinship to the imperial project (including its least noble aspect, the slave trade). His zealous Christian acquisitiveness is also demonstrated by his mania for numbers and statistics: he compiles charts of "ghastly figures" (29–30); he sizes up "three millions as representing the total strength of the destitute army (31);[20] he includes an appendix detailing "The Position of Our Forces: October, 1890" (299). At times, *In Darkest England* reads like a missionary balance sheet or shareholder report intended to woo investors of both economic and spiritual capital to a new and promising market. Which, of course, it was.

Not only the "denizens" of the East End have their counterparts in Darkest Africa; the equivalent of Booth's army of social reformers can be seen there, too. Stanley's expedition, comprised mostly of Africans who had been recruited as guides, began as an optimistic group:

> "We entered the forest," says Mr. Stanley, "with great confidence; forty pioneers in front with axes and bill hooks to clear a path through the obstructions, praying that God and good fortune would lead us." But before the conviction of the forest dwellers that the forest was without end, hope faded out of the hearts of the natives of Stanley's company. The men became sodden with despair, preaching was useless to move their brooding sullenness, their morbid gloom.
>
> "The little religion they knew was nothing more than legendary lore, and in their memories there dimly floated a story of a land which grew darker and darker as one travelled towards the end of the earth and drew nearer to the place where a great serpent lay supine and coiled round the world." (16)

Stanley's natives have been exposed to religion and Western ways, but when they are back in the interminable forest they slip back into their old ways and believe their old myths. Eventually, the Zanzibari guides leave the expedition. Stanley imagines that they "wander and stray in the dark mazes of the woods, hopelessly lost" and that some will soon be "carved for the cannibal feast" (16–17). Only Stanley (Booth's Stanley) can resist the "sullenness" and "gloom" produced by the forest. He rallies the weak of heart.

In Booth's vision of Darkest England, these native assistants have their doubles among the Salvation Army's convert-soldiers. "And just as Mr. Stanley's Zanzibaris lost faith, and could only be induced to plod on in brooding sullenness of dull despair, so the most of our social reformers, no matter how cheerily they may have started off, with forty pioneers swinging blithely their axes as they force their way into the wood, soon become depressed and despairing" (16). At an early stage of his missionary career, Booth had come "to realize the value of enlisting the aid of converted drunks, gamblers and so on, in addressing their own kind, and began to include their testimonies in [his] services."[21] Later, Catherine Booth would argue that the work of conversion was best carried out "by people of their own class, who would go after them in their own resorts, who would speak to them in a language they understood, and reach them by means suited to their own tastes."[22] The ranks of his army are filled with religious converts for whom there is always the danger of regression when they reenter the urban jungle from which they earlier were saved. For Booth, such backsliding breeds an omnipresent contagion of despair in the battle against an implacable foe.

Although Booth sees both jungles as primarily natural or divine foes, at times the evil takes on a human guise. In his reading of Stanley, he notes the presence of bad imperialists in the guise of the supposedly civilized Arab traders who have devastated the innocently passive primitive Africans. "Upon the pygmies and all the dwellers of the forest has descended a devastating visitation in the shape of ivory raiders of civilization. The race that wrote the Arabian nights, built Bagdad and Granada, and invented Algebra, sends forth men with the hunger for gold in their hearts, and Enfield muskets in their hands, to plunder and slay. They exploit the domestic affections of the forest dwellers in order to strip them of all they possess in the world" (17).

Booth wholeheartedly buys Stanley's depiction of imperialism in Africa. In Stanley's narrative, the Arabs are the ruthlessly imperial bad guys, driven solely by the profit motive, who contrast with the benevolent European explorers and missionaries. Perhaps, in his allusion to a "race" that has declined over time, from the writers of great literature and builders of great cities to capitalistic slave traders, Booth launches an attack against those imperialists who are driven by profit, not God. Stanley, the white European, is not the first intruder of a pristine, untouched natural community. Rather, he finds that the Arabs have come before to "plunder and slay." There is, of course, no mention of the more recent and more devastating European and American slave trade. Stanley represents the archetypal second-coming, the benevolent imperialist who will right the wrongs of previous imperialist exploitation and free the natives from domination and Arab captivity. This "better us than them" strategy of representation has been typical in twentieth-century imperialist discourse, from Conrad's indictment of Belgian imperialism in *Heart of Darkness* (contrasted implicitly with a kinder and gentler English version) to Cold War rhetoric about stopping Soviet expansion in the Third World. Against those who would oppose imperialism with a "live and let live" attitude, Stanley and Booth argue that it is too late—the Serpent is already in the Garden. Thus, imperial and missionary work, in both the African and urban jungles, announce themselves as secondary reform or correction.

For Booth, the urban jungle is also a Garden that has been poisoned by his powerful predecessors. In Darkest England, the bad imperialists wear many guises. The worst kind are the pub-keepers. "The ivory traders who brutally traffic in the unfortunate denizens of the forest glades, what are they but the publicans who flourish on the weakness of our poor?" (18). For Booth, alcohol is the unhealthy stream that nourishes the decay of the urban jungle: "As in Africa streams intersect the forest in every direction, so the gin-shop stands at every corner with its River of the Water of Death flowing seventeen hours out of the twenty-four for the destruction of the people" (21); "Darkest England has many more public-houses than the Forest of the Arumwi has rivers, of which Mr. Stanley sometimes had to cross three in half-an-hour" (32); "Many of our social evils, which overshadow the land like so many upas trees, would dwindle away and die if they were not constantly watered with strong drink" (55). Needless to say, alcohol was taboo among Salvationists.

Booth also sees an analogy to the African slave trade in widespread prostitution. "The lot of a negress in the Equatorial Forest is not, perhaps, a very happy one, but is it so very much worse than that of many a pretty orphan girl in our Christian capital?" (20). Both classes of women are prey for the hunters who would enslave them. Booth would have been highly aware of the proliferation of white slavery in the metropolis, for his organization was involved in the events of the Maiden Tribute scandal in 1885, at the center of which stood his ghostwriter W. T. Stead.[23] The Salvation Army offers shelter to those who escape their barbaric slave drivers. In this sense, Booth resembles Doyle's Jefferson Hope, who rescues Lucy Ferrier from the polygamous Mormon harem. In Booth's case, urban civilization is now measured by how well it treats its "helpless" women. Like the heroes of Rider Haggard's *King Solomon's Mines,* Booth and his soldiers come to the jungle to free captives from a ruthless class of publicans and white slave masters who are no better than cannibals and beasts of prey. They do not see themselves as the invaders of a barbaric urban culture, but rather as the rescuers and restorers of a nobly simple primitive culture.

The one analogy left unspoken by General Booth, but that seems to underlie the whole narrative purpose, links him to Stanley, the resolute, courageous African adventurer. But in adopting this role, Booth is not simply an egotist, for he invites others to adopt it as well. He tells his audience that each one of them is a potential Stanley with his or her Emin and heart of darkness only a stone's throw away. I say "his or her" because the Salvation Army was progressively open to enlisting women in its ranks. In fact, one key to its success was that it provided women a place to adopt the exotic imperialistic roles from which they had been excluded in Victorian adventure fiction. Booth proudly proclaims that "our Slum Brigade is composed of women. I have a hundred of them under my orders, young women for the most part, quartered all of them in outposts in the heart of the Devil's country. . . . Some are ladies born and bred, who have not been afraid to exchange the comfort of a West End drawing-room for service among the vilest of the vile. . . . They are at the front; they are at close quarters with the enemy" (166). The most famous female Salvationist was the fictional heroine of Shaw's play *Major Barbara* (1907); a more realistic fictional account of life for women in the Salvation Army is offered in Margaret Harkness's novel (discussed in chapter 1) *In Darkest London* (1891); in the world beyond literature, Booth's wife and daughters occupied high-ranking and highly visible positions within the Army. In reading Booth's boast that he has a hundred young women from all social classes "under [his] orders," one is tempted to join Booth's detractors and see him as a type of despot; at the same time, the Army afforded new opportunities to women of all classes.

Anyone—male or female—who heeds Booth's call can become an

urban Henry Stanley. This vicarious participation was the source of the Salvation Army's popularity.

> Talk about Stanley and Emin! There is not one of us but has an Emin somewhere or other in the heart of Darkest England, whom he ought to sally forth to rescue. Our Emins have the Devil for their Mahdi, and when we get to them we find that it is their friends and neighbors who hold them back, and they are, oh so irresolute! It needs each of us to be as indomitable as Stanley, to burst through all obstacles, to force our way right to the center of things, and then to labor with the poor prisoner of vice and crime with all our might. But had not the Expeditionary Committee furnished the financial means whereby a road was opened to the sea, both Stanley and Emin would probably have been in the heart of Darkest Africa to this day. This Scheme is our Stanley Expedition. (164)

Booth points the way to an African adventure to which the more affluent can contribute and from which they can obtain salvation. Anyone unwilling to commit their person to the effort is invited to fund it. Booth ends *In Darkest England* with an appeal for £100,000, hoping to tap into the philanthropic urges that supported African missionaries and explorers.

Many listened and contributed, even if they did not heed Booth's invitation to become urban missionaries. By February 1891, Booth had exceeded his goal and received £108,000.[24] The ten thousand copies of the first edition of *In Darkest England* reportedly sold out on the first day of publication. Within a month, a second edition of forty thousand copies sold out and, within a month, yet another forty thousand copies had been sold. One year after its publication, more than three hundred thousand copies had been sold and the text had been translated into Japanese, German, French, and Swedish.[25] Booth was so successful that, indeed, some of his greatest detractors in the press were fellow urban missionaries who were jealous of his success and fearful that he was sucking up the funds that were necessary to their own endeavors. In *Life in Darkest London: A Hint to General Booth* (1891), the Reverend A. Osborne Jay writes of Booth's book that "the new scheme, even if it be all its contrivers seem to think, can by no means take the place of existing work. Let it go side by side with it, but it must not uproot it. Even the Salvation Army cannot properly claim *all* the alms of the Church."[26]

In Darkest England stirred a passionate debate in the London press. According to Herman Ausubel, "within a few months of the publication of the General's proposals, England had become divided into Boothites and anti-Boothites."[27] One anti-Boothite was Bernard Bosanquet, who titled his rejoinder to Booth, '*In Darkest England*': *On the Wrong Track*. The most prominent anti-Boothite was the social philosopher T. H. Huxley. In Booth's narrative, Huxley had actually been invoked to strengthen the parallel between the East End and another primitive society. "When Professor Huxley lived as a medical officer in the East of London he acquired a knowledge of the actual condition of the life of many of its populace that led him long afterwards to declare that the surroundings of the savages of New Guinea were much more conducive to the leading of a decent human existence than those in which many of the East-Enders live" (166). But while Huxley may have shared Booth's vision of the East End as no better than the "surroundings of the savages of New Guinea," he strongly opposed General Booth's scheme for deliverance.

From December 1890 through January 1891, Huxley wrote a series of letters to the *Times* that scathingly attacked Booth's scheme.[28] Huxley, an atheist, abhorred the work of the Salvation Army as a modern version of religious fanaticism. He wrote, "Few social evils are of greater magnitude than unobstructed and unchastened religious fanaticism, no personal habits more surely degrade the conscience and the intellect than blind and unhesitating obedience to unlimited authority. Undoubtedly, harlotry and intemperance are sore evils, and starvation is hard to bear or even to know of; but the prostitution of the mind, the soddening of the conscience, the dwarfing of manhood are worse calamities."[29] Elsewhere in his letters, Huxley compares Booth and the Salvation Army to the Mormons, the Jesuits, the Sicilian Mafia, "The New Papacy," "the 'Ranters' and 'Revivalists' of undesirable notoriety in former times," and a society of covert socialists. "Who is to say," Huxley asks, "that the Salvation Army, in the year 1920, shall not be a replica of what the Franciscan order had become in the year 1260?"[30] Huxley also attacks Booth's originality, pointing out that in posing as the "Columbus" or "Cortez" of the East End, Booth ignores the work of predecessors like Mayhew, Charles Booth, and Carlyle.

For several decades, such criticism continued to surround discussions of the Salvation Army and its leader. In 1910, for instance, H. Rider Haggard published a highly sympathetic study of the Salvation Army titled *Regeneration*. In addition to his fiction for boys, Haggard authored several documentary studies of rural England and deeply shared Booth's back-to-the-land politics. In his introductory remarks, Haggard articulates the typical view of the Army that his book seeks to dispel.

> What is the Salvation Army? If this question were put to the ordinary person of fashion or leisure, how would it be answered? In many cases thus: "The Salvation Army is a body of people dressed up in semi-military uniform, or those of them who are women, unbecoming poke bonnets, who go about the streets making a noise in the name of God and frightening horses with brass bands. It is under the rule of an arbitrary old gentleman named Booth, who calls himself a General, and whose principal trade assets consist in a handsome and unusual face, and an inexhaustible flow of language, which he generally delivers from a white motor-car wherever he finds that he can attract the most attention. He is a clever actor in his way, who has got a great number of people under his thumb, and I am told that he has made a large fortune out of the business, like the late prophet Dowie, and others of the same sort. The newspapers are always exposing him; but he knows which side his bread is buttered and does not care. When he is gone no doubt his family will divide up the cash, and we shall hear no more of the Salvation Army!"[31]

Throughout his career as Salvation Army leader, Booth was attacked for his religious zeal and his strong-handed, authoritarian leadership. His fanaticism has its origins in his own childhood and religious conversion. Like Henry Stanley and Jack London, Booth came from working-class origins. He was born in Nottingham in 1829 and was exposed at an early age to the worst ravages of the industrial revolution. In the preface to *In Darkest England,* he recalls how his own impoverished childhood profoundly influenced his later missionary crusade. "When but a mere child the degradation and helpless misery of the poor Stockingers of my native town, wandering gaunt and hunger-stricken through the streets droning out their melancholy ditties, crowding the Union or toiling like galley slaves on relief works for a bare subsistence, kindled in my heart yearnings to help the poor which have continued to this day and which have had a powerful influence on my whole life" (5).

As a child, Booth was an avid reader. Like Doyle, he was particularly drawn to the heroically historical novels of Fenimore Cooper and Walter Scott.[32] At age thirteen, Booth was apprenticed to a pawnbroker, where he undoubtedly became even more acquainted with the daily struggle for existence of the poor. Two years later he was converted to

Christianity, as a Methodist. Booth would later describe this conversion as the substitution of the Christian narrative for his earlier literary favorites: "Rather than yearning for the world's pleasures, books, gains, or recreations, I found my new nature leading me to come away from it all. It had lost charm for me. What were all the novels, even those of Sir Walter Scott or Fenimore Cooper, compared with the story of my Saviour?"[33] For the mid-Victorian youthful Booth, Christ was a better kind of hero. Until he left Nottingham at age nineteen, Booth held open-air meetings in the streets. Often, he dragged groups of working-class youths into Sunday church meetings, much to the consternation of middle-class ministers and their respectable congregations. Throughout his life, Booth would be chastened by the middle classes, who loathed his means, if not his ends.

When Booth arrived in London, he was funded by a wealthy Methodist reformer and continued to preach in the streets and public parks. In 1858, he was ordained a Methodist minister but, always an outsider, a few years later he left that church because he was not given enough freedom to pursue his own work among the urban poor. Booth and his wife Catherine, another outsider who flaunted the gender mores of her time by preaching, continued to hold tent meetings and increasingly became involved in the Home Mission Movement. In Whitechapel in 1865, Booth began the "Christian Mission to the Heathen of our Own Country." In 1878, the Booths' "East London Christian Revival Society" was renamed as "The Salvation Army" of Christian volunteers. In the 1880s, the "Army" adopted a whole series of militaristic accouterments—a flag, a motto ("Blood and Fire"), a newspaper (the *War Cry*), articles of faith, uniforms, a highly visible marching band, and military ranks.[34] The militarization of missionary work became a guiding metaphor for later social-welfare programs, such as the Peace Corps and the War on Poverty in the United States of the 1960s.

Booth's class origins and his discomfort with official or organized Methodism are important for understanding his later conflicts with middle-class intellectuals like Huxley. In Begbie's sympathetic *Life of William Booth*, Huxley is portrayed as "the middle-aged comfortable Professor in his Eastbourne villa," while Booth "cried out, not rhetorically from a student's library, but with authentic piteousness from the very abyss itself."[35] Although Huxley's strongest criticisms are aimed at "religious fanaticism," he is also aesthetically repulsed by the Salvation Army's secondhand uniforms, loud and brassy marching bands, genderless and classless uniforms, and the rag-tag crowds that assemble at their open-air meetings. On the one hand, the Army's greatest financial support came from those who saw it as a mechanism of working-class containment. But on the other, there were the materialists, like Huxley, who despised the Army's urban jungle warfare because they feared a disciplined army of Salvationist converts advancing the cause of religious fanaticism.

In the warfare of the urban jungle, Booth's chief foe was modernity itself. For him, all the misery of modern existence could be traced to the migration of agricultural laborers from the countryside into the city. The city is a place of disease that "reeks with malaria" (20), a place of slavery where the inhabitants are "enslaved to taskmasters as merciless as any West Indian overseer" (31), and, in the tradition of Henry Mayhew, a place of homelessness traversed by the "nomads of civilization" (37). Worst of all, Darkest England lacks any Christian sense of community. In the slums, all neighborly ties have disappeared. Just as Stanley found isolated tribes scattered throughout the immense jungle, Booth finds families without ties to one another in overcrowded tenements.

In opposition to the jungle, Booth proposes an antiurban vision of a Garden. His romantically conservative solution is to recreate the conditions of small-town life by reversing the flow of population. He wishes "to restore the missing element in modern civilization" (225) by attempting to "restore to the masses of humanity that are crowded together in cities, the human and natural elements of life which they possessed when they lived in the smaller unit of the village or the market town" (284).[35] In contrast to Marx, who saw industrialism as a necessary progression to better ways of life and forms of community, Booth believed that smaller is better. His plan, then, is a late-century version of those experimental utopian communities proposed by early-nineteenth-century romantic thinkers such as Fourier, Saint-Simon, and Owen (not to mention Joseph Smith and Brigham Young). His scheme, however, is much grander than those of earlier utopians because, although his ideal social unit is the small town, his plan is to produce a rationally ordered empire of small towns that will eventually cover a Christianized earth.

Part 2 of *In Darkest England,* "Deliverance," articulates Booth's carefully detailed back-to-the-land scheme for the "rescue" and salvation of the urban savages. "As the race from the Country to the City has been the cause of much of the distress we have to battle with, we propose to find a substantial part of our remedy by transferring these people back to the country, that is back again to 'the Garden!'" (100). Booth so firmly believed in the therapeutic effects of the country that one of his proposals—Whitechapel-by-the-Sea—was merely an attempt "to make it possible for every man, woman and child, to get, now and then, a day's refreshing change by a visit to that never-failing source of interest" (245). Booth's grand "Scheme," which became widely known as the Darkest England Scheme, envisions a three-stage series of utopian communities, significantly named Colonies: The City Colony, The Farm Colony, and The Colony-Over-Sea.

Inside the front cover of *In Darkest England*, there is an illustrated chart showing the pathway that the "victims of vice and poverty" must travel to reach the utopian Oversea Colony. One might see it as the road map that makes good on the promise implicit in the second half of Booth's title . . . *and the Way Out.* At the foot of the illustration, ship-wrecked souls founder in a turbulent sea (the "morass"). On the surface of the sea floats wreckage, foundered souls with only their heads above water, and a series of words that describe life in the sea: "prison," "homeless," "betting," "Black Maria," "want," "anarchy," "separation," "sweating," and so forth. At the very bottom, in bold print, the chart proclaims "3,000 IN THE SEA" and "STARVATION." On either side, Salvation Army officers pull out "the lost" and point to an uphill path.

At the top of this path, we see the City Colony, a better-lit place. Here, in the midst of the East End and "in the very center of the ocean of misery," Booth proposed a number of institutions that would "act as Harbors of Refuge for all and any who have been shipwrecked in life, character, or circumstances" (100). On the chart, we see the programs that the Salvation Army has already implemented or planned to implement in the East End. These include, among others, a "poor Man's Bank," "Rescue Homes," "Cheap Food Depots," the "Prison Gate Brigade," "Salvation Factories," "Lodgings for Single Women," and "A Preventive Home for Unfallen Girls When in Danger." The City Colony is comprised of branches that provide food, temporary shelter, and temporary employment. They encourage the virtues of sobriety, industry, and discipline. In the Scheme, those who spend time in the City Colony would either be placed in more permanent employment or "sent home to friends happy to receive them on hearing of their reformation"

(100). Of course, this happy goal presents a problem because the lack of "permanent employment" is what made the East Enders desperate and homeless in the first place. Few of the saved have "happy" friends to go home to. Many of them remained with the Salvation Army, which provided them a home and family of sorts.

As the work of salvation proceeds, Booth realizes that he needs a place to send "all who remain on our hands." He proposes that they be sent out to the Salvationist Farm Colony where their reformation would continue as they learned agricultural skills. Booth desires that all his reformed converts will want and be able to find permanent employment in the country, again seeming to forget that most left the countryside in the first place because there was simply not enough work. He hopes to alleviate this by settling people in "cottages on a small piece of land that we should provide" and by promoting "Co-Operative Farms," pictured on his chart. However, he does realize that this will not suffice to employ all the souls he hopes to save and, thus, he envisions the Salvation Army Colony-Over-Sea.

Like most Victorians, Booth envisioned the world as so much surplus land that could absorb the surplus populations of England and Europe, especially the population of the urban jungle. Thus, at the top of his chart, one can see the extremities of Foreign Lands and dotted shipping routes that proceed from the British coast. "All who have given attention to the subject are agreed that in our Colonies in South Africa, Canada, Western Australia and elsewhere, there are millions of acres of useful land to be obtained almost for the asking, capable of supporting our surplus population in health and comfort, were it a thousand times greater than it is" (100). Emanating out from Darkest England, his converted enlightened natives will colonize the planet's other places of Darkness and Jungle. Booth's passive victims of industrial urbanization will serve as the regenerated agents of a far-flung Christian empire.

Booth's Scheme is that grand in scope: "Forwarding them from the City to the Country, and there continuing the process of regeneration, and then pouring them forth on to the virgin soils that await their coming in other lands, keeping hold of them with a strong government, and yet making them free men and women; and so laying the foundations, perchance of another Empire to swell to vast proportions in later times. Why not?" (101) In Booth's vision, civilization's outcasts and victims will be the builders of a heaven-on-earth. Ultimately, Booth's regeneration of the urban jungle was idealized as a scheme to regenerate the rest of the empire by reforming it in the image of a utopian Boothite Christian Empire.[37]

In Booth's appendix, "The Position of Our Forces: October, 1890," he reports there are already Salvationist corps or societies in most North and West European countries, the United States, Canada, Australia, South Africa, India, Ceylon, and the Argentine Republic.[38] According to Rachel Tolen, "India was the Salvation Army's first mission territory outside England. Salvation Army mission activities were begun by Frederick de Latour Tucker (Commissioner Booth-Tucker), who had originally been with the Indian Civil Service but had resigned his post after becoming acquainted with the Salvation Army on a trip to England. There he had met and married Emma Booth, the daughter of the Salvation Army's founder."[39] The commencement of Salvation Army activities in 1882 in India is recalled in Army literature as the "invasion." General Booth was heavily involved in this colonial expansion. Four years after the "invasion," he writes to instruct his colonial soldiers in "the methods that should be followed in carrying on the Indian War." After encouraging each soldier to "fix your eye, your heart and your aim upon the Indian, and go for his Salvation with all your might!" Booth lays out a four-part plan: "(1) To attract their attention; (2) To gain their confidence; (3) To save their souls and (4) To train them up to live and fight for God and the Salvation of their fellows."[40]

Tolen notes that the Army faced resistance from the British colonial government, who feared the strategy of open-air meetings because they encouraged street crowds. The government also strongly disagreed with the Army's decision to adapt "Salvation Army practices to customs familiar to the peoples of India," especially their adoption of Indian clothing as their official uniform. Booth was an early proponent of the colonial strategy of adapting one's tactics and persona to the "native" situation, one made famous by T. E. Lawrence in *The Seven Pillars of Wisdom*. Booth writes to his followers in India "that perhaps in no other country will there be a louder call, and a wider opportunity, for the display of that principle of adaptation that is a fundamental principle with the Army everywhere. In order to conquer you must stoop, becoming with the Apostle all things to all men, in order that you may win them to your Master. This must mean, if anything at all, that to the Indians you must be Indians."[41]

Frederick Booth-Tucker published *In Darkest India,* which caused "several native gentlemen of wealth" to promise ten thousand rupees "to enable The Salvation Army to commence and carry out this eminently Christian work among their own unchristianized people."[42] The repetition of the Stanley title provides an excellent example of how colonial metaphors circulated. Following Edward Said's work on orientalism, we can say that the conjunction of *In Darkest Africa* and *In Darkest India* exemplified a British tendency to generalize about their racial or colonial others. Yet more interesting here is the role played by the East End as a middle term in the comparison. In the chain of titles— Africa, England, India—India occupies Africa's slot only because the Booths liken both of them to "Darkest England." Africa and the missionary discourse is appropriated to represent the East End: that representation is then, later, redeployed to talk about India. To move from Africa to India, the discourse must journey first through London's East End and the imagination of General Booth. In the work of the Salvation Army, the imperial plot moves from empire to metropolis and back to empire.

Booth's life and work uncannily resemble the plot of typical Victorian fantasies like, for instance, those of Dickens. With the "great expectations" of one from a working-class background, General Booth envisioned himself as the founder and head of an empire that might someday "swell to vast proportions" (101). In examining this rhetoric, it is easy to see why the Salvation Army was attacked for being autocratic and the "General" upbraided, by Huxley and others, as an egomaniacal tyrant. Like Conrad's Kurtz, his desire to save and enlighten the brutes is closely allied to personal aggrandizement and a lust for power. *In Darkest England* reads, as one can only imagine, like Kurtz's eloquent unpublished "Report to the International Society for the Suppression of Savage Customs." Although there is no evidence that Booth ever scrawled or uttered "Exterminate all the Urban Brutes," it is not hard to imagine that some readers were inspired to slash and burn or, more likely, gave up on the possibility of reforming the urban jungle and supported its clearance.

While I certainly do not mean to downplay Booth's accomplishments in alleviating real suffering, I also do not want to forget how his rhetoric produced a discourse that cast the urban poor as brutish. I suspect that Booth's motives were a complicated mix of sympathy (instilled by his Nottingham childhood of the 1830s and 1840s), a desire to dominate and control his Army and master the chaotic jungle he perceived around him, and a need to place a racial distance between himself and the poor from which he had "risen." But whatever Booth's noble motives and real achievements, *In Darkest England* functioned as an act of literary brutalization. Booth's vision of the East End as an African jungle and the East Enders as primitive savages was no less crucial in producing West Enders' perceptions of their neighbors than were the fictions of Haggard, Doyle, and Conrad for instantiating "truths" about Britain's colonial others.[43] And we should note, in the century that has followed the publication of *In Darkest England,* Booth's representations of "Darkest England" and its "natives" have continued to shape our perceptions of inner cities and those "natives" who continue to inhabit them.

CHAPTER FIVE

WRITING LONDON

East End Ethnography in Jack London's
The People of the Abyss

In August 1902, twenty-six-year-old Jack London arrived in England for a brief stay while en route to South Africa. He had recently completed his most successful novel to date, *The Call of the Wild,* and had been asked by the American Press Association to travel to South Africa and report on the aftermath of the Boer War. Upon arriving in London, however, he learned that his commission had been canceled. Turned away from Africa, London ventured incognito into that "Darkest England" Booth had chronicled twelve years earlier.

While Booth was interested in naming the East End an "urban jungle" and colonizing it in order to create a more far-flung Christian empire, Jack London ventured into the East End as an explorer, an unemployed writer, and a committed socialist interested in reform. London's narrative of London—*The People of the Abyss* (1903)—starkly exposed the hunger, homelessness, suicide, alcoholism, prostitution, overcrowding, degradation, and danger that he found on his seven-week journey. What is equally interesting is that it presents the adventurer as an ethnographer. In *The People of the Abyss,* London applies ethnographic methods, especially participant-observation and photography, to describe the urban Heart of Empire. In this sense, his narrative continues a pattern we have already seen in Doyle and Booth: the empire comes home at the turn of the century.

However, London's narrative is neither simply a portrayal of a "savage" culture within the metropolitan center nor a presentation of the urban adventurer as ethnographer; in addition, it reveals the deeper (abysmal?) motivations of the (Western) self who writes (about) another culture—in this case, the culture of London's poor. London's ethnography encourages us to explore connections between the American "London" who writes and the English "London" that is written. It encourages us to ask: What is the relationship between man and city, subject and object, narrator and narrated, outsider and insider, writer and working class, West and East, self and other, in a book where both terms have the same name—*London*?

At the beginning of his preface, London writes: "I went down into the under-world of London with an attitude of mind which I may liken to that of the explorer. I was open to be convinced by the evidence of my eyes, rather than by the teachings of those who had not seen, or by the words of those who had seen and gone before."[1] Yet despite London's firmly empiricist statement, those "eyes" have been profoundly constructed by the "teachings" of those who went before him. As a self-taught and well-read socialist, London had no doubt read Engels's *The Condition of the Working Class in England in 1844,* which had been translated into English for the first time in 1887 by Florence Kelley-Wischnewetsky. London's account also indicates his familiarity with T. H. Huxley's comparison between East Enders and South Sea Islanders and Arthur Morrison's *Tales of Mean Streets.*[2] In addition, London was most likely familiar with the work of his fellow American, Stephen Crane. During the early 1890s, Crane spent time among the urban proletariat of New York in order to experience life from the "native perspective." His most famous sketch was *Maggie: A Girl of the Streets.*[3] And finally, as we shall see below, London's narrative betrays the deep influence of James Greenwood's "A Night in the Workhouse" (1866).

When London decided to go to the East End, he very consciously saw himself not as a casual tourist but as a more serious, purposive "explorer." He wanted to investigate the living conditions of the urban lower classes and find things out for himself, rather than trusting accounts written by his predecessors in the field of social exploration. His own experiences were to serve as the final authority—not those of others. Although London's account begins by declaring a fundamental mistrust of other accounts, he does not suspect the validity of others' knowledge as much as he discounts the *method* by which they obtained knowledge. For London, the best way to know something is to become a part of it and experience it immediately. He emphasizes the self and its sensations—"the evidence of my eyes."

This emphasis on "presence" was also becoming increasingly important for his ethnographic contemporaries. As other turn-of-the-century ethnographers were coming to believe, London believed the new road to knowledge involved joining the culture—mixing with it, learning the language, participating in it, meeting it "face to face"—rather than observing it from a detached distance.[4] Historians of anthropology have named this modernist ethnographic methodology "participant-observation" and cite its origins in the work of Bronislaw Malinowski, specifically his *Argonauts of the Western Pacific* (1922). London's narrative predates Malinowski's account by twenty years and the latter's fieldwork experience by a decade.[5] Indeed, London's text is not a classic example of participant-observation. London's voice upsets what James Clifford has called the "delicate balance of subjectivity and objectivity" characteristic of participant-observation.[6] In *The People of the Abyss*, despite the objectivist intentions, the subjectively autobiographical voice still tends to dominate. However, I will argue that London's attempts to inhabit the native point of view move urban ethnography in the direction of what will come to be called participant-observation. London addressed an audience that increasingly believed that to know something was to know it experientially. Knowledge was becoming the privilege of the (supposedly) naked eye.

But despite his claim to rely solely on the new "evidence of [his] eyes," London structures his narrative according to traditional ways of perceiving others and of explaining primitive cultures. He appropriates tropes foreign to the city—the abyss, the sea, the battlefield, the jungle —and applies them to the urban culture in order to produce a "new" discourse on the East End.[7] In a historical sense, London's account is not yet an example of those postcolonial narratives in which the "empire writes back." Yet London, like Booth, prefigures later accounts by inverting the tropes of colonialist discourse and deploying them to understand the culture of the modern city and its "natives." Because he can assume that his audience is familiar with tales of "savage" lands, these older narratives become a lens through which the slum can be safely spied.

Despite its more metaphoric or literary qualities, *The People of the Abyss* does not purport to be a fiction. Instead, it claims to be a work of realism, description, autobiography, and science. The form of the book is that of the collage; many chapters interweave London's "face to face" experiences, clippings from newspapers, selections from court transcripts, photographs, and comparisons between the East End and other cultures. It claims to represent another culture with a pure representation that does not construct reality but reflects it. London deploys a set of rhetorical strategies that we can label "ethnographic": an account of his trip to the field site, a claim to the epistemological privilege of the participant-observer, his retreat to a "safe house" where he can write and relax, a collection of photographs taken by the author that implicitly promise the reader unmediated access to "native" culture, and references to the difficulty of translating the "alien" experience. All these strategies strengthen London's claim to the authority of immediacy, presence, and objective truth. In using them, London implicitly tells the reader: "I went into the Heart of Darkest England and I have lived to tell about it."

London opens with an account of the preparations for his trip and his first foray into alien territory. His first chapter is filled with warnings from friends, experts, and authorities. In discussing his plans, he has difficulty in making himself understood. The chapter's blend of danger and humorous confusion supply the mood or atmosphere for the more "objective" descriptions of the East End and its inhabitants that will fill subsequent chapters.

Such an autobiographic opening is typical of ethnographic writing. Although ethnography claims to be objective and primarily concerned with the objective descriptions of remote cultures, it also cannot totally purge itself of information that is subjective. The latter, more personal aspect of the narrative is necessary to give the work the authority of empirical presence. For the writer of ethnographies, Mary Louise Pratt tells us, the first chapter is always a personal narrative and, for the reader, invariably the most interesting. Accounts of how the ethnographer got to the field site, while often amusing, serve the crucial purpose of "anchoring" the experience as truth.[8] They also function, by placing a brief space of readerly time between the opening of the book and the arrival at the descriptive work of the text, to first distance the reader from the objects of the study, before placing one on the far side of the gap between the reality one leaves behind and the textualized culture at which one arrives. Such a distancing function is especially germane in a text where the geographical distance between West and East is virtually negligible—a stone's throw, a brief stroll. Finally, the opening personal account, especially when extensive like London's, leaves no doubt that the ethnographic text is, above all, an instance of self-fashioning. That is, the most important identity on display here is that of the protagonist of the opening chapter: Jack London.

London's journey is mapped for the reader before the author ever sets out. The clues that orient the reader can be found in the book's title (*the Abyss*) and that of the first chapter ("The Descent"). In London's ethnography, "going out," or, horizontally, into the East End, is imagined as "going down": "I went down into the under-world of London" (vii). The title of chapter 1 invokes the journey into Dante's Infernal "Abyss" and the evolutionary heritage of Darwin *(The Descent of Man)*. In describing his movement across the spatial boundaries that demarcate two cultures, London's discourse immediately invokes descents of Christian and biological hierarchies. Later, he will descend other hierarchies of class, nationality, race, and gender. Here, there is also an analogy to Conrad's *Heart of Darkness,* in which going up the river is seen as going back in time. In London, spatial movement is not necessarily temporal (though it is in terms of personal history, as we shall see below), but, as in Conrad, is always caught up in other kinds of journeys: between classes, nationalities, sexualities, and races.

Before he ventures into the East End, London's West End friends try to dissuade him from taking the trip. There is a paradoxical nature to their warnings. On the one hand, they seem quite knowledgeable about the dangers of the East End. They warn London not to undertake such a dangerous trip: "[Y]ou can't do it" (1); "'You don't want to live down there!' everybody said, with disapprobation writ large upon their faces. 'Why, it is said there are places where a man's life isn't worth tu'pence'" (2). On the other hand, when he solicits information about how to begin, their persuasive knowledge gives way to ignorance— they cannot supply the merest detail. "We know nothing of the East End. It is over there somewhere" (2–3). Curiously, this paradoxical state of knowledge and ignorance about the East End entails a split in spatial relationships. When thinking vertically—"You don't want to live down there!"—London's informants seem to be speaking from a position of knowledge. Conversely, when thinking horizontally—"It is over there somewhere"—they claim to "know nothing." The depths are confronted with mythological certainty; the peripheries are unintelligible.[9]

London meets with a similar response when he asks a travel agent, well known for sponsoring exotic journeys and African safaris. A modern Dante, London unsuccessfully seeks guidance. In response to his "strange" request, Thomas Cook & Son are no help at all.

But O Cook, O Thomas Cook & Son, pathfinders and trail-clearers, living sign-posts to all the world and bestowers of first aid to bewildered travellers—unhesitatingly and instantly, with ease and celerity, could you send me to Darkest Africa or Innermost Thibet, but to the East End of London, barely a stone's throw distant from Ludgate Circus, you know not the way!

"You can't do it, you know," said the human emporium of routes and fares at Cook's Cheapside branch. "It is so—ahem—unusual." (3)

Frustrated, London explains his plan to Cook's agent so that he can be identified in case he gets into trouble. Upon doing so, he receives not reassurance, but another hint of the dangerous world he wishes to visit:

"Ah, I see; should you be murdered, we would be in position to identify the corpse."

He said it so cheerfully and cold-bloodedly that on the instant I saw my stark and mutilated cadaver stretched upon a slab where cool waters trickle ceaselessly, and him I saw bending over and sadly and patiently identifying it as the body of the insane American who *would* see the East End. (4)

Seeking reassurance, London receives a premonition of himself as "cadaver." His active imagination enhances the travel agent's images for the reader. The agent's "corpse" is translated, in London's mind, into a "mutilated cadaver." Similarly, what Cook's agent labels "unusual" behavior becomes, in London's discourse, the mission of "the insane American." Although London's trip is seen by others only as bizarre or "unusual," it reaches new degrees of danger in his own rhetoric.

London's depiction of his narrated self as "insane" serves a twofold rhetorical purpose. On the one hand, it casts him as a stubborn adventurer who is braver than the average travel agent, London clerk, or tourist. On the other hand, the narrator who writes from a later position of experience, actually gains authority by poking fun at his earlier "insane" self. In laughing at his former self, London establishes his writing voice as one who knows better now. Through experience, he has come to knowledge and established his authority. Humor is crucial to the success of the narrative. Although we laugh *at* London, more crucially, we are laughing *with* a more knowledgeable him. And in doing so, a bond of trust develops between reader and author. In the eyes of both the narrating self and his readers, the "naive" London is viewed as akin to those "insane" travelers who, decades before, ventured into the jungles of Africa, South America, and the South Seas. It is worth noting that, at this historical moment, a journey to the East End is imagined as less sane and less safe than visits to the more conventionally imagined ends of the earth.

Although Cook's will not take responsibility for him, the U.S. consul-general does agree to keep track of him. This greatly relieves the would-be adventurer, who wants to minimize the dangers of his undertaking: "I breathed a sigh of relief. Having built my ships behind me, I was now free to plunge into that human wilderness of which nobody seemed to know anything" (5). Here, London depicts himself not as a potential Henry Stanley but instead as a Dr. Livingstone. He wants the civilized world, represented by the U.S. consulate, to know where he is going. If he is not heard from or disappears, presumably a Stanley will be sent in to find, rescue, and bring him back from the urban heart of darkness. London bravely asserts he does not fear being killed, but instead fears he might end up in jail without anyone to identify him and bail him out. That is, he fears getting stuck ("lost") in the jungle without any means of escape. London's desire to "go native" coexists with the fear he will not be able to come back—a fear that casts his journalistic venture as risky business.

This opening evocation of danger and suspense carefully establishes what Pratt calls "the initial positionings of the subjects of the ethnographic text." The ethnographer writer may be seen as a little bit crazy, but he is also brave and determined. While we do not know much about the natives, we do discover that they are violent and, perhaps more importantly, unknown. Finally, the reader is offered a number of positions from which to view London (both city and writer)—London's own more knowledgeable eyes, his friends' eyes, the eyes of the Cook's agent, the eyes of the U.S. consul. The reader's possible responses are structured by all these points of view that are established before the "explorer" ever enters the East End. Several visions of the East End pre-date what will become "the evidence of [London's] eyes." They suggest the East End is, to a great extent, already written for London and by London before he ever goes there.

If London's behavior seems odd or lunatic to the West Enders, it is even more inexplicable to his native, East End subjects. On his first foray into the East End, London confuses his lower-class cabdriver by giving orders that are so general that they are meaningless.

"Drive me down to the East End," I ordered, taking my seat.
"Where, sir?" he demanded with frank surprise.
"To the East End, anywhere. Go on."
The hansom pursued an aimless way for several minutes, then came

to a puzzled stop. The aperture above my head was uncovered, and the cabman peered down perplexedly at me.

"I say," he said, "wot plyce yer wanter go?"

"East End," I repeated. "Nowhere in particular. Just drive me around, anywhere."

"But wot's the haddress, sir?"

"See here!" I thundered. "Drive me down to the East End, and at once!"

It was evident that he did not understand, but he withdrew his head and grumblingly started his horse. (5–6)

In this exchange, the middle-class London speaks in the imperative while his confused conductor constantly interrogates his passenger. London "thunders;" the "puzzled" cabbie "grumbles." And as the temper mounts on London's side, a deferential confusion mounts on the other. These two people obviously cannot understand one another.

London, the outsider, gives what he understands to be perfectly specific directions because, for him, the East End is all the same ("East End," "nowhere in particular," "anywhere"). The cabman, a frequenter and perhaps inhabitant of the East End, cannot understand the foreigner. He responds with "frank surprise," "puzzle[ment]," "perplexion," and miscomprehension. "Wot's the haddress?" London posits ignorance or lack of understanding on the part of the cabdriver. He never thinks that perhaps his utterance and his directions are at the root of the confusion. But is it not he who "did not understand?" At this stage of his acquaintance with the East End, the idea of an "address" in Darkest London strikes him about the same way Stanley might have been struck if one of his African bearers had asked for Dr. Livingstone's "haddress."

Upon setting out, London imagines the East End as one immeasurable, undifferentiated place, with no organization or distinguishable variety of people, occupations, sights, and sounds. It is constituted as difference, as other, yet it contains no differences within itself. Here, London's discourse resembles that of the orientalist as described by Edward Said. Said demonstrates how ignorance of other cultures leads to a tendency to generalize or universalize. For the orientalist, one Oriental represents all Orientals. Or in London's case, one place in the East End is as good as any other, one East Ender represents, and speaks for, all. Elsewhere, London tells us that West Enders see it the same way and have named it "The City of Dreadful Monotony" (211). The East

End is "one unending slum," "miles of bricks and misery," and "filled with a new and different race of people, short of stature, and of wretched or beer-sodden appearance" (7). London is frightened by his encounter with a new race and place that can be understood only in terms of past fearful encounters with another alien element—the sea: "for the first time in my life the fear of the crowd smote me. It was like the fear of the sea; and the miserable multitudes, street upon street, seemed so many waves of a vast and malodorous sea, lapping about me and threatening to well up and over me" (8).

London's account is structured by a metaphorical linkage of "crowd" and "sea" that was common in middle- and upper-class accounts of the industrial proletariat. The "fear of the crowd" is likened to the fear of drowning. Earlier, London described his readiness to "plunge into that human wilderness" (5)—a mixed metaphor that shows that both "sea" and "wilderness" are interchangeable for the "crowd" in London's mind. Like the wilderness and sea, the crowd threatens to destroy, to consume, to engulf, to obliterate individuality and boundaries between people (class, nationality, gender). For London, there is neither pleasure nor rapture amid "the waves of a vast and malodorous sea" that threaten to annihilate him. The only pleasure available here is to survive or stay afloat.

Marianna Torgovnick has described how later modernists use a notion of the "oceanic" to metaphorically articulate a fusion of the individual and the collectivity. She defines the "oceanic" as "a dissolution of boundaries between subject and object and between all conceived and conceivable polarities."[10] In *Civilization and its Discontents*, Freud uses *the oceanic* to describe religious sentiment and the subject's desire to participate in an identity greater than the self. For Freud, such ego dissolution is a dystopian form of regression to a pre-Oedipal state. On the other hand, Virginia Woolf, in her novel *The Waves*, explores *the oceanic* as a metaphor by which the subject can transcend individuality and participate in more collective, transindividual, or natural identities. It is my belief that this modernist turn to the use of *oceanic* is related to the individual's experience of and relationship to the urban crowd. At roughly the same period in which she composes *The Waves*, Woolf wrote her essay "Street Haunting," which compares the experience of London crowds and streets to an adventure in the jungle. Clearly, these two responses to the urban oceanic are gendered responses. Jack London's reaction to the East End oceanic is much closer to Freud's masculinist fear than Woolf's feminist notion of transcendence. Yet it might be wrong to choose sides here. Perhaps a dual notion of the oceanic (Freud and Woolf) can explain London's oscillating attraction to and repulsion from "the people of the abyss."

London's desire for a life preserver enables him to give his perplexed driver more explicit instructions. He instructs him to find an old clothes shop. By this point, the cabdriver doubts he will ever collect his fare. Yet, his disbelief cannot match that of the shopkeeper, who at first refuses to bring London the kind of clothing he requests. Only "after fruitless attempts to press upon [London] new and impossible coats and trousers," does he bring "light heaps of old ones" (10). London selects "a pair of stout though well-worn trousers, a frayed jacket with one remaining button, a pair of brogans which had plainly seen service where coal was shovelled, a thin leather belt, and a very dirty cloth cap." This clothing carries the signs of labor and filth by which London wants to be read by the "miserable multitudes." He is now outfitted for his adventure in the wilds, except for the gold sovereign that he later sews "inside [his] stoker's singlet." When he dons his purchase, the clothes feel uncomfortable—they are his closest bodily contact with proletarian life—but this discomfort is necessary. London is "confident that the most rigourous of ascetics suffer no more than did [he] in the ensuing twenty-four hours" (13). The sacrificial ethnographer and would-be saint suffers for his knowledge.[11]

This dressing-up or dressing-down, though uncomfortable, is perceived as a means to both liberation and knowledge. London believes his "seafaring" costume allows him to move across class barriers, allows the outsider to become insider, allows him to belong, and by changing his identity allows him access to the "native" point of view. He becomes, so he argues, "one of them."

> No sooner was I out on the streets than I was impressed by the difference in status effected by my clothes. All servility vanished from the demeanor of the common people with whom I came into contact. Presto! in the twinkling of an eye, so to say, I had become one of them. My frayed and out-at-elbows jacket was the badge and advertisement of my class, which was their class. It made me of like kind, and in place of the fawning and too-respectful attention I had hitherto received, I now shared with them a comradeship. . . .
>
> . . . For the first time I met the English lower classes face to face, and knew them for what they were. When loungers and workmen, on street

corners and in public houses, talked with me, they talked as one man to another, and they talked as natural men should talk, without the least idea of getting anything out of me for what they talked or the way they talked. (13–15)

London enters a different world in which he is "of like kind." The masks are gone as the interlocutors meet "face to face." The communication is pure or "natural"; there is no visible self-interest or ulterior motive on either side. This is the way "natural men" talked before the days of civilized conventions and class divisions. For London, it is the most positive benefit of his "descent"—the talk of men who can cut through the civilized frills and get down to business.[12] London and the English lower classes have become comrades—birds of a feather. Meeting them "face to face" offers a privileged means to knowledge: "[knowing] them for what they were." In London's mind, his costume is not connected with falsehood, but with enabling truthful or "natural" behavior.

In his new identity, all kinds of things change quickly. He no longer has to tip. He has to be more careful and hurry when crossing the street. Forms of address change: he becomes "mate" and no longer "Governor" (14). As London is quick to point out, this experience is unique and, certainly, not that of the typical tourist. It is "delight"-ful. It is also cost-effective. "This brings me to a delight I experienced in my rags and tatters which is denied the average American abroad. The European traveller from the States, who is not a Croesus, speedily finds himself reduced to a chronic state of self-conscious sordidness by the hordes of cringing robbers who clutter his steps from dawn till dark, and deplete his pocketbook in a way that puts compound interest to the blush" (14).

London's changed identity may offer pleasures not known by American tourists, but such delight can hardly be akin to the consciousness of the poor, his desired "native point of view" ("[knowing] them for what they were"). I doubt his new comrades spent much time feeling good about the fact they were never approached by beggars, or saw their neighbors as "hordes of cringing robbers" who "clutter" the steps. London's pleasure is afforded by his passage to native garb, yet it is hardly a pleasure that derives from access to native consciousness—because, for him, civilization is always a mere change of clothes away. His thrill derives from looking like them but not from thinking and feeling like them.

London's ability to "go native" by dressing down empowers him and dissipates his fears of the working-class crowd and the lapping and engulfing sea. The clothes are not just disguise; they are also a security blanket, a life jacket or, perhaps more accurately, a scuba suit: "And when I at last made into the East End, I was gratified to find that the fear of the crowd no longer haunted me. I had become a part of it. The vast and malodorous sea had welled up and over me, or I had slipped gently into it, and there was nothing fearsome about it—with the one exception of the stoker's singlet" (15). The crowd, the malodorous sea, is only dangerous when one stands outside of it and casts it as other, or different. In this passage, there has been a miraculous sea change: the formerly passive London, to whom the sea does things, has become an active agent in control. Formerly "the sea had welled up and over me"; now he, as actor, has "slipped gently into it." Ironically, London's costume ("seafaring" clothes) mark him as an out-of-work American seaman. His garments, which enable him to survive in this sea, are already associated with putting out to other seas. Thus, London's costume is not disguise but simply the appropriate outfit for the job. Furthermore, his unemployed pose is not really a pose since London is literally "out of work." Despite his recent literary success, he apparently had taken up his original journalistic commission because he was "three thousand dollars in debt."[13]

London not only survives the crowd but also gains a different knowledge of it by adapting, by fitting in, by becoming one with it, by giving up his West End identity for an East End one. By the end of the opening chapter, London has overcome warning, fear, confusion, difference, and has "slipped gently" into the alien culture. The process of his initiation (and ours) is complete. In the urban jungle, he has gone native and is ready to meet the other natives "face to face." And as readers, we are prepared to hear the strange stories and facts of what he finds there.

London's participation in East End culture is not simply a matter of changing clothes. It also includes bodily degradation. In *The People of the Abyss,* London aspires to the native point of view by abjectly subjecting himself to hunger and revolting food, to vermin, to nights on the streets, to the casual wards and workhouses. He writes, "I must beg forgiveness of my body for the vileness through which I have dragged it, and forgiveness of my stomach for the vileness into which I have thrust it." London's experience of bodily suffering is undoubtedly genuine. However the crucial point here, and one that marks the distance between the writer and his East End subjects, is that London controls the suffering—he is always free to leave at any time, always free to eat or not to eat, always free to take out the piece of gold he has sewn into his clothes in case of emergency, always free to exchange the identity of the participant for the middle-class stranger. This is not suffering so much as a theatrically staged suffering, one that seeks to understand it and cope with it by playing it out safely.

During one encounter with two elderly homeless men, London is overcome with pity for their condition and discloses his "true" identity. He offers to buy a meal for the two men, who up to this point have been very talkative, friendly, and informative. But when the two grudgingly accept his alms, the relationship undergoes a profound change. "Of course, I had to explain to them that I was merely an investigator, a social student, seeking to find out how the other half lived. And at once they shut up like clams. I was not of their kind; my speech had changed, the tones of my voice were different, in short, I was a superior, and they were supremely class conscious" (86). London's native informants mistrust him once they discover he is "not of their kind." The relationship changes from "man to man" to "man to clam" as class-consciousness is figured as an oceanographic species-consciousness. In London's view, they have learned through a hard life of exploitation and servility not to trust their class betters. Of course, it is also likely that they mistrust London because they feel betrayed—he had pretended to be someone else. As an insider, London cannot pay for a meal and express the compassion and humanity these old men evoke in him. But as an outsider, he cannot get the "face to face" knowledge he wants.

Despite the occasional moment of revelation that destroys "face to face" communication, London, like other ethnographers, maintains the fiction of participant-observation by separating the sites where he *experiences* the other culture and the site where he *writes* about it. Ethnographers typically accomplish this division in one of two ways. First, they wait and write about their trip after returning home. Secondly, and perhaps more commonly, they write in a "safe house," a place near, or on the margins of, their native village. This place not only serves to obscure or closet the ethnographer's "foreign" identity as writer or outside investigator, but also, perhaps more crucially, functions as a space where they can escape back into the identity of their former literate and "civilized" selves. The "safe house" saves the ethnographer from the dangerous possibility of identifying too closely with his subjects and the possibility of becoming one of them. Here, he can remember who he is (or was) and reassure himself that civilization still exists and is available to him.

In another episode, London's narrative reveals the impossibility of participating in a culture and attaining the native point of view when his escape from that culture is constantly an option. London has just spent a night and day in a casual ward, where in return for a day of hauling medical waste down several flights of stairs, he received two nights' room and board. However, he cannot stand the thought of another night of miserable food, vermin-infested bedding, and dirty bath water. While near an open gate, London invites a companion to split before they have to spend a second night in this circle of the East End Inferno. But the East Ender will not join him; if the escapees are caught, they will receive fourteen days in jail; but even worse, if they are successful, they will never be allowed to come back, which, as London fails to comprehend, they may someday want to do. He alone has the luxury to leave, and he cannot pass the opportunity up. "'No bloody fear,' said I, with an enthusiasm they could not comprehend; and, dodging out the gate, I sped down the street" (112).

Again, we should note where the miscomprehension occurs. For London, it is "they" who lack understanding and behave "cowardly," enabling London to appear heroic in flight. "Straight to my room I hurried, changed my clothes, and less than an hour from my escape, in a Turkish bath, I was sweating out whatever germs and other things had penetrated my epidermis, and wishing that I could stand a temperature of three hundred and twenty rather than two hundred and twenty" (112). "Knowledge" is not the only thing this explorer contracts. London escapes in order cleanse his body of the diseases and filth with which he fears he has come into contact as a result of his so-called participation. Fortunately, the contamination that accompanies his investigation can be cleansed away, by merely changing the clothes that cover his skin, or going to the Turkish bath to sweat out those carriers of foreignness that may have penetrated below the surface of his skin.[14]

In order to ensure periodic escapes from the East End, London carefully planned and built bridges when he first arrived there. His room is in a house on the borders of the slum, in a street described as "a veritable oasis in the desert of East London" (16). The house belongs to a police detective, provocatively named "Johnny Upright," to whom London had been referred by a West Ender. "Johnny Upright" is an East End name, "given him by a convicted felon in the dock" (20). In him, London detects "Shades of Old Sleuth and Sherlock Holmes" (21). One senses Holmes's strong presence in London's account. For instance, the image of the safe house or oasis recalls Sholto's description of his apartment in *The Sign of Four* as "an oasis of art in the howling desert of London." "Johnny Upright," whose space London will inhabit, also functions as an alternative identity for London himself. There is a kinship between "Johnny" and "Jack"—both being nicknames for John. In going to the safe house, the robust adventurer Jack steps back into the character of the more civilized Johnny. Spatially, London the writer comes out of the "abyss," back from his "descent," to assume a role that is more Upright. This latter point is especially relevant in a narrative that continually calls attention to the slack and hunched bodies of the slum dwellers. London has to ascend to the safe house, periodically, to remind himself that he is one who stands "upright." The name also introduces issues of gender difference: London emerges from the cavernous abyss to assert his phallic upright-ness.

London confides his intentions and plans for costumed excursions to Upright and his family in order to provide an escape route. In a narrative filled with metaphors of the sea, Upright's room will be his port to civilization. "While living, eating, and sleeping with the people of the East End, it was my intention to have a port of refuge, not too far distant, into which I could run now and again to assure myself that good clothes and cleanliness still existed. Also in such port I could receive my mail, work up my notes, and sally forth occasionally in changed garb to civilization" (19). The obsessive need for safety and "assurance," for building bridges between his West End and East End identities, heightens the sense of danger attached to London's journey into the urban jungle. This "port," "safe haven," or "room of one's own," can be reached by London whenever he wants comfortable rest, better food, clean clothes, a quiet moment in private, a place to write, or reassurance that an alternative world—one with "good clothes and cleanliness"—still exists. Such a "room of one's own" stands out as a class privilege in a narrative filled with accounts of overcrowded buildings in which several families often occupy a single room. This overcrowding often leads him to think of America and "[his] own spacious West, with room under its sky and unlimited air for a thousand Londons" (32). London's ethnography compares the East End not only with the West End but also with the (American) West that is London's home. In London's clean and spacious refuge, he is physically reminded of those wider, open spaces of his former self.[15] In one letter from the abyss, London writes, "There's no place like California, & I long to be back."[16]

London apparently spent quite a bit of time in this room (and a lot less time on the streets) than the narrative would lead one to believe. In a letter to Anna Strunsky on 21 August 1902, London reveals how much time he spent writing the narrative that would get him out of the wilds and back to civilization. When he wrote, the book was one-fifth done, but he was frenetically moving ahead: "Am rushing, for I am made sick by this human hellhole called London Town. I find it almost impossible to believe that some of the horrible things I have seen are really so."[17] In this sense, the room represents "escape" as both a sanctuary and in its function as a place where London can write the narrative that will financially enable him to leave the abyss or "hellhole."

In the space of Jack London's London, writing is a decidedly Western activity. First, it is writing that allows London to step out of the East. Second, only back in "port" can he can find the privacy that allows him to write. Third, the act of writing immediately marks London as a foreigner. He would disrupt his secret exploration if he were to take out a notebook and start writing. As we have already seen above, when London lets on that he is a writer, he fundamentally changes his relationship with his subjects and loses his desired epistemological privilege. By itself, this factor is enough to require the ethnographic "safe house" as a guarantor of London's authority.

But if he must retreat or ascend to Johnny Upright's in order to maintain his disguise, we should wonder how London maintained his disguise when he took the seventy-seven photographs that powerfully enhance the book's documentary quality.[18] Some of the photographs show us a particular scene that London is describing in his narrative—"Petticoat Lane," "The East India Docks"—while others have captions that are direct quotes from the text—"In the shadow of Christ's Church I saw a sight I never wish to see again." The photographs lend authority to London's representation of the East End. Although London appears in only one of the photographs, each one testifies to London's presence, reminding the audience that his eye has been "there." The photographs downplay London's presence as mediator all together; they introduce the possibility of unmediated access for the audience to the East Enders. The photographs offer a fantasy of readerly presence in the dangerous world of East London.

However, while the photographs give the narrative an authority of presence, they also serve to undercut London's claim to epistemological privilege. How, we should ask, does he photograph his poor subjects and maintain an appearance "of like kind?" While London tells us so much about his trip, he never tells us anything about taking pictures, the sheer number of which suggest that he shot scenes fairly often. London cannot tell his reader about his photographic activities because to do so would be to admit that every time he took out the camera, he literally took off his disguise and revealed himself as an outsider. Any claim to show East End life "as it really is" is subverted by the behavior that the camera produces. The introduction of the camera caused people to stop what they were doing, in some cases out of curiosity for this new-fangled, alien device and in others to actually pose for the pictures. In almost every one of London's photographs, at least one (and sometimes many) of the figures looks directly into the camera's lens. These photographed "natives" turn the gaze of the ethnographer back on him and, in so doing, disrupt the subject-object relations between ethnographer and natives and between reader and characters, on which the text is structured.

This reversal again reminds us that the ethnographic text is, among other things, an act of self-fashioning; one of the most important objects being constructed by the text is its authorial subject. London could not play "candid camera" for one obvious reason—because the size of cameras in 1902 would not allow such concealment. While we cannot fault him for blowing his cover in order to obtain such evidence (albeit "tainted" evidence), we might wonder why he tells us, in great detail, about the old clothes he wears, but not about the camera he totes around. London seeks to gain authority through "documentary" photography, without calling our attention to his manifest presence as an outsider in the urban jungle.

London, the urban participant-observer, is involved in a double concealment. On the one hand, he must conceal his identity from his subjects in order to maintain "pure" interaction. On the other, he must also conceal from his reader moments when the natives see through his disguise. If he reveals those apparently plentiful moments when the subject-object relations are ruptured, he would effectively discredit the authority of the photographic evidence that purport to display objectively how the other half lives. London's photographs both offer an immediately "real" window to the East End and, in so doing, obscure the text's imaginative qualities. The novelty of photography in an account of urban exploration tends to overshadow the messages of London's many imaginative visions and representations.

Toward the end of the book, he abandons the voice—adopted after the opening—of social reporter, statistical recorder, and man-in-the-street for a voice that immediately sounds more poetic. The narrative assumes an explicitly dreamlike (or visionary) quality; this London sounds at times like Coleridge on opium, at times like Marinetti wandering the Futurist streets, at times like Eliot gazing over the Wasteland. His "untellable" tale is a chapter titled "A Vision of the Night."

At first, London anchors his experience in reality by giving it a definite location—"Last night I walked along Commercial Street from Spitalfields to Whitechapel, and still continuing south, down Leman Street to the docks" (283). The geographic positioning lends the ethnography an air of objectivity. By providing street names, in effect, he says, "Dear reader, you too can see what I saw, hear what I heard, smell what I smelled; that is have my experience. The vision I am about to give you is available, provided only that you come to this place." While London provides a specific geographic location, he is less careful with respect to time. "Last night" could have been any night. By being less specific about time, London implies that the "when" of his experience is insignificant. The entire narrative—*The People of the Abyss*—shares this chapter's emphasis on specific places and lack of emphasis on time. As an ethnographer, he cannot admit that this experience is unique, that it has an irreducible moment in history, because that would highlight its subjective and ephemeral qualities. To highlight his vision's historicity would be to subvert his authority.

In London's other introductory sentence, he positions his narrative against other narratives: "And as I walked I smiled at the East End papers, which filled with civic pride, boastfully proclaim that there is nothing the matter with the East End as a living place for men and women" (283–84). Since we already know that London does not share this rosy view, his mention of the East End papers functions to remind us yet again that we are on the verge of moving from textual falsehood (the newspapers) to textual truth (his visions in *The People of the Abyss*).

London is compelled to reproduce his realistic ethnographic authority through geographic anchoring at this particular point in order to set up the text's most clearly imaginative or fictional passage—the most bizarre tale London has to tell. Yet it is also the most crucial part of his story. "It is rather hard to tell a tithe of what I saw. Much of it is untellable. But in a general way I may say that I saw a nightmare, a fearful slime that quickened the pavement with life, a mess of unmentionable obscenity that put into eclipse the 'nightly horror' of Piccadilly and the Strand. It was a menagerie of garmented bipeds that looked something like humans and more like beasts, and to complete the picture, brass-buttoned keepers kept order among them when they snarled too fiercely" (284). It all seems like T. S. Eliot's Unreal City, or at least an inhuman one, a collection of "garmented bipeds" that is more bestial than human. London feels no kinship to these creatures; his figure of "garmented bipeds" calls attention to his distance from this species.

Here, he is not even an anthropologist any more; he becomes a naturalist who classifies. His East Enders are clothed animals; like London they wear the costume of something they are not. However, there is a difference: whereas London's costume enables a metaphorical descent, the "costumed" East Enders use clothing to enact a metaphorical ascent. The scene disorients him, causing him to let his guard down for a moment when he reveals he is composing a "picture." In placing a painterly distance between himself and this vision, he admits that his representation is produced or constructed, not simply reflective. Similarly, the labeling of the vision as a "nightmare" calls attention to his imaginative intervention: one doesn't see nightmares, one's unconscious produces them. This story has to be painted or narrated; for London is not in the presence of what the camera can capture.

London survives his "nightmare" because keepers ("brass-buttoned policemen") hold the snarling beasts in check. In fact, it is the keepers who ensure the safety of the narrating London, who experiences this scene as if naked or, in this context, wearing the costume of civilization. "I was glad the keepers were there, for I did not have on my 'seafaring' clothes, and I was what is called a mark for the creature of prey that prowled up and down" (285). London's revelation that during the night vision he is out of costume seems curious. Has he not already told us back in chapter 1 to discredit any knowledge he obtains while wearing the garb of civilization?

London gains so much comfort and excitement from viewing the police as keepers that he extends the zoo trope to every other object in view:

> At times, between keepers, these males looked at me sharply, hungrily, gutter-wolves that they were, and I was afraid of their hands, of their naked hands, as one may be afraid of the paws of a gorilla. They reminded me of gorillas. Their bodies were small, ill-shaped, and squat. There were no swelling muscles, no abundant thews and wide-spreading shoulders. They exhibited, rather, an elemental economy of nature, such as cave-men must have exhibited. But there was strength in those meagre bodies, the ferocious, primordial strength to clutch and gripe and tear and rend. (285)

Although there are women present, his attention is caught by the "males," whose penetrating gaze is felt "sharply." Here, there is another reversal. As in the photographs, the gaze is reversed. The "social investigator" becomes an object of cannibalistic curiosity. In this instance, he is not just an object for the eyes but, in his imagination, an object for their hunger—a piece of meat. He is also an object for their hands, to which he pays special attention. The narrative lingers not just on the hands themselves, but also on their nakedness. For London, they represent the threat of violence—clutching, gripping, tearing, rending—and simple physical contact. These hands catalyze a complex combination of fears, including fears of death, working-class contamination, "primordial" masculinity, and homosexual panic.

In this scene, London cannot even decide whether the East Enders are animals or people, gorillas, gutter wolves, or cavemen. But whether beast or savage, they suggest to him a primitive, "primordial" power. In London's fantastic "nightmare," their "strength" overrides the evidence of the merely visible world. In the passage above, these men actually *lack* "swelling muscles," "abundant thews," and "wide-spreading shoulders," and their bodies are "meagre." In calling attention to *what* these men lack and not the fact of lack *itself,* London evokes a presence that creates a fearful impression and contradicts or subsumes the visual evidence that a camera might have captured. As he struggles to tell the "untellable," like Marlow in *Heart of Darkness,* the invisible becomes more powerful than the visible.

Once he conjures an imaginative vision of their "ferocious, primordial strength," London can flesh out his tale of potential, though unrealized, terrors. This is, after all, the neighborhood where the Ripper murders occurred fourteen years earlier. He begins his walk, presumably, from the Flower and Dean Street lodgings (adjacent to Commercial Street in Spitalfields) in the vicinity of the location of the Ripper murders. The men who people London's vision are also Ripper-like predators. "When they spring upon their human prey they are known even to bend the victim backward and double its body till the back is broken. They possess neither conscience or sentiment, and they will kill for a half-sovereign, without fear or favor, if they are given but half a chance. They are a new species, a breed of city savages" (285). The people of his abysmal vision are "a new species, a breed of city savages." This formulation is crucial. The terrors experienced in this vision do not signify racial regression or degeneration. Instead, they mark the emergence of a "new" type, a people with a unique physiognomy, and without morality. The dangers are great because they will kill with little to gain (a mere "half-sovereign"), randomly, and, presumably, at risk to themselves (they require only "half a chance").

London's vision of the East End as a zoo without cages gives way to a vision of the "urban jungle." Once we have "a new species, a breed of city savages," it doesn't take long to see that we need a jungle for them. "The streets and houses, alleys and courts, are their hunting grounds. As valley and mountain are to the natural savage, street and building are to them. The slum is their jungle, and they live and prey in the jungle" (285). The slum dwellers are "city savages" in the urban "jungle." And Jack London is the explorer-hero who has emerged from this savage land to urge this truth. He is like J. Habakkuk Jephson, the protagonist in Doyle's fantasy, who warns civilized Europe about future invasions by the dark races of Africa. But in Jack London's "realist" account, the barbarian invaders are neither fantasy characters nor waiting outside the city gates. Rather, they are "real" people who live right next door. London pleads with the West Enders, who are as innocently naive as he was before his adventure, to recognize the dangerous possibilities he sees festering in the urban jungle.

> The dear soft people of the golden theatres and wonder-mansions of the West End do not see these creatures, do not dream that they exist. But they are here, alive, very much alive in their jungle. And woe the day, when England is fighting in her last trench, and her able-bodied men are on the firing-line! For on that day they will crawl out of their dens and lairs, and the people of the West End will see them, as the dear soft aristocrats of Feudal France saw them and asked one another, "Whence came they?" "Are they men?" (285–86)

London hints that a future like the one envisioned by H. G. Wells in *The Time Machine* is not all that distant. Like the peasants of the French

Revolution, the "new species . . . of city savages" will travel Westward (and Upward) in order to avenge themselves. In this light, his ultimate plea for socialism should be seen in the light of both sympathy and fear and as calls for both working-class betterment and working-class containment.

In "A Vision of the Night," crucially placed near the book's conclusion, London extends his ethnographic insight that the culture of the East Enders is "different" or other. Now, the inhabitants of the East End are to be seen not simply as "the other half" or the "lower class," but as a new species, a new breed, and a new "savage" race. The introduction of a more "poetic" vision into a text of scientific "investigation" indicates that London's text is, in the final analysis, not just discovery but also invention, not just recognition but also naming, not just reflective but also creative, not just descriptive but also imaginative.

Once we recognize the poetic qualities of the ethnographic text, we can ask the following questions: What is it about London that makes him inclined to tell *this* story, to paint *this* picture, to see *these* sights? Why does London write London as the urban jungle? the East Enders as "savages"? What does he have to gain? We can find one answer to these questions in London's self-proclaimed socialist politics. His description of the urban "savages" is supposed to elicit sympathy in the reader. They are not to blame for their own degradation; the responsibility lies with capitalism.

As he writes in his preface, London's Londoners attest to the failure of the "political machinery": "I measure manhood less by political aggregations than by individuals. Society grows, while political machines rack to pieces and become 'scrap.' For the English, so far as manhood and womanhood and health and happiness go, I see a broad and smiling future. But for a great deal of the political machinery, which at present mismanages for them, I see nothing else than the scrap heap" (viii). London's ethnography builds toward a concluding chapter in which he condemns "The Management." His survey of a particular locale (the East End) has implications for capitalist society as a whole. Capitalism has stunted growth, destroyed bodies, and produced competitive predators. Each East Ender discussed by London—"every worn-out, pasty-faced pauper, every blind man, every prison babe, every man, woman, and child whose belly is gnawing with hunger pangs" (316)—testifies to the failure of "management." As an optimistic socialist, Jack London is convinced that "it is inevitable that this management, which has grossly and criminally mismanaged, shall be swept away" (316). Yet by the time we reach this point in the narrative, it is difficult to share his faith in the inevitable logic of capitalism's demise. His portrait of the degraded "savages" has been too convincing; they cannot be capable of sweeping anything away; even if one were to grant the "gutter-wolves" of London's night vision the power to sweep away existing conditions, surely these beasts would be incapable of replacing them with a new civiization.

London's "urban jungle" and "city savages" are rhetorically necessary for his politics. Like the dying Africans Marlow confronts at the company station in *Heart of Darkness,* the emaciated bodies of the East Enders serve as evidence with which the writer can condemn the "machine" that produced them. For London, this machine has committed the ultimate horror in spawning a "new breed." It is a crime not only against them but, more importantly, against Nature. "As they drag their squat, misshapen bodies along the highways and byways, they resemble some vile spawn from the underground. Their very presence, the fact of their existence, is an outrage to the fresh bright sun and the green and growing things. The clean, up-standing trees cry shame upon them and their withered crookedness, and their rottenness is a slimy desecration of the sweetness and purity of nature" (168). For London, the production of this "race" is a crime worse than genocide: "it is far kinder to kill a strong man with a clean-slicing blow of singing steel than to make a beast of him, and of his seed through the generations, by the artful and spidery manipulation of industry and politics" (169). London's socialism has a decidedly Darwinian twist to it in his concern not just with living instances but also with "seed." He is very much concerned with the body and its function in reproducing the race. Yet he is not simply concerned with the body as an instrument of healthy reproduction. He also focuses on it as an aesthetic object—a locus of "natural" beauty.

While London's attention to the East Enders' bodies reinforces the socialist politics and sympathy for the working classes that London brought with him to the East End, they also point to a more personal concern with issues of race, nationality, gender, and his own class origins. It is my conviction that London's deepest motivations in writing the "urban jungle" do not stem from a sympathetic desire to describe another culture, but rather derive from his desire to construct his own identity and body in racial and nationalist relation to the East Enders. Or better still, the false problem of ascribing relative value to his motivations (surface versus depth, politics versus personal) can be avoided if we see how London's two projects are the same: In writing London (the city), he writes London (the man). The culture of the East End and individual East Enders function as touchstones against which London defines himself.

As we have already seen, London sees a close link between economics ("the machine") and the bodies of his "natives." In his narrative, London shows a remarkably constant attention to the East Enders' bodies and frequently puts them on display. This is especially true with regard to male bodies. He reacts with repugnance at the urban jungle's effects on his subjects. But while capitalism is the responsible culprit, he never doubts that the new race has become a biological or genetic fact. London's disgust with a generalized and naturalized urban body ultimately has far-reaching racial (Anglo-Saxon) and national (English and American) significance. This body is at the heart of his narrative and the photographs that accompany it.

Although the photographs are London's vehicle for introducing us to the urban savages ("face to face" and "face to physique"), in one case they also allow a most direct look at the author and what he is up to. "Bert and The Author Ready to Pick Hops" shows London beside one of his "natives." It is the only photograph in which London himself appears. In the photograph, the author dwarfs "a young East End cobbler" named Bert (172). Despite London's claims about Bert's youth, he actually appears quite a bit older than the youthful London. This discrepancy is only the beginning of the contrast. Bert is shorter, thinner, his shoulders stoop, and his jacket seems sizes too big. He stands with legs together and thumbs in pockets. His clothes are markedly wrinkled and seem to be all there is to him. His head tilts forward slightly and his eyes seem shy—he is unable or unwilling to make direct contact with the camera. In marked contrast, "The Author" is more handsome and robust. He is bigger and well-balanced. His clothes fit better than Bert's. He does not seem to be ashamed of his body—several buttons on his shirt are undone, exposing his chest. But most importantly, he gazes straight into the camera. There is no embarrassment or diffidence. In this pose, he looks like one who fears nothing. Although neither of the pair occupies the center, London certainly takes up more of it; Bert has been elbowed closer to the margins.

In this photograph, we see the usually inconspicuous "Author" at his most conspicuous. Although we might read London's self-denomination in the caption—"The Author"—as yet another attempt to erase his own subjectivity from the text, it is also a moment in which his own individuality is subsumed in his function. He becomes a type, or species, and, more importantly, an object for our (and his own) gaze and study. He wants readers to pay attention to both Bert's body and his own. The photo encourages us to compare outsider and insider, London and the Londoner, the writer from the American West and the cobbler from the East End. The photograph is the most stark comparison London makes in a narrative that is full of such comparisons—a comparison that is carefully composed.

Its composition can be seen in the pose adopted by the author and read in the text accompanying the photo. London had asked Bert to join him on an expedition into the countryside to pick hops. Bert agrees to join him, but not before London gives him careful instructions. "Acting on my advice, he had brought his 'worst rags,' and as we hiked up the London Road out of Maidstone he was worrying greatly for fear we had come too ill-dressed for the business" (172). Bert, the "native," is clearly uncomfortable with the costume that he has been told to don. In fact, it is this discomfort that might be responsible for his slack pose and avoidance of the camera eye. In a practice that will become increasingly common in ethnography, the native is told how to dress and how to act before the camera. Better off than many of London's East End acquaintances, Bert joined London not because he needed employment, but because "he yielded to the lure of adventure." Bert's curiosity and desire for adventure are just like Jack London's— while the photo is composed to communicate their difference, the contradictory message of the text indicates that its two subjects are not all that different.

When London encounters "evidence" contradicting his paradigmatic East Ender (Bert), he reads it as part of a tragic plot about noble, but "doomed," savages. He describes one atypical East Ender as follows: "His head was shapely, and so gracefully was it poised upon a perfect neck that I was not surprised by his body that night when he stripped for bed. I have seen many men strip, in gymnasium and training quarters, men of good blood and upbringing, but I have never seen one who stripped to better advantage than this young sot of two and twenty, this young god doomed to rack and ruin in four or five short years, and to pass hence without posterity to receive the splendid heritage it was his to bequeath" (39). Like James Greenwood in "A Night in the Workhouse," Jack London, the student of male physique, finds a "young

god," a "noble savage," who is all beauty.[19] Those features that defy
bodily perfection, do so because of their exposure to a harsh existence—the youth's "sweet" mouth and lips are "developing a harsh
twist." In the slum, the ethnographer discovers his ideal "type," but
upon finding him, immediately condemns him to a future of doom, of
"rack and ruin," of wasted posterity. London must accommodate the
exception to the rule, the diamond in the rough, the god among the
savages, the shapely in the midst of the misshapen, by relocating it in
the country or relegating it to the vanishing past.

Beside the deterioration of the racial stock that occurs in the city,
London cites one other reason for the development of the new "breed"
of urban savages: the drainage of Anglo-Saxon blood from the national
center to the colonies. For London, the essence of Englishness is no
longer to be found in England. Rather, "the erstwhile men of England
are now the men of Australia, of Africa, of America. England has sent
forth 'the best she breeds' for so long, and has destroyed those that
remained so fiercely, that little remains for her to do but to sit down
through the long nights and gaze at royalty on the wall" (184). When
Jack London comes to visit the English, it is as if he found them absent
and someone else ("savages") occupying their homes. A popular evolu-
tionist, London laments the passing of old Britain. In a discussion of
British naval prowess, London writes,

> The true British merchant seaman has passed away. The merchant
> service is no longer a recruiting ground for such sea dogs as fought with
> Nelson at Trafalgar and the Nile. Foreigners largely man the merchant
> ships, though Englishmen still continue to offer them and to prefer for-
> eigners for'ard. In South Africa the colonial teaches the Islander how to
> shoot, and the officers muddle and blunder; while at home the street
> people play hysterically at mafficking, and the War Office lowers the
> stature for enlistment.
>
> It could not be otherwise. The most complacent Britisher cannot
> hope to draw off the life blood, and underfeed, and keep it up forever.
> (184)

In civilizing the world, Britain has been drained of its "true" seaman
(semen) and blood.

In writing his ethnography of the East End, London never fully gave
up his original goal of reporting on the aftermath of the Boer War.
Originally seeking knowledge about why the British suffered a national

embarrassment in a fight over a colonial possession, London finds his answer in the abyss of Darkest England. Darkest England contains "a deteriorated stock left to undergo still further deterioration" (221). "Those who are lacking, the weak of heart and head and hand, as well as the rotten and hopeless, have remained to carry on the breed. And year by year, in turn, the best they breed are taken from them. . . . The wine of life has been drawn off to spill itself in blood and progeny over the rest of the earth. Those that remain are the lees, and they are segregated and steeped in themselves. They become indecent and bestial." London's interest in the bodies of the urban savages and his discovery of "a new and different race" in the East End is confirmed by an evolutionary tale of English national decline. The "life blood" has been drained off; the stock has deteriorated; all that remains are the "lees." London offers us the sad end of this story in the photograph of Bert. He can even read such degeneracy in the body of the beautiful country youth who is a "young god doomed to rack and ruin" without progeny. And most importantly, he demonstrates it by way of comparison with his own robust self. For it is the son of the American West, the London of the photograph, who exemplifies the characteristics of the true British line, the untainted blood, and the pure stock.

London's Anglo-Saxonism is also evident in his choice of a wife. In 1899, London had met Anna Strunsky, a Russian Jew, at a socialist lecture. The two were passionately drawn to each other and collaborated on an epistolary dialogue about the nature of love, published as *The Kempton-Wallace Letters* in 1903. "Yet," according to biographer Earle Labor, "despite his great affections for Anna, Jack married Bessie Madern the following spring [1900]—not because of romantic love but because he wanted 'seven sturdy Saxon sons and seven beautiful daughters'" (90). In addition to the debts that drove him to write of the East End, Lundquist suggests, London's trip was "partly to escape from his marriage."[20]

The People of the Abyss can best be understood in the context of London's better-known work on the American West, where he was raised. It is a hybrid work of both British and American literature, like Eliot's *The Waste Land*. For London, the venture into the East End is a return to origins—part of the anthropological and modernist project of looking at peoples and cultures as examples of previous moments in a narrative of racial progress and Civilization. When London (the city) produces a new race of urban savages, London (the author) registers both a disappointment that his ancestral culture is one of squalor, filth, ugliness, and an "outright" denial of kinship. Instead, his true ancestors are the "wine" that has been drained off to the colonies. The "city savages" are not his ancestral people who have left and gone elsewhere. These people are someone else—"a new and different race." Having established this convenient fiction, London can then envision himself and his own American culture as examples of the true stock and the main racial line. In returning to his origins, London finds not himself but a savage other. For him, civilization—the true Anglo-Saxon stock— is now to be found in Australia, Africa, and, one suspects most importantly, America.

If we see Jack London's trip to London's East End as a frustrated search for his racial origins, it is also a return to class origins. Jack London was the child of working-class parents in northern California. As a youth, his family constantly moved from one home to another because his stepfather could not remain long at any one job. Paternal "origins" were also a highly confusing yet charged issue for London. He did not know his biological father; his patronym came from his stepfather. When he later learned the name of his probable father, he decided to keep the name London that allusively tied him to the capital of the Anglo-Saxon world. If not self-named, he is at least someone who has chosen his name from two possibilities. The same can be said of his first name: he was very careful to renounce John for Jack, a name that carries more masculine, boyish, and, perhaps, working-class connotations. The youthful London was self-taught. He worked among the lower classes on the San Francisco docks, aboard fishing boats, as a prospector during the Yukon Gold Rush, and traveled as a hobo throughout America during the 1890s. San Francisco, as the center of West Coast and Pacific trade in London's youth, was, like London Town, a cosmopolitan crossroads. In San Francisco, the most significant immigrant group was the Chinese, but, because of the midcentury gold rush, the city was full of immigrants from the Eastern United States and Europe. Most likely, the East End of London was not, for Jack London, a foreign city, but rather one that uncannily reminded him of his youth among the docks and urban jungle of 1890s San Francisco.

By the time he published *The People of the Abyss,* the twenty-six-year-old London had become a successful writer of fiction and nonfiction. Financially, he had transcended his class origins. He still feels the urge of upward class mobility (ascent) and fears slipping back into poverty (descent). This fear may be impossible for him to escape and is certainly present during his East End exploration, a project resulting from sudden unemployment. Yet, at the same time, his journey into the East End is, at some level, a nostalgic trip back to the place from where he had come. As an act of self-fashioning, London's ethnography of the East End constructs another culture in terms of which he can define his own culture and self, while also constructing a portrait of his own racial and class origins. While we should not doubt London's genuine sympathy for the urban savages and his commitment to their salvation through socialism, neither can we discount the consequences of defining the urban poor as a separate race and species. In returning to the self from which he believes himself to have ascended, London's "descent" into the abyss measures the distance that he has already climbed.

In the next chapter, I explore how another out-of-work seaman, Joseph Conrad, also imagined London as an abyss, an urban jungle, and a site of metaphorical descent. Unlike Jack London, whose depiction of the dark urban jungle structures a romantic vision of a vibrant Anglo-Saxon race thriving in the open spaces of the American West, Conrad's vision of the urban jungle is the very unromantic sign of a more universal darkness.

CHAPTER SIX

WHERE DOES THE EAST END?

With Conrad in Darkest Soho

Of all quarters in this queer adventurous amalgam called London, Soho is perhaps least suited to the Forsyte spirit. . . . Untidy, full of Greeks, Ismaelites, cats, Italians, tomatoes, restaurants, organs, coloured stuffs, queer names, people looking out of upper windows, it dwells remote from the British Body Politic.

—John Galsworthy, *In Chancery* (1920)[1]

No discussion of literature, metropolitan London, and the discourses of empire would be complete without treating Joseph Conrad. And any treatment of Conrad's vision of the urban jungle must come to terms with the most London of his novels, the fictional cityscape of *The Secret Agent* (1907). The rather-not-so-simple question this chapter poses to a novel whose deceptive subtitle is "A Simple Tale" is, simply, Why Soho? Or, to put the matter more fully, given a well-established discourse that locates the urban jungle and darkest England in London's East End (William Booth, Arthur Morrison, Israel Zangwill, Margaret Harkness, Jack London, and others), why does Conrad, in 1906, choose to focus most of his dark narrative gaze elsewhere?

In light of the authors listed above, Conrad's turning away from the East End, rather than a turn toward Soho, should be what immediately strikes us as the significant oddity. Such a departure is clear when we map the geographic references of the entire novel, as Robert Hampson has done at length elsewhere.[2] The prominent feature in his account is not simply the extent of the cityscape covered by Conrad, but the utter exclusion of an East End that had figured so prominently in the 1880s and 1890s. Hampson's topographical narrative is too lengthy to quote in full here, but includes the following specific London locales: Vauxhall Bridge Road; 1 Stratton Street, Piccadilly; Verloc's shop at 32 Brett Street, Soho; Islington; Whitehall; Westminster; various locations in Greenwich; Old Kent Road; Knightsbridge; Chesham Square; Bridge Street and the Embankment; Waterloo Station; South London; "across Westminster Bridge and past 'the towers of the Abbey,' the 'lights of

Victoria,' Sloane Square and 'the railings of the park'" (presumably Hyde Park). Though Hampson correctly comments that "*The Secret Agent* is Conrad's most wide-ranging engagement with London," what he and others have missed is that its range seems to stop at the amorphous boundaries of the East End; *The Secret Agent* takes us no farther east than Waterloo Bridge and the Embankment. While Greenwich is no doubt east, it is more suburban than urban and was never within the domain of East End mythologizing.

This omission of East London is far from a matter of Conradian ignorance and is especially curious given Conrad's personal biography; as a sailor, the area of the docks in the East End would have been the stuff of his earliest London memories, and, as Hampson's own essay demonstrates, they are prominent locales in other Conradian narratives such as *Victory, A Personal Record, The Nigger of the 'Narcissus,'* and *Chance.* Indeed, the prominence of the East End in *Chance* seems especially pertinent, given that the earliest drafts of that novel were begun in 1905, just before Conrad began working on *The Secret Agent.*[3] But while Hampson argues that "it is clear that an exactly conceived topography underlies both *The Secret Agent* and *Chance,*"[4] I want to argue that, because of the absence of the East End in *The Secret Agent,* these are markedly different urban topographies.[5]

In 1967, Avrom Fleishman launched his discussion of "The Symbolic World of *The Secret Agent*" by asking us to consider "why Conrad bothered to take up anarchism at precisely the time (1906) that he did."[6] My argument buttresses Fleishman's claim that the novel is "not as much a novel about political anarchism as it is a novel about social anarchy," at least insofar as one might want to keep the political and social domains separate.[7] But it is now time to ask a slightly different question, one that puts the emphasis on space rather than time: Why did Conrad bother to take up anarchism at precisely the place (Soho, London) that he did? While Galsworthy's Forsyte wants to imagine that anarchic Soho "dwells remote from the British Body Politic," even a cursory glance at a map of London proves otherwise, at least spatially, or geographically. To begin then, let us leave behind *The Secret Agent* and discern what sort of "untidiness" (following Galsworthy) Soho and, indeed, London have to offer to Conrad's evolving modernist imagination.

In 1907, *Strand Magazine,* a publication whose career is inextricable from that of Sherlock Holmes, asked several eminent gentlemen the question, "Which is the most interesting street in London?" Some of the worthies suggest those grand national monuments such as White-hall and Pall Mall; others refer to centers of global finance and commerce such as Lombard and Leadenhall Street; still others point to the Strand and Fleet Street artery that connect the centers of government and commerce. Two chroniclers of the late-Victorian East End, Arthur Morrison and George Sims, single out important streets in their own haunts. Morrison speaks with the voice of nostalgia in selecting the Ratcliff Highway "in its old days. It is interesting still to those who remember it in its glory and can still detect the scattered and blackened traces of its ancient state. Otherwise it is rather dull." For Morrison, the author of *Tales of Mean Streets* and *A Child of the Jago,* interesting London streets are unavailable to our senses in the here and now; they exist only as traces that can activate the historical imagination of long-time Londoners.

Strand Magazine then turns to Sims, "No one can speak with a more intimate knowledge of our great Metropolis than Mr. George R. Sims." Sims's interest is in the modern-day street as a linguistic cauldron, even as he, too, echoes Morrison's nostalgic gaze. For him,

> The most interesting street in London to me is the Mile End Road. From morning till night it is packed with pages from the Book of Life written in many European tongues. . . . Here Asia jostles Europe and the dominant Oriental note carries you back to the Picture Bible of your childhood. Here are Abraham and Isaac, Jacob and Esau, Aaron and Miriam, the bearded Patriarchs and the children of Israel, who have come through the wilderness to a Canaan that, if it does not flow with milk and honey for them just when they enter it, has promise of a golden harvest to be reaped in the fat years to come. . . . Both the Ghettoes—the old Ghetto and the new Ghetto—pour strange streams of humanity into the Mile End Road. The English-speaking Jews are in the minority. Everywhere the world jargon of the Ashkenazim, which is 'Yiddish,' salutes your ear, and salutes it somewhat harshly if you have no familiarity with the German tongue.[8]

For Sims, "the most interesting street in London" seems worlds and tongues away from the more official national sites of Westminster and the City that might normally be seen as anchoring "the British Body Politic." But, if we think about this for a moment, Sims's Mile End Road is an equally important site for the constitution of linguistic and national identity. It contains the domiciles and language of an instantiated "other," one readily available for visitation, exploration, colonization, and conversion by the English. A recently settled Canaan, it is populated by a people who have just "come through the wilderness," a wilderness from which it and its natives seem just barely removed. There one can hear a "world jargon" that helps define a uniquely English language. The Mile End Road of London's East End becomes, if not the locus of the urban primitive, at least a village, available to and against which the more affluent West Enders can identify themselves as civilized, modern, urbane, and English. As a renowned chronicler expert on the intimacies of the East End, Sims can pinpoint an extremely precise locale for the late-Victorian urban jungle. Whether his audience might want to visit or avoid it, they know where to find it.

Several months before the *Strand* piece, a fracas had broken out over another street's claim to metropolitan distinction and infamy, this one not quite so far from the fashionable West End. Reporting to a royal commission in 1906, a police inspector—an Inspector MacKay—had claimed that "Greek-street, Soho, is one of the very worst streets I have to deal with. In fact, it is the worst street in the West End of London. Crowds of people gather there nightly who are little better than a pest. I will go further and say that some of the vilest reptiles in London live there or frequent it."[9] If the Mile End Road is the new domain of the oriental linguist, then Greek Street, Soho might be the proper laboratory for the Edwardian naturalist, at least according to one local policeman. The citizens of Soho, led by their champion, the Reverend Cardwell, the vicar of the Parish of Saint Anne's, fired back and claimed that the inhabitants of Soho, while mostly foreigners, were by-and-large moral, hard-working, law-abiding citizens. Certainly, their street did not deserve MacKay's negative accolades.

Despite MacKay's ultimate retraction of the remark, he was on to something. If Soho was not one of the "very worst" locales in turn-of-the-century London or its West End, it was certainly one of the most interesting in ways that the *Strand*'s panel of worthies seems to neglect. This notoriety is especially true for reasons similar to those that attracted Sims to the Mile End Road. For instance, here one might hear an even more polyglot "world jargon" than the still recognizable Yiddish of the East End ghettoes. In August 1900, a reporter for *Cassell's Saturday Journal* had described Soho as "more Continental than it is English."[10] His remark appears as part of an interview with the abovementioned Reverend Cardwell. The reporter is especially interested in two aspects of Soho: its cosmopolitan character and its reputation as a haunt for political anarchists. Both qualities might be seen already, as they were later by the Galsworthian Forsyte (1920), to threaten the integrity of the British body politic. In response to the charge of anarchism, Cardwell admits that Soho is the home of many anarchists, many of them refugees from France after the defeat of the Commune in the 1870s. But contrary to popular conception, "they are, for the most part, decent, moral-living people." Karl Marx—not, of course, an anarchist—lived for many years in Dean Street, Soho, a site whose Continental reputation as a haven for political radicals dates back to the late seventeenth century, when French Huguenots settled there.[11]

In response to the charge that it is "more Continental than it is English," Cardwell lovingly rhapsodizes on the heterogeneity of his congregation, cataloging his parish as if it were his special collection: "[E]very European nationality is represented in this parish. We have Austrians, Belgians, Danes, Dutchmen, Frenchmen, Germans, Greeks, Hungarians, Italians, Norwegians, Poles, Portuguese, Roumanians, Russians, Servians, Spaniards, Swedes, Swiss, and Turks, to whom may be added Armenians, Persians, and Africans. The Italians alone number over 650." In a similar interview three years later (1903), Cardwell reports that while "12 years ago, the foreign population was little more than half," now "there are 7,396 persons" in his district and "nearly all of these are foreigners."[12] For Cardwell, Soho was experienced as a picturesque, multicultural, working-class "village," an image that still colors late-twentieth-century images of Soho, as we can see in the title of Judith Summers's recent *Soho: A History of London's Most Colourful Neighbourhood* (1989). Looking back on late-Victorian and Edwardian Soho, Summers suggests that "for the international community of Soho-ites, daily life contained all the small pleasures of and intimacies of living in a village at carnival time, and despite their poverty most children who grew up there enjoyed an almost idyllic life." I must admit a strong skepticism about Summers's late-1980s multicultural nostalgia for the happy urban village, doubts fueled by another image of Soho that emerges from the historical record. This alternative tendency is to see Soho as London's center of vice and pollution—sexual, political, linguistic, and artistic. Indeed, Summers herself describes this Soho elsewhere in her account; then as now, it was the locale of "clip joints where 'unwary men' were 'lured by innocent young girls imported from the Continent'—only to be robbed on the staircase by souteneurs who were 'the very incarnation of a "bounder."'"[13] For us to decide whether Soho was an immoral inferno or a Disney-esque exemplar of liberal British tolerance is beside the point. What seems more significant is the duality of representation of this urban locale, a duality not unlike the writing about the primitive we have seen throughout this study.[14]

Whether Soho is conceived of as an inferno or utopian colorful "village," one can imagine the variety of sounds to be heard while walking down the streets of the parish described by Cardwell. At least the ethnological voice of Sims had been able to identify, if not understand, the sounds of Yiddish in his East End Canaan. Here, however, according to another writer, the sounds of the street were a complete "babel" of tongues, a frightening counterpoint to its "picturesque" visual qualities: "No city in Europe has quite such a cosmopolitan area. The sights one sees in Soho are often picturesque as each nation retains its own method of living. . . . Sometimes this district is invaded by a stray Englishman who happens to pass through one of the markets. Frightened by the fearful babel of languages which assault his ears he quickly makes his way to the nearest large thoroughfare, where he again finds himself in his own country."[15] For Sims, an excursion down the Mile End Road had been a pleasurably exotic excursion through a region remote in time and place. But for this writer, the encounter is not with an identifiable and, thus, manageable Jewish village but with the "babel of languages" spoken by the peoples listed above by Cardwell.

Though we should not be quick to dismiss this writer's claim to ethnic separation and the prevalence of urban subcultures—"each nation retains its own method of living"—it is difficult to imagine these various immigrants remaining in tidily hermetic compartments. Looking back on a document like Cardwell's list and others like it, we should note the curious dearth of hyphens that, in ethnic descriptions, have become so common to our postmodern eyes.[16] His catalog seems to tidy things up too much; we need look no further than Conrad's protagonist Verloc, the offspring of an Anglo-French parental alliance, as evidence that things were a bit more complicated. One can imagine the difficulty, and perhaps impossibility, of orienting oneself in the audible dimension of this Soho. Note how the writer fails to identify any specific language and how the experience is not Sims's "salute" from the "Book of Life," but rather a violent "assault" from which the writer takes flight back to the safety of "his own country."

Of course, even in this passage, all is not a fearful fright; there is also attraction, especially for the sensations of the palate. The writer admits that, "on the other hand, numbers of Englishmen lunch or dine at the Soho restaurants."[17] While the literati, such as Sims and Morrison, continue to focus on an East End they documented during the 1880s and 1890s, popular attention in the first decade of the twentieth century, at least as reflected by journalists, seems to be gravitating toward the streets of Soho as a new locus of the urban jungle—a place that is "picturesque," an "assault," and an appealing place to dine.

Why? Although there were many reasons for a turn toward Soho, four seem especially crucial. The first two I have already mentioned: Soho's reputation as a refuge for anarchists and its cosmopolitan character ("more Continental than it is English"), both of which are reflected by the anarchic babel heard on the streets.[18] Another reason is Soho's long-standing associations with the vice trade, deviant sexual practices, and an atmosphere of moral pollution. The Reverend Cardwell launched the first "Clean Up Soho" campaign in 1892, bringing suits against keepers of disreputable lodging houses and restaurants, an activity that seems to have peaked in 1895 and 1896. For Walter Besant, writing in 1898, there is an "interest, known to the fullest extent only by those who work in the place, that attaches to the vice and poverty of Soho," a district that he defines as the "modern centre" of "profligacy."[19] And, in case one might be ignorant of its local reputation, the London visitor is warned by Baedekker in 1902 "against going to any unrecommended house near Leicester Square [on Soho's fringes], as there are several houses of doubtful reputation in this locality."[20] Indeed, a locality of "doubtful reputation" is perhaps an apt encapsulation of Soho's place in the metropolitan imagination. It is, I would argue, far from accidental that we find this nexus of concerns about impurity—political anarchy, ethnic heterogeneity, and sexual profligacy—all concentrated in one location.

Finally, the appeal of Soho as a new locale of the urban jungle has to do with a most complicated phenomenon that can best be articulated as a "crisis in mapping"—a difficulty in representing the urban landscape that is, ultimately, also a crisis in mapping the self. Soho becomes the solution to a problem in the geographic representation of early-twentieth-century London, a crisis that we can see evidenced in a number of places in the two decades prior to the date of *The Secret Agent*'s composition. First, we can see it in Morrison's evocation of Ratcliff

Highway "in its old days" as London's most interesting street. For the author of *Tales of Mean Streets,* interest is located in the past, a nostalgia for the vanished streets he wrote about only a decade before. The exotic London street can no longer be found on any current map; its existence is neither historical nor fictional.[21] In another vein, we have already seen the crisis of mapping in the competing metaphorics of Jack London's *The People of the Abyss,* a text whose geography shifts from two dimensions to three. That is, London's London is organized around oppositions both horizontal (West End versus East End) and vertical (one descends into the "abyss" of London's East End). In London's text, horizontal and vertical divisions coexist, and indeed complement each other, even though they now include a new cartographic dimension. But in other places, most notably, H. G. Wells's *The Time Machine,* we are asked to look forward to a future where the only significant difference is between those who live above and those who live below.[22] Both of these imaginative reconfigurations—the pastness of the exotic and its movement underground—suggest the unfitness of the geography of the 1880s.

This metaphoric crisis signals a new understanding of the geography of metropolitan London, one instigated by the pioneering sociological investigations of Charles Booth in the late 1880s. Booth's *Descriptive Map of London Poverty* (1889) was based on his street-by-street investigations of relative wealth throughout the vast extent of London. These colored maps articulated a spectrum of wealth from the black and dark blue of the "lowest class" and "very poor" to the red and yellow of the "well-to-do" and "wealthy." Booth's seven-color gradations complicated the gulf between categories of rich and poor such as Disraeli's idea of "two nations" or the division of London into East End and West End. Given the dominant discourse of West and East now being undermined, one might expect to see Booth's color spectrum unfold in an orderly way across the map of London. And, to a certain extent, this is how the map looks from a distance. However, closer analysis reveals finer, yet significant, differentiations. In close proximity to the wealthy West End streets, one sees, usually in backstreets, pockets of blue and black; conversely, one sees a surprising amount of reds and pinks ("working-class comfort") along the more prosperous, major East End thoroughfares, like the Mile End Road.

Although one does not want to say that the city mapped by Booth was an irrational jumble, clearly the order of it was a more complexly sophisticated one than that suggested by the imaginative division of

East and West London in the decades before Booth's survey. As David Reeder succinctly puts it, "Booth's map brings out the complexity in the social patterning of late-Victorian London to great effect."[23] For instance, "it is possible to locate on the map examples of districts exhibiting almost the entire spectrum of colours in the space of a few streets." Booth's maps were a revelation for late-Victorian Londoners, including Booth himself. In 1902, Charles Masterman noted that Booth's work and maps reveal a London "beyond the power of individual synthesis, a chaos resisting all attempts to reduce it to orderly law."[24] Clearly, the older representation of the sharp boundary between a modern West End and a darkly primitive East End needed fine-tuning, if not wholesale revision.

One other incident signals the geographical and epistemological confusion I seek to describe. In May 1910, the bishop of Kensington, during a parish ceremony in Soho, echoed the growing sentiment about Soho's cosmopolitanism and estrangement: "I do not suppose there is any city in the world—I am sure there is not another diocese in the kingdom—which has a more strangely varied population than that confined within these limits." For the bishop, this presented "the very real danger . . . of there arising in West London a sort of East London."[25] This rhetoric demonstrates the unsuitability of his older conceptual map of London to a new situation that can be described only as, illogically, the East in the West.

At this point, we should cast a brief glance ahead to *The Secret Agent* in order to mention that it is a walk westward, to the Kensington embassy of Mr. Vladimir, that starts the trouble in the novel. The emissary of some unspecified East European power, Mr. Vladimir demonstrates that the East End and the Mile End Road are not the only London addresses where one can find transplanted Eastern Europeans. Verloc, in heading West, actually goes East.[26] The title of the present chapter is meant to raise the question of both the decline and "end" of the East End as the imaginative locale of the urban jungle and, echoing the bishop of Kensington, to suggest that this ending of the East raises a new problem; namely, "Where does the East end?" when "there aris[es] in West London a sort of East London."

The urban jungle was now more difficult to locate; like East London, it had become, paradoxically, nowhere and everywhere. Gone was the comforting imaginative containment granted by the fictive East End of earlier decades. Enter Soho. What Soho provided or supplied was a locale to meet the needs of this imaginative geographic crisis.[27] On the one hand, it was a place in close proximity to the West End, a pocket of poverty, vice, foreigners, and sexual exoticism separated from fashionable Mayfair only by the width of Regent Street. The urban jungle was no longer "over there somewhere," as Jack London had been told, but, for West Londoners, practically right here. On the other hand, despite its encroaching proximity, Soho still offered the pleasing containment of an *other* locale. While perilously closer to a West End imagined as the height of civilization, it was still markedly separate on the map.[28] By the early years of the twentieth century, Soho offered a new locale, dangerously proximate, for those primitive qualities formerly situated in East London; but it was still an attempt to contain them imaginatively in an exotic place called Soho. Even when not looked at darkly, but rather as a lightly pleasant medieval or traditional village, Soho is imagined as a primitive community that remains, relic-like, in the heart of central London.

It is, then, for these four interconnected phenomena—political anarchy, ethnic cosmopolitanism, sexual pollution, and a crisis in metropolitan mapping—that the urban jungle resurfaces in central London, in Soho, in the first decade of the twentieth century. The journalists seem to anticipate the literary voices in noticing this shift. Until Conrad. Until, more specifically, *The Secret Agent*.

Conrad's vision of a more generalized or greater London as "one of the dark places of the earth," as a heart of darkness, certainly pre-dates his preoccupation with Soho in *The Secret Agent*. London has been a place of darkness, of "cold, fog, tempests, disease, exile, and death" conquered centuries before by "the decent young citizen" of Rome. But the darkness of London is not merely a thing of its past. Looking back toward London from the ship *Nellie,* the late-Victorian Marlow of *Heart of Darkness* notes a darkness "condensed into a mournful gloom, brooding over the biggest, and the greatest, town on earth."[29]

In his treatment of London and other places, Conrad refuses the kind of polarities—civilization versus savagery, light versus darkness—that infuse the works of his predecessors in the genre of imperial fiction (Haggard, Conan Doyle, and others). Or, to put this more accurately, Conrad reverently invokes these Manichaean dualities only to empty them, cynically, of their efficacy.[30] His narrative voice clings to them as its "saving illusion" even as it rejects their correspondence with his world. Thus, his ambiguous title *Heart of Darkness*, here, vague as to its referent, is equally applicable to the interior of the African continent and the heart of the British metropolis. The "urban jungle" is a kindred Conradian concept, a phrase that paradoxically invokes opposites at the same time it refuses their difference.

In his autobiographical work *The Mirror of the Sea* (1905), Conrad describes a journey up the Thames in a passage resembling a venture into the African jungle.

> This stretch of the Thames from London Bridge to the Albert Docks is to other watersides of river ports what a virgin forest would be to a garden. It is a thing grown up, not made. It recalls a jungle by the confused, varied, and impenetrable aspect of the buildings that line the shore, not according to a planned purpose, but as if sprung up by accident from scattered seeds. Like the matted growth of bushes and creepers veiling the silent depths of an unexplored wilderness, they hide the depths of London's infinitely varied, vigorous, seething life. In other river ports it is not so. . . . But London, the oldest and greatest of river ports, does not possess as much as a hundred yards of open quays upon its river front. Dark and impenetrable at night, like the face of a forest, is the London waterside. . . . The lightless walls seem to spring from the very mud upon which the stranded barges lie; and the narrow lanes coming down to the foreshore resemble the paths of smashed bushes and crumbled earth where big game comes to drink on the banks of tropical streams.[31]

In this extended metaphor, Conrad depicts a "jungle"-like London, at least the London of a specific stretch of docklands riverside that would have been the first sight of many visitors before the age of air travel. It is a vision that, in its analogical attention to seemingly every detail, reminds us of General Booth's extended metaphor in *In Darkest England*. Of course, Conrad's vision of the African jungle does not come exclusively, like Booth's, from reading Henry Stanley, but also from his own first-hand knowledge of Stanley's jungle.

Gazing at the London waterside, Conrad offers an urban vision of the irrational, the untidy, and that which defies knowledge and insight, the "dark and impenetrable." The dense veil of the waterfront obscures a richly organic life in the streets behind it that, growing out of the mud, is "infinitely varied, vigorous, seething." This London is not the outcome of a rational plan; it is not like a cultivated "garden." Instead, it is like an "unexplored wilderness" and "virgin forest," still like that London that the Roman citizen first gazes upon in the opening pages of *Heart of Darkness*. To discover its secrets, the adventurous speaker must enter those jungle depths by plunging or, as we shall see, descending into them.

It is perhaps not all that curious, but indeed significant, that Conrad uses this "stretch of the Thames from London Bridge to the Albert Docks" to introduce his readers to London. If he had described the riverside upstream, from Blackfriars Bridge west, he would have had to tell a quite different tale of London. That is, he would have had to present the quite different vision of the Embankment, one of Victorian London's most visible and acclaimed signs of metropolitan improvement and human progress. But he does not. Instead, his narrative turns back from London Bridge toward the older docks of the port of London: Saint Katherine's, East and West India, Blackwall, and the Victoria and Albert Docks.[32] Perhaps we can see what Conrad offers here as a mirror image of the river journey in *Heart of Darkness*—to journey up this river is to move forward in time from the "virgin forest" to the "cultivated garden," from the jungle to the urban. Thus, the London waterside offers a panorama that recapitulates human history. But this cannot be the whole story. For such a narrative of progress should immediately strike one as un-Conradian.

What is important here for Conrad is to strike a blow for a more balanced understanding of the urban jungle, one that calls attention to the "vigorous, seething life" of the London waterside because this "stretch" is what typically goes unnoticed in those Victorian accounts in which the Embankment steals the show. To point to an analogous situation in *Heart of Darkness,* if Kurtz's "Exterminate the Brutes" is the phrase that leaps off the page and stays with us as readers, it is not because Conrad wants us to forget Kurtz's more enlightened, paternalistic goal to improve the savages, but because he wants us to see the two attitudes, like the urban and the jungle, as coterminous.

Conrad wrote *The Mirror of the Sea* in 1905, in the period between the composition of *Nostromo* and *The Secret Agent.* In his 1920 author's note to the latter novel, he describes how a vision of the urban jungle came to him in a moment of narrative genesis. He had just finished a long, imaginative project set in South America, when "the vision of an enormous town presented itself, of a monstrous town more populous than some continents and in its man-made might as if indifferent to heaven's frowns and smiles; a cruel devourer of the world's light. There was room enough there to place any story, depth enough for any passion, variety enough there for any setting, darkness enough to bury five millions of lives."[33] This vision of a seemingly infinite town of darkness, with "room enough" for countless ("any") stories, passions, and settings is a source of inspiration, but more importantly an almost insurmountable problem for a creative artist like Conrad. For here there is simply too much to tell in "any" one narrative. Conrad's response, to focus his attention on Soho and, even more locally, on the domestic plot of the Verlocs, is more firmly in the tradition of his recent predecessor Gissing, who locates *The Nether World* within a few streets of Clerkenwell and the lives of a handful of families, than Dickens, who in novels like *Bleak House* and *Our Mutual Friend*, plots far-reaching connections between Leicestershire and Tom All Alone's or Cavendish Square and Limehouse.

The intense localism of *The Secret Agent* is evident in Cedric Watts's description of one evening in the life of Conrad's assistant commissioner of police. This character manages to accomplish quite a bit in a short period of time because of the dense compactness of his urban universe. "In one evening, the Assistant Commissioner can walk from police headquarters in Scotland Yard to the Home Secretary's office, can take a cab to Soho, walk to Verloc's nearby, take Verloc to the Continental Hotel for a forty-minute conversation, take a cab to the House of Commons to report again to the Home Secretary, 'walk slowly home' to change his clothes, visit the fashionable mansion of an aristocratic lady, and walk from there with Vladimir to the Explorers' Club: all before 10:30 P.M."[34] Although this series of walks and cab rides take the assistant commissioner to many different kinds of places, his metropolitan journey is nothing like the extensive one made by Inspector Bucket in *Bleak House.*

Geoffrey Galt Harpham suggests that Conrad, in composing his text, must inevitably find it necessary to resist the challenge to his powers posed by anarchy, in this case an anarchy figured as a "monstrous town."[35] Conrad must impose coherence upon that which defies comprehension and, thus, rescue it from epistemological darkness. His artistic response to his vision, the local and domestic plot of *The Secret Agent*, can be seen as a way of managing or coping with the horrific magnitude of a metropolis conceived of as almost infinite urban jungle. Narrative becomes Conrad's own distancingly ironic and "saving" response to the "monstrous" urban jungle in which he lives.

Elsewhere in the author's note, Conrad describes the process of writing as not so much a matter of getting close to the urban jungle, but rather keeping it at bay. He writes, "I had to fight hard to keep at arm's length the memories of my solitary and nocturnal walks all over London in my early days, lest they should rush in and overwhelm each page of the story" (xiii). Conrad's writing becomes a "fight" or struggle with his own memories and experiences of London streets at night. Like Dickens, Conrad's art depends upon nocturnal walks in the streets of London; indeed, the novel seems inconceivable without this kind of experience.[36] But his relationship to these memories is a paradoxical one; Conrad must achieve a distance from the material of his memories, creatively forgetting the experiences on which his work depends. Perhaps a more appropriate model here would be the Jack London we saw in the preceding chapter. London first descends into the abyss and, later, uses writing as a distancing means of escape, of keeping the memories at least at the "arm's length" of the page on which he records them. Thus, the ironic voice and language of the novel, that which literary critics from F. R. Leavis onward celebrate as *The Secret Agent*'s major achievement, can be seen as Conrad's way of putting distance between the self who writes and the self who walked the night streets of the urban jungle.

Thus, our ironic twist is that this novel where the narrative voice seems so cynical, so distanced, so unsympathetic, actually contains the material to which Conrad is uncomfortably closest. Like the "stray Englishman" in the account of Soho discussed earlier, Conrad-the-writer flees back to "his own country," away from "this queer adventurous amalgam called London." But we must not forget the other moment either: something attracted Conrad to foray into the urban jungle in the first place, even if it was, like the stray Englishman described by the journalist, only lunch in a Soho restaurant. In fact, Conrad and his literary circle spent lots of time doing just that. According to Richard Tames, "the Mont Blanc restaurant at 16 Gerrard Street served as the gathering-place for a loose literary network whose members included the essayists Hilaire Belloc and G. K. Chesterton, the novelists John Galsworthy, Joseph Conrad and Ford Maddox Ford, and the poets John Masefield, W. H. Davies and Edward Thomas."[37] In *The Secret Agent,* then, Conrad is not like the Marlow of *Heart of Darkness,* who, more familiar with foreign parts, is in strange waters when he turns to the metropolitan scene. Rather, he is in his own familiar element that has to be kept at arm's length. Yet he is also unlike Verloc, whose home and various livelihoods fix him immovably in Soho. Conrad the writer and aspiring middle-class gentleman has the Forsyte-like freedom to come and go in Soho, visiting for lunch and a plot before returning to his Kensington desk.[38] Here, we can see the distance between a claustrophobic novel like *The Nether World,* in which Gissing's narrative refuses us any escape or distance from Clerkenwell, and *The Secret Agent,* in which Conrad's narrator, like the assistant commissioner, can playfully take us in and out of Soho and offer us the thrill of vicarious slumming and a distanced recovery of composure.

Writing for Conrad, though it may be the means to class ascent, depends upon, and maybe even legitimates, those other darker moments figured by so many chroniclers of the urban jungle as descent. That is, while we might be more inclined to see the act of writing as a desirable way of redeeming and/or distancing Conrad's journey through the infernal urban jungle, we might also want to see it as the mask he dons to revisit and sanctify an otherwise illicit desire to experience the urban primitive. In the first case, the act of writing would resemble that of Kurtz's famous document. Whether we focus on Kurtz as the paternalistic writer of the seventeen-page report to the International Society for the Suppression of Savage Customs or, alternatively, as the genocidal writer of the line "Exterminate the Brutes!" we are in both instances seeing a writer who objectifies the savages. In so doing, he masks the savage Kurtz, who totally "lacked restraint in the gratification of his various lusts."[39] In the present instance, the Conrad who ironically distances himself from Soho in the anonymous, unplaced narrative of *The Secret Agent* might be seen as masking the Polish immigrant Conrad. The immigrant Conrad, though he speaks English (with a thick accent) and so desperately wants to be a British middle-class gentleman, still identifies, at some level, with the inhabitants of the immigrant ghettoes of Soho. Soho is, for Conrad, too close to home, too threatening as the locus of an unwanted point of identification. The heart of London becomes a place of darkness and, for Conrad, an uncanny home of non-English peoples and tongues.

With regard to the language, we should note that the distanced location of the ironic narrator is not simply a matter of establishing a self distanced from Soho—that is to say, securely within the British body politic—but also about establishing an unmistakably English voice. To distance one's voice from the babel of tongues heard on the streets of Soho is a project bound up with the process of becoming English. Yet becoming an English speaker is a habit Conrad finds it difficult to acquire. While writing *The Secret Agent,* Conrad wrote to his friend Marguerite Poradowska that "English is . . . still a foreign language to me, requiring an immense effort to handle," a tongue difficult to inhabit.[40] Leo Gurko notes that Conrad's "favorite image for his art was that it was like quarrying in the depths of a coal mine."[41] In this guiding metaphor, literary creation becomes an act of descent, like the pleasurably evil "descent" of the assistant commissioner into the "slimy aquarium" of the London streets (147). If the London streets, the habitus of raw and varied cosmopolitan and English tongues, are like a mine, then writing and "art" become the place where the raw materials are mastered and refined. Writing is Conrad's most important saving work, labor that transforms the babble of the streets, a babel most Babel-like in Soho, to the eloquent Conradian English that flows from the novel's ironic narrative voice. In fixing Soho through narrative, Conrad is attempting to flee a Soho that powerfully calls him (home). In writing the novel, he must get close (descend) in order to get away (ascend).

Like Kurtz, the writer of *The Secret Agent* might be seen in the guise of colonizer, bringing order to London's "infinitely varied, vigourous, seething life," or as a kind of policeman who enforces the law by seeking out and making known the agents who foster anarchy. This writerly alliance with an ordering principle is why many critics of *The Secret Agent* have seen the assistant commissioner of police, a figure with previous experience in distant colonial work, as an apt biographical and artistic analogue for Conrad himself.[42] The assistant commissioner of police has, like his creator, lived two lives: a colonial past of exciting, unalienated work; and a metropolitan present of writing, domesticity, and drudgery. Conrad is attracted to such figures; recall how, in *Heart of Darkness,* Marlow tells his audience that London has also been "one of the dark places," seated in "the pose of a Buddha preaching in European clothes."[43] He is an amalgam of insider and outsider, Londoner and stranger, native and visitor, a modern-day Marco Polo whose life and work have taken him from Europe to the ends of the earth and back again. Marlow also shares this placelessness and hybridity with Sherlock Holmes, who reportedly spent the years of his death (or disappearance) traveling in Tibet and learning from the head lama, as well as visiting Mecca and Khartoum.[44]

Like these predecessors, the assistant commissioner cut his law-enforcement teeth while working "in a distant part of the globe" (113).

But now, as a condition of his recent marriage, he has been forced back to modern London and is thoroughly bored by his desk job at Scotland Yard, the police headquarters. Like Holmes, he is frustrated by the "commonplace" character of London life, but, unlike the amateur consulting detective who chooses his own cases and plays by his own rules, he is "debarred by his position from going out of doors personally in quest of secrets" (117). His police work prohibits contact with criminals and danger; he depends upon subordinates and their "hearsay" information.

In this sense, the assistant commissioner's type does not look back so much to the cowboy as much as he anticipates the bureaucratic "organization man" of the 1950s. Imprisoned at his desk amid a "litter of paper" (113), he longs to break free and have real experiences like he did during his previous life as a colonial policeman in India. There, he had been able to exercise his talents: "The police work he had been engaged on in a distant part of the globe had the saving character of an irregular sort of warfare or at least the risk and excitement of open-air sport" (113). When work has a "saving character" in Conrad, life is about as good as it can get, despite the highly cynical inflection of its redemption.[45] In the colonies, the "work" was saved and, even, glorified by its risky, exciting, sporty, and playful elements. There, he found the kind of unalienated labor that is not available in the metropolis, or, rather, available only in a fictional urban universe like that created by Doyle. Although he now sits at the center of a vast web of information, he feels powerless and constrained in a place with an "apparent lack of reality" (133). As we saw in discussing Holmes, work that lacks such reality is increasingly common in a metropolitan world Eliot will soon name the Unreal City.

In the middle of the novel, the assistant commissioner breaks out of his bureaucratic prison and ventures into the metropolitan streets of nearby Soho in order to acquire intimate, firsthand knowledge. But the goal here is not only knowledge; knowledge serves as the pretense for the escapist excursion itself. While the divide between the assistant commissioner's two lives invokes the city/colony distinction crucial to Victorian imperial fiction, his escape is not back to his past in the colonies but actually out to the streets of the urban jungle—with one significant difference. Now, the urban jungle is no longer across town in the East End explored by General Booth and Jack London; instead, it is only a few blocks north of Whitehall, in Soho. Actually, it is even closer.

For the narrative suggests that the crucial geographic distinction is no longer between West and East or even between different regions of the metropolis, but between the "unreal" place of the office desk and the reality of the street. "His descent into the street was like the descent into a slimy aquarium from which the water had run off" (147). Gazing out from behind the window of his metropolitan outpost of progress into the precivilized aquarium of the streets below, the assistant commissioner had maintained a safe, dry, and clean, if also boring, professional distance.

But now, propelled by civilization's boredom, he plunges into the destructive, liberating, and restorative element of London street life. "A murky, gloomy dampness enveloped him. The walls of the houses were wet, the mud of the roadway glistened with an effect of phosphorescence, and when he emerged into the Strand out of a narrow street by the side of Charing Cross Station the genius of the locality assimilated him. He might have been but one more of the queer foreign fish that can be seen of an evening about there flitting around dark corners" (147). In this passage, there are a number of things worth commenting on. First, we can see a wonderful early modernist conflation of mythic and contemporary urban landscapes, one that pre-dates Joyce's conflation of Dublin and the Mediterranean of the *Odyssey*. The "descent" into a wet, dark, phosphorescent abyss invokes the topography of heaven, hell, and Dante's Inferno, so common in nineteenth-century writing about London (from Blake, through Thomson's "City of Dreadful Night," and on to Jack London). But at the same time, the infernal action is also carefully located "by the side of Charing Cross Station," one of London's major crossroads for international, national, and metropolitan travel. The streets about Charing Cross would not only have been full of commuters at this early-evening rush hour, but, more importantly, would have been full of the strangers represented here as "queer foreign fish."

Although the description pushes toward the more imaginary realm of Dante, this narrative is also intensely local. While it is certainly not incorrect to think in terms of a somewhat abstract opposition between *the* office and *the* street, we must also remember that for Conrad these were not mythic abstractions; instead they were specific buildings (Scotland Yard and Charing Cross Station) and streetscapes (the Strand). Conrad's novel, as I show in more detail below, alerts us to the importance of concrete places such as Charing Cross Station, as well as the Soho Italian restaurant and pornography shop that are the assistant commissioner's destinations. These localities can be read and visited as sites of imperial encounters and stages for the performative transformation of the actors who pass through. While late-Victorian writers worked with larger imaginative realms such as the Orient, the East, the East End, Darkest England, and the urban jungle, Conrad reminds us that these abstractions were home to more intimate encounters in less abstract places on the London map such as railway stations, observatories, museums, exhibitions, theaters, coffee houses, hotels, brothels, restaurants, and department stores. It is such institutional sites as these that comprise the microgeography of the urban jungle.

The assistant commissioner's "descent" into the urban aquarium recalls the dominant metaphor around which George Gissing and Jack London structure their own investigatory narratives of London poverty—that of going down into the "nether world" or the "abyss." These descents invoke other metaphorical descents, some of which I have already mentioned: (1) Dante's moral descent into the Inferno; (2) Darwin's evolutionary descent—the assistant commissioner, with his sea change, travels down the evolutionary ladder to become one of those "queer foreign fish";[46] (3) a communal descent from his settled, stationary desk to a "flitting" nomadic existence; (4) a national descent as the English policeman is transformed into a "foreign" fish; and (5) a professional descent as the assistant commissioner usurps the lower-level duties usually delegated to bureaucratically inferior inspectors or chief inspectors (in this case, the coolly detached assistant commissioner takes over the tasks of an inspector with the passionate surname of Heat).

All of the hierarchies here are mapped onto actual physical locations. In the office, the assistant commissioner has one moral, national, professional, species identity and, when he ventures out into the damp, slimy world of the Strand, the "genius of the locality" assimilates him to another, lower, more fluid (yet more primitively real) identity (147). In Conrad's urban jungle, identity is ideally a function of one's place or position in carefully articulated bureaucracies and hierarchical schemes, as well as geographically differentiated urban locations. Like a naturalist in the jungle, his narrator is more concerned with classifying species or identifying types than with individuality. Thus, he seldom identifies characters by proper names, and most of those who do possess proper names are best known in terms of their function—the secretary of state (Sir Ethelred), the chief inspector (Heat), the ticket-of-leave apostle (Michaelis), and the professor. Although this structural or locational identity is more fluid than an essentialist or humanist one, it retains a certain stability in a world where places—like the Strand, Charing Cross Station, and Soho—have definite associations and assign concrete meanings to those who pass through them. However, as I questioned in the above discussion of mapping, the urban topography is now losing such stability, is being drained of its placefulness, and becoming converted into anonymous, abstract "space."

With the assistant commissioner, Conrad structures an opposition between the civilized writer stuck behind a desk and the more primitive walker in the streets of the urban jungle. To see that the metaphorics of "descent" into the streets of the urban jungle has larger significance as a lasting modernist trope, we can look ahead to an essay entitled "Street Haunting: A London Adventure," published in 1930 by Virginia Woolf. As one might expect, Woolf's urban ramble along the Strand is a much more pleasant and light-hearted escape from the daily drudge of writing and the litter of paper than the darkly brooding, heavy Conradian one. But nevertheless, the same kind of imagery is present. "As we step out of the house on a fine evening between four and six, we shed the self our friends know us by and become part of that vast republican army of anonymous trampers, whose society is so agreeable after the solitude of one's own room. For there we sit surrounded by objects which perpetually express the oddity of our own temperaments and enforce the memories of our own experience." Quite obviously, Woolf needs more than the concentration afforded by a room of her own in order to write; she also needs the soul-expanding experience of street-haunting, in which she can, reptile-like, shed her skin, become anonymous, and even flee the confines of the embodied self for the disembodied, ghostly experience of street-haunting. In seeking Conradian antecedents, we might here recall that the narrator of *The Secret Agent* is thoroughly disembodied and that Marlow is often figured as ghostly. For Woolf, "what greater delight and wonder can there be than to leave the straight lines of personality and deviate into those footpaths that lead beneath brambles and thick tree trunks into the heart of the forest where live those wild beasts, our fellow men? . . . to escape is the greatest of pleasures; street haunting in winter the greatest of adventures."[47] In Woolf, an urban experience—the London street adventure—and jungle experience—the encounter with "wild beasts" in "the heart of the forest"—are one and the same. Like the Conradian night rambles, Woolf's experience of street-haunting is intimately linked to her artistic vocation. On the one hand, streets provide relief and psychological refreshment from her work. On the other, it supplies material support, both the material content of the essay and the "lead pencil" that is both the excuse that underwrites her quest and the physical means with which she records it.

For the assistant commissioner, the same thing seems to apply. The specific goals of his quest—following up on a clue, solving the case, or even eating his dinner—are less important than the process of the adventure itself. What is more important for him is the opportunity to descend from a fixed identity into one that is lower, more primitive, and more fluid. This last quality is crucial. The assistant commissioner will discover, like Woolf's street-haunter, that the thrill is not in the exchange of identities, the unreal for the real, but rather in the flight from stable identity all together—a regression to a fluidity that turns out to be a type of transcendence. As I mentioned above, such processes are not abstract; they take place in specific sites, whether street or interior, which assign concrete meanings to those who pass through them. Such, anyway, is the lure of the Soho Italian restaurant that is the assistant commissioner's first stop.

Conrad's particular Italian restaurant is dangerous because it threatens to expose and, thereby, explode the "fraudulent" character of the symbolic order of place on which stable structural identity depends. Such a destabilization of the symbolic order is what the novel's anarchists sought to accomplish by plotting to blow up the Greenwich Observatory and destroying the first meridian. But in the Conradian metropolis, symbolic anarchy is not the matter of such intentionally cosmic and grandiose terroristic acts. Instead, it is a matter of relatively simple, everyday acts being raised to the level of the cosmic and grandiose by what might appear to be a quirky Conradian use of inflated diction. But such diction, for Conrad, is not hyperbolic. Anarchy, the great fear of the conservative Conrad, is the insidious and uncontainable by-product of everyday life that results from the secret agency of deceptively innocent acts, like eating plates of spaghetti. It is on those plates that lurk the wildest beasts of the Conradian urban jungle.

How so? Let us step away from the Italian restaurant, described by the narrator as "a peculiarly British institution," and for a moment consider earlier Victorian scenes of imperial and national spectacle, such as the Great Exhibition of 1851. In the Crystal Palace, the products and technologies of Britain were displayed alongside those of Britain's foreign competitors and colonial possessions. Here, the visitor learned through carefully staged exhibits what was British and what was "other." The exhibition's message was that Britain was the most technically advanced and modern nation. Perhaps an even better example would be a later event like Imre Kiralfy's Empire of India Exhibition at Earl's Court (1895–96), a fusion of science and theater, educational exhibition and elaborate theatric spectacle, where one could walk the streets of a reconstructed Indian city, watch imported native craftsmen at their work, and walk through a garden enclosed by fifty-foot painted scenery that "shuts [the visitor] out from London, and leaves him to luxuriate amidst Indian scenes."[48] The colonial exhibitions of the nineteenth century, along with a whole range of other cultural venues such as spectacle plays, museums, panoramas, Wild West shows, and department stores enacted an urban version of an imperial dialectic of national selves and others.[49] These sites, whether their focus was knowledge, entertainment, commercial profit, or all of these, offered passages to India and other exotic locales and escapes from modern London. It is alongside these institutions that I want to read the site of Conrad's Italian restaurant, ethnic restaurants being a relatively new phenomenon in turn-of-the-century London. Such encounters can either instantiate the difference between the English and their others or afford the visitor the chance playfully to slum and go native. However, these possibilities for self re-creation are precisely what Conrad resists and undercuts. This Conradian turn of events suggests, in ways that Woolf's "Street Haunting" will echo, that the ultimate satisfaction of the urban jungle is not in any playful reaffirmation or exchange of identities, but the ability to transcend identity and become an "anonymous tramper." While such a transcendence is itself at the same time for Woolf and the assistant commissioner a refreshing lark, restoring them for the daily work they pursue behind their desks, it is for Conrad's narrator "the horror." Where we might want to position Conrad himself on the spectrum between delight and dread is a much trickier question.

Conrad's narrator describes this particular Soho Italian restaurant as "one of those traps for the hungry, long and narrow, baited with a perspective of mirrors and white napery" (148). At first, the interior landscape is, if not comforting, at least intelligible. We have entered a place recognizable by type; it is one of "those" places, suggesting its kinship

or affinity with others we can recognize and with which we are probably familiar. At the outset, the place seems relatively anonymous and
dull—"white," colorless, and blank. Rather than a room offering a view
of Italy, the assistant commissioner encounters mirrors; looking for
exotic others, he is instead given a vision of himself. There's also something in this sterile introduction to make us wary; it is after all a trap,
"baited" to ensnare the unwary beasts who roam the streets of the urban jungle. This trap offers nourishment, indeed exotic nourishment,
while preying upon an unsuspecting public.

But how does it prey? The restaurant is described as a place "without
air, but with an atmosphere of [its] own—an atmosphere of fraudulent
cookery mocking an abject mankind in the most pressing of its miserable necessities. In this immoral atmosphere the assistant commissioner,
reflecting on his enterprise, seemed to lose some more of his identity.
He had a sense of loneliness, of evil freedom. It was rather pleasant"
(148). This Italian restaurant is neither quaint nor picturesque like the
spectacle spaces of the exhibitions, panoramas, or department stores.
Its duplicitous status as "trap"—long, narrow, full of mirrors and white
napery, instead of exotically furnished—is reinforced by the "fraudulent cookery" and "immoral atmosphere."

How fraudulent? The Italian restaurant is a place of both physical
and symbolic reproduction. In the first case, patrons exchange money
for a meal in order to satisfy the "most pressing" of their "miserable
necessities": the reproduction of the self through the consumption of
food. But additionally, the patrons reproduce themselves symbolically,
as at the colonial exhibitions, in either of two ways (or both). First, by
an encounter with an exotic national other, the patron can reconfirm a
sense of national self, a rediscovery of what it means to be British and
what it means to be, in this instance, Italian. Or, as we saw in the East
End slumming narratives, the Italian restaurant can offer playful participation in another identity; it is the stage for an urban drama of going
native or Italian.

While Italy may not have been the "heart of darkness" of the Belgian
Congo, it was a powerful locus of otherness and touchstone for self-
definition in the Victorian and Edwardian imagination. Though one
could cite countless examples, I will mention here Ruskin's reverent
homage to "the stones of Venice," Pater's invocation of Renaissance
culture, and Forster's novelistic excursions to Florence, a place of picturesque "rooms with a view" and a locale "where angels fear to tread."[50]

My references above to the stage and the theater are not gratuitous. A significant number of Soho restaurant patrons were there because of its proximity to the theater district around Leicester Square and Covent Garden. While the two types of business occupy proximate locales for obvious economic reasons, we might also reflect on how the two reinforce each other, offering their diner-spectator patrons an evening of almost seamless theatricality whose real intermission takes place between dinner and show. This dialectic of symbolic recreation, familiar to readers of imperial romances like those written by Rider Haggard, or even of urban romances like those of Doyle, is what one expects to occur in the Italian restaurant. But this is not the Conrad way. Conrad, a writer well known for draining imaginatively exotic locales such as Africa of all romantic possibility, is not the exuberant prophet of liberatory elsewheres; his depiction of the Italian restaurant is no less ironically cynical.

In the Conradian restaurant, the symbolic exchange is not working; it is producing the cultural and geographic anarchy of the urban jungle instead of producing reauthenticated Britons, newly metamorphosized Italians, or even proto-postmodern hybrids. Its reproductive failure signals the breakdown of oppositions that enable the Victorian exoticizing plot, a breakdown that Conrad unflinchingly delineates as "the horror" in more explicitly imperialist narratives such as *Heart of Darkness* and *Lord Jim*. In the former, the famous "horror" is not Kurtz's evil; rather, it is Kurtz's inability to map himself in terms of inherited schemes of good and evil, the terror of the Nietzschean superman. Similarly, the "horror" of *The Secret Agent*'s Londoners can be seen as a shocking moment of recognition that one can no longer map places and peoples. The doubleness of characters such as Verloc, Mr. Vladimir, and even Winnie, demonstrate the failure of traditional norms as indices that might help one decisively map character. It is not that characters turn into their opposites, becoming one thing instead of the other —bad instead of good, agent provocateur instead of anarchist, terrorist instead of ambassador, murderess instead of devoted sister. Instead, they are both, and thus ("the horror, the horror!") neither. While the Italian restaurant promises a new identity to be conferred by theatric play in an authentically Italian place, the assistant commissioner, "in an atmosphere of fraudulent cookery," seems only to "lose" identity without any corresponding gain.

What he receives instead is freedom from identity altogether, "a sense of evil freedom"—feelings that admittedly are "rather pleasant" (148). He also detects this liberation from identity in the other patrons. With "frequentation," they have lost "all their national and private characteristics." "These people," muses the assistant commissioner,

> were as denationalized as the dishes set before them with every circum-
> stance of unstamped respectability. Neither was their personality stamped
> in any way, professionally, socially or racially. They seemed created for
> the Italian restaurant, unless the Italian restaurant had been perchance
> created for them. But that last hypothesis was unthinkable, since one
> could not place them anywhere outside those special establishments.
> One never met these enigmatical persons elsewhere. It was impossible to
> form a precise idea of what occupations they followed by day and where
> they went to bed at night. And he himself had become unplaced. (149)

This sense of being unable to place others and, consequently, becoming "unplaced" oneself, is central to what I have already called a crisis in
mapping.

Here now, we can see how an inability to map others also makes it
impossible to locate one's self. The Italian restaurant, like other metropolitan sites, holds out the promise of symbolic reproduction for the
slumming assistant commissioner but fails to function as a place. Here
in the restaurant, place becomes unplace or space, and the city, as
Horkheimer and Adorno would say, reverts to barbarism. According to
Paul Walker Clarke, "the capitalist creation of *space* is the homogeniza-
tion of a locale, and the discursive identification of *place* is the distinction of locale. Clearly *space* has the potential to become *place*. Likewise,
place can be divested of human discourse and be rendered as *space*."[51]
To extrapolate, place confers identity, while space lacks character. This
disvesture of human discourse is precisely what has happened in the
Italian restaurant—place has become space—and the consequences for
the assistant commissioner are that he has "become unplaced," cut
loose in a landscape "divested of human discourse," quite literally lost
in space.

The people he gazes upon cannot be distinguished by nation, work,
class, blood, or sexual orientation. They are "denationalized," not, as
one might have expected (or hoped), renationalized. One cannot place
them in any occupations or professions. Nor can anyone tell where
and with whom "they went to bed at night." In this Italian restaurant,
the symbolic function has broken down because of the "atmosphere

of fraudulent cookery" in which the "dishes" fail, metonymically, to stamp their consumers. To focus on the politics of nationalism, the food does not function to reconfirm or strip one of British identity and replace it with an Italian one—the delights and dreads of going native, of escapism, of invasion. Rather, the food threatens to strip one of identity all together because it is a "fraud"; that is, the dishes are not authentically Italian (or anything) enough. Like the generic atmosphere or space (one can hardly call it an ambience or place) of an Italian restaurant that is only "one of those," the dishes themselves have become "unplaced." In Conrad, we can see a metropolitan phenomenon analogous to Walter Benjamin's diagnosis of "the work of art in the age of mechanical reproduction," one that we might call "the plate of spaghetti in the age of mechanical reproduction."

Food or cuisine as a "work of art" was certainly not a remote idea, at least for wealthier late-Victorian Londoners. In a 1901 preface to *Dinners and Diners,* a collection of reviews originally published in the *Pall Mall Gazette,* a Lieutenant-Colonel Newnham-Davis argues that one adopt a refined and aestheticized attitude toward one's daily bread. Newnham-Davis writes, "the connoisseur of pictures does not look at the work of only one painter, and musicians turn with pleasure from Wagner to Sullivan, from Sullivan to Offenbach, and from Offenbach back to Wagner. So should it be with gourmets."[52] The London dining experience need not be one of "commonplace" Holmesian monotony, nor one of random, unmapped chance. Instead, *Dinners and Diners* invites one to adventure by offering "a little incentive to sometimes move out of the groove we are apt to fall into of going night after night to the same restaurant and eating dinners conceived always on identical lines." Newnham-Davis, a culinary dilettante, further reveals that "not only France, but countries much farther afield are systematically pillaged that Londoners may dine, and I do not despair of some day eating mangostines [an exotic East Indian fruit] for dessert." The London culinary landscape is becoming so complex that one needs a guide to find one's way around. Its international diversity requires a guide like Newnham-Davis, a retired soldier who knows the cuisines of the Orient and who, not unlike Conrad's assistant commissioner, had been involved in intelligence work in India and China. Indeed, the complexity of dining is not just a matter of cultural diversity, but also one of class stratification, ranging from the "really artistic dinner" for which one must pay on "the higher scale" to the cheaper "pot-boiler." The culinary scene of London was becoming no less differentiated by distinctions of high and low than the novel or musical entertainment (opera and music hall). In the restaurants of central London, concentrated in and around Soho, there were tremendous opportunities to live out fantasies of class and geographic mobility, for those who have the money to pay.

Clearly, the assistant commissioner has not entered the realm of the "really artistic," but rather that of the "pot-boiler," one of those "many cheap foreign restaurants" that abound in Soho, according to late-Victorian Baedekker's.[53] But whether "high" or "low," the Benjaminian premise still applies. As he argues, "the presence of the original is the prerequisite to the concept of authenticity."[54] However, such authenticity is lost in an age in which new technologies have made objects reproducible and new systems of communication and migrations of populations have made them transportable. As objects are pried from their shells, sites, and places, they become part of a commodity system of universal equality in which their "aura" is destroyed. Using Clarke's distinction between *space* and *place,* we should also note that this process transforms not only our experience of reception but also our experience of *sites of reception*—our relationship not just to *things* but to *wheres.* Benjamin's loss of "aura" occurs consequently with a loss of "placefulness." That is, as the sacred "work of art" becomes a reproducible commodity, its place gives way to homogenized space "divested of human discourse."

As David Harvey has pointed out, the dynamic of commodity exchange in a world market is crucial to the transformation of significant urban places into hollow space. Harvey locates the late-nineteenth-century revolutions in transport and communication as key moments in this process.

> The world market ultimately defines the "community" of exchange interactions, and the money in our pocket represents our objective bond to that community as well as our social power with respect to it. Here, too, money is the great leveler and cynic, the great integrator and unifier across the grand diversity of traditional communities and group interests. Commodity exchange and monetization challenge, subdue, and ultimately eliminate the absolute qualities of *place* and substitute relative and contingent definitions of places within the circulation of goods and money across the surface of the globe.[55]

It should go without saying that such an elimination of "the absolute qualities of place" would be felt first and most intensely in a metropolis like London, where commodity exchange as a way of life is lived at its greatest intensity. Money, and thus power, is in the pockets of the West Enders, and therefore they can bring the "East" ever closer (Soho, as well as department stores like Liberty's and Harrod's), until distance and the absolute difference of the exotic is no more. In this process, there is for Harvey, as for Benjamin, a hint of the utopian—money is "the great integrator and unifier." But ultimately, this process eradicates the "grand diversity of traditional communities and group interests." The result is a community of blandness, monotony, the commonplace, the same—not the romantic version of the urban jungle but its hollow counterpart. As William Booth echoes Henry Stanley, so might Harvey, Benjamin, and Conrad say of the urban jungle, "As in Africa, it [London] is all trees, trees, trees with no other world conceivable."[56] In such a landscape, devoid of any points of orientation, one cannot find one's bearings—one becomes lost in blank, empty space.

Such is the London of *The Secret Agent*. After jilting Winnie at Waterloo Station, Comrade Ossipon walks through a city devoid of place. "He walked through Squares, Places, Ovals, Commons, through monotonous streets with unknown names where the dust of humanity settles inert and hopeless out of the stream of life" (300). This is a city divested of human discourse. Ossipon walks through a cityscape where the streets have no names—no individuality, no specificity, no identity—and space is simply constituted by the anonymous abstractions of geometry. In leaving Winnie behind, he has left behind a commitment to a place in the social order (marriage to Winnie), a commitment to relationship, for the loneliness and alienation of city space. If, as Harvey argues, commodity exchange has transformed the city from place to space, it would seem that Stevie's aimless, yet intense, drawings represent not madness but realism. Or, if not madness, then the insanity of an all-too-real engagement with his environment. While the politicians sit in one room of the Verloc household plotting anarchy, Stevie sits in the adjoining room representing the anarchy that is already London, "drawing circles, circles; innumerable circles, concentric, eccentric; a coruscating whirl of circles that by their tangled multitude of repeated curves, uniformity of form, and confusion of intersecting lines suggested a rendering of cosmic chaos, the symbolism of a mad art attempting the inconceivable" (45). Thus Stevie's art. Thus London.

Benjamin argues that technical reproduction—commodified art and aestheticized commodities like ethnic food—"enables the original to meet the beholder halfway, be it in the form of a photograph or a phonograph record. The cathedral leaves its locale to be received in the studio of a lover of art; the choral production, performed in an auditorium or in the open air, resounds in the drawing room."[57] While for Benjamin there is loss (of the "aura") and gain (democracy) in this "halfway" space of meeting, for Conrad, there is only horror or "an evil freedom." For him, to meet things "halfway" is to occupy an "unplace." Just as in *The Sign of Four* we observed the presence of India and the Orient in a suburban apartment, here a reproduced Italy is only a short walk from Charing Cross Station. But the two moments are worlds apart, for the Conradian London is not the Holmesian one. The horror of the Conradian metropolis is the absence of any authentically exotic aura or locales, despite the abundant offering of fraudulent traps or lures, like those constantly being discovered and visited by earlier urban heroes such as Sherlock Holmes, General Booth, and Jack London. Rather than a kaleidoscope or panorama of cosmopolitan difference, the Conradian metropolis is experienced as a monstrous series of undifferentiated or "unstamped" dishes and sites that, because they are not authentic "places," render their inhabitants placeless and the social landscape an unreadable map. One character, Ossipon, believes he can still read the social landscape, not by reference to place but by attending simply to anatomy. He is a devout follower of the Italian criminologist Lombroso, a popular writer in the late nineteenth century who believed that one could read people's physiognomy in order to discern their place on the moral map. Conrad, however, has little patience for the reliability of the Lombrosan social map; his view cannot be very far from that articulated by Karl Yundt: "Lombroso is an ass" (47).

In Conrad's Soho, the only site less arousing than the Italian restaurant is Verloc's pornography shop; that is, the only thing less arousing than food is sex (except, perhaps, for crime and politics). In Soho, these commodities live in extremely close proximity. Verloc's shop is also a realm of depreciated artistic exoticism. A man of shady business, as well as politics, Verloc sells pornographic reproductions brought back from his visits to the Continent. His business, which is also his home, is as depressing and nondescript as the Italian restaurant visited by the assistant commissioner. On the first page of the novel, we are shown "one of those grimy brick houses which existed before the era of reconstruction dawned upon London. The shop was a square box of a place, with the front glazed in small panes." Again, the generic atmosphere of the built environment is emphasized; it is another "one of those"—a plainly geometric "square box of a place" (3). The narrator does not exude the excitement of an urban explorer. In fact, he does not exude at all. He drones. This is the locus of a distinctly Benjaminian "mechanical" sexual encounter. Here, pornography exists alongside a whole range of debased commodities:

> The window contained photographs of more or less undressed dancing girls; nondescript packages in wrappers like patent medicines; closed yellow paper envelopes, very flimsy, and marked two and six [two shillings and sixpence] in heavy black figures; a few numbers of ancient French comic publications hung across a string as if to dry; a dingy blue china bowl, a casket of black wood, bottles of marking ink, and rubber stamps; a few books with titles hinting at impropriety; a few apparently old copies of obscure newspapers, badly printed, with titles like the Torch, the Gong—rousing titles. (3)

The equation of such proximate commodities is telling. One can only imagine that the dancing girls are about as sexy as the patent medicines are effective; they fulfill as much as the "dingy blue china bowl" satisfies the quest for the oriental objet d'art. While the lure of the newspaper titles might be rousing, one suspects that the politics within are about as refreshingly original as texts and novels produced by rubber stamp. The "closed yellow paper envelopes" tease with all the seductiveness of numbers "marked . . . in heavy black figures." Though the sex for sale in Soho might be tantalizingly foreign (in most cases, like the restaurants, French),[58] the exotic pleasures for sale in Verloc's shop can hardly be more refreshing and recreative than the "fraudulent cookery" served up in the Italian restaurant nearby. In its commodified form, an exotic sexuality of the rubber stamp is an unstamped pleasure at best. For Conrad, one is tempted to extrapolate, the sexual atmosphere of Soho is an immoral one, not because of extramarital liaisons or the flourishing of illicit sexual practices, but because it is a space of prostitution and pornography, a practice and commodity that fail to stamp their consumers. Politics in this world, I will briefly add, also signal a commitment that runs no deeper than the market; Verloc is anarchist and reactionary agent provocateur, on the payrolls of both liberal Britain and an East European power. He is politically overstamped and, thus, unstamped; overplaced and, thus, unplaced; he has too many lives and, consequently, by the novel's end, no life at all.

According to Benjamin, the techniques of reproduction that "[detach] the reproduced object from the domain of tradition" eventually cause "a tremendous shattering of tradition." For Benjamin, the social base for the decay of the aura and the "shattering of tradition" is "the desire of contemporary masses to bring things 'closer' spatially and humanly, which is just as ardent as their bent toward overcoming the uniqueness of every reality by accepting its reproduction." In the late nineteenth century, this erasure of distance would have been experienced first, and in an especially acute fashion, at a metropolitan crossroads of empire like London, but more specifically in localities like Soho and in sites like Italian restaurants and porn shops. If we follow Benjamin's logic, the incursion of the foreign into the metropolis is not figured here as an invasion of Britain (like in *The Sign of Four*'s cannibal plot), but rather as the fulfillment of a British desire to "bring things closer" and "overcome their uniqueness" (as Holmes attempts in *The Sign of Four*'s cocaine plot).

The dishes, then, neither convert their consumers into Italians nor reestablish their British identity. As a city filled with sites of inauthentic foreignness, the Conradian metropolis fails to reproduce Britain not because it allows in the foreign, but because by doing so it destroys the aura of symbolic difference that made the objects desirable in the first place and renders that first place as undifferentiated and unidentifiable space. In the scene we have been analyzing, the "secret agent" of the destruction and "shattering of tradition" is not an anarchist's bomb but a more pervasive agency whose symptom is the unstamped food. In fine organicist fashion, Conrad's passage suggests that the consciously artificial reproduction of tradition (for example, "fraudulent cookery") actually debases and "shatters" tradition.

Conrad offers no sense of an outside to this commodity culture; the East is at an end, or, rather, the East End has disappeared in the fulfillment of Western ends. As a good detective, the assistant commissioner of police uncovers the fraud perpetrated by these dishes. But is he any different from the patrons he and Conrad place at ironic distance? Might they also know they participate in a fraud? And if so, how then does the fraud satisfy? Why would they continue to pay homage to a symbolic order and undifferentiated cityscape that they know to be fraudulent?

I want to suggest two ways in which the fraud, known as fraud, can still satisfy its patrons. Only one of these (the second), I believe, is satisfying to Conrad; but it is this second reason that redeems the "monstrous town" by lending it a "saving character." First, it is the discovery of the fraud that initiates the "loneliness," the "evil freedom," and the pleasures of being "unstamped," "unplaced," and anonymous. The fraud offers its consumer "that pleasurable feeling of independence" felt by the assistant commissioner when he left the restaurant. "Independence," or the freedom from identity, is what he originally craved, when he left his desk for the streets of the urban jungle. In a roundabout way, this is what he gets at the Italian restaurant. There, he discovers a more potentially fluid, variable, and multiple identity.

Along with this more plastic form of identity, the assistant commissioner discovers two new kinds of community. First, a community that is transitory or ephemeral—a community of the Italian restaurant that patrons enter, leave, and reenter; a community constantly in flux, forming, and reforming; a community of those who flit about. In this sense, the Italian restaurant and the dishes anchor what Clifford Geertz, following Erving Goffman, calls a "focused gathering":

> a set of persons engrossed in a common flow of activity and relating to one another in terms of that flow. Such gatherings meet and disperse; the participants in them fluctuate; the activity that focuses them is discrete—a particulate process that reoccurs rather than a continuous one that endures. They take their form from the situation that evokes them, the floor on which they are placed, as Goffman puts it; but it is a form, and an articulate one, nonetheless. For the situation, the floor itself is created . . . by the cultural preoccupations . . . which not only specify the focus but, assembling actors and arranging scenery, bring it actually into being.[59]

We can see metropolitan identity as increasingly constituted by one's flow through a series of sites that enable "focused gatherings" (like Conrad's restaurant), rather than places inscribed by histories and discourses. The community that it brings into being is one that existentially "reoccurs" rather than a platonically "continuous one that endures."

Secondly, the assistant commissioner's musings suggest a community shaped by a shared experience of placelessness, a default community of those who belong simply by virtue of not belonging anywhere else. This is a community of wanderers like Marlow, the assistant commissioner, Conrad, and other immigrants. The assistant commissioner can no longer place the patrons according to his system of classification, but he realizes that he, too, cannot be placed. At this moment, he becomes one of them, lonely but not alone. The fraud-begotten satisfaction of street-haunting may be pleasurable for the assistant commissioner and Woolf, but it is not a terribly satisfying one for Conrad.[60] This is where the two part company, as Conrad ironically distances the ghostly narrator from his policeman: the feeling is "rather pleasant," but it is evil.

However, Conrad does gain some satisfaction from the "fraud," and he partially redeems metropolitan commodity culture, lending it a "saving" character. For him, the "fraudulent cookery" satisfies because it presupposes and, thus, guarantees the existence of an authentic. Here, we can see Conrad's lingering romanticism hard at work. In the Italian restaurant, the assistant commissioner experiences the "fraudulent." Yet this discovery depends upon the continued existence of an original somewhere. There cannot be fraud without authenticity, no fake without the original, or, to put it in Benjamin's terms, no "depreciated aura" without the notion of a genuine one. The "fraud" is ultimately a satisfying fiction because it enables the consumer to retain a notion of authentic or real experience, even if it located only in the past or only in the notional realm of disembodied ideas. Though the fraud presupposes an authentic that it is only an absent fiction, the notionally authentic is sustenance that fills the symbolic belly very nicely.

The assistant commissioner leaves the Italian restaurant with a strange feeling of satisfaction and a "pleasurable feeling of independence" (150). Back on the streets, he has been liberated and transported back to another existence. He feels at home. "He felt light-hearted, as though he had been ambushed all alone in a jungle many thousands of miles away from departmental desks and official inkstands" (150). For office workers like the assistant commissioner, it is far better to imagine oneself under attack in a faraway jungle than to feel "oppressed" by the rigmarole of a London office. Luckily for him, the jungle is now only a short cab ride away, or even closer, at a distance of only a flight of stairs.

But this urban jungle is, crucially, not the romantic place of the Holmesian metropolis. Its identity with the colonial jungle is a matter not of content, but form. In the scene I have analyzed, the assistant commissioner does not leave the place of his desk for the more exotic place of the street or Italian restaurant. Instead, he flees to a site that does not function as place—one that has become unplace or blank, homogenous space. In this nonplace, he loses his bearings, his symbolic markers, his points of identification, and, ultimately, himself. This Conradian urban jungle, thus, formally resembles those monotonous empty spaces—deserts, oceans, and jungles—where earlier explorers had lost their ways. In this sense, London is the mirror of the sea, a city-scape of endlessly repeated forms, devoid of any landmarks. For those who inhabit the London of *The Secret Agent,* the city has become unmap-pable. While we should be cautious about labeling this "evil pleasure" as a manifestation of Conrad's own urban dreadful delight, we should not dismiss the possibility of a Conradian unconscious, kept at arm's length, but not completely silenced in or by the novel.

The quote from Galsworthy that appears as the epigraph to this chapter, though written more than a decade after the publication of *The Secret Agent,* nevertheless bears an intimate connection to Conrad's novel. Galsworthy was a close friend of Conrad, perhaps his closest; *In Chancery,* the second of his Forsyte novels, is dedicated to Joseph and Jessie Conrad. Although *In Chancery* is not the artistic work of high modern-ism that Conrad's novel had been, it, too, demonstrates the shifting location of the urban jungle to Soho that we saw in *The Secret Agent.*

Galsworthy's dramatis personae are almost exclusively wealthy resi-dents of South Kensington, Bayswater, Park Lane, and suburban Lon-don estates (the novel's events take place around the turn of the century). For Galsworthy, as for Conrad, the urban jungle is Soho, a locale that "dwells remote from the British Body Politic." His central character, Soames Forsyte, is a staunchly upper-middle-class barrister and avid collector of art. He is forty-five and had separated from his wife ten years before. A wealthy man, Soames's most nagging concern is that he has no heir on whom to settle his immense property: "property with-out any one to leave it to is the negation of true Forsyteism." Soames is clearly on the lookout and, certainly, in the market for a wife—one who can both please his collector's eye and fulfill his desires to reproduce himself.

Thus, he seems to be stepping quite out of character when he seeks to acquire a girl in the marketplace of a Soho "least suited to the Forsyte spirit." The object of Soames's desires is Annette Lamotte, who lives in Malta Street, Soho, where, with her mother, she runs the Restaurant Bretagne. The French Lamottes are "Catholic and anti-Dreyfusard."

They do, indeed, seem to "dwell remote from the British Body Politic." Despite his rigidly held principles of Forsyteism, Soames cannot stay away. With him, Galsworthy makes explicit connections among upper-class, male slumming, the politics of reproduction and sexuality, and concerns about national character that underlie earlier narratives of the urban jungle, including *The Secret Agent*. Because of his wealth, Soames can get what he wants, and the novel leaves no doubt that the acquisition of Annette is a transaction where sexual attraction and commercial investment are indistinguishable. In a comic twist, Soames must take Annette to Paris for several months in an attempt to reauthenticate her Frenchness before reintroducing her to his family. In no instance does he want others to know that his new wife and child are lower-middle-class Sohoites. The outcome of his plots to conquer, capture, and reproduce with Annette is a daughter, Fleur Forsyte. The combination of the child's aesthetically French forename and British surname indicate that she is more a creature of the urban jungle (Verlockian), more akin to that "queer adventurous amalgam called London," than she is an embodiment of the true "Forsyte spirit." Galsworthy's novel, then, demonstrates the fantastical nature of desires for purity and containment in an increasingly cosmopolitan metropolis.

The urban jungle spreads with the desire to bring the exotic closer. Because of his wealth, Soames can easily move throughout the topography of London acquiring what his heart desires. His surreptitious ventures into and out of Soho are like those of the assistant commissioner. But in doing so, he brings Soho into his home and transforms both. Fleur Forsyte is a metropolitan hotchpotch, a child whose identity further confuses the boundary between Soho and South Kensington, between Britain and the urban jungle, between West and East. She is, like those denationalized patrons of Conrad's Italian restaurant, difficult to place. She is, perhaps, unplaceable. Who, we ask, is Fleur Forsyte and where does she belong? Does she dwell "remote from the British Body Politic" or is she its emerging type? To these questions we will return in the next chapter, where we will ask them of Eliot and the narrative voice of *The Waste Land*.

CHAPTER SEVEN

"WHAT ARE THE ROOTS THAT CLUTCH?"

Money, Migration, and *The Waste Land*

In this study, we have covered much ground in London. We have seen Holmes at home in Mayfair and visiting murder scenes south of the Thames. We have accompanied General Booth and Jack London into the dark abyss of the East End. And with Conrad we have moved westward to the haunts of darkest Soho. The invasion of the foreign into the metropolis has been seen in many of its neighborhoods. Now we venture into what might be the heart of it all, the City, with T. S. Eliot: "over London Bridge . . . up the hill and down King William Street / To where Saint Mary Woolnoth kept the hours" at the corner of Lombard Street, into the precincts of the Bank of England, the Royal Exchange, and Lloyd's Bank.

From 1917 until 1925, years during which T. S. Eliot published his most influential poetry and criticism, he held a nine-to-five job at Lloyd's Bank. During this period, he wrote his epic *The Waste Land,* published his collection of essays *The Sacred Wood* (including "Tradition and the Individual Talent"), and founded and edited the influential journal *Criterion.* I like to imagine this Eliot—mild-mannered banker by day, cultural savior by night—along the lines of another modernist icon, Superman. I find this comparison particularly apt because, like Clark Kent, whose job as a reporter for the metropolitan media conglomerate the *Daily Planet* provided unique access to global information, Eliot worked in the Foreign and Colonial Department of Lloyd's Bank, at a crossroads of global finance and information. This career, along with his immigrant status in London, contributed to structuring his special relationship to an emerging global culture, a relationship whose roots are the subject of this chapter.

In a 1917 letter to his sister, Eliot expressed keen excitement for his new job. "Lloyd's is one of the banks with largest foreign connections, and I am busy tabulating balance-sheets of foreign banks to see how they are prospering. My ideal is to know the assets and liabilities (of every bank abroad Lloyd's deals with) for ten years in the past! You will be surprised to hear of me in this capacity, but I enjoy it. Incidentally, I shall pick up scraps of the Spanish and Portuguese, Danish, Swedish, and Norwegian languages. Russians, fortunately, manage to produce their reports in English or French. Anything to do with money—especially foreign money—is fascinating, and I hope to learn a little about finance while I am there."[1]

Throughout this book, I have described London as a crossroads of empire and global capitalism where products, peoples, and styles from around the world are brought into contact. In addition, London was the clearinghouse for two other important commodities: currency and information. At this historical moment, London and Lombard Street were the heart of the global capitalist economy in ways that New York and Tokyo were to become later in the century. As information and capital flowed in and out of London, they were constantly being compared, exchanged, translated, and converted. In Eliot's own life, the economy of imperialism and the economy of culture mimicked one another. As someone with a great deal of cultural capital (Eliot was educated at elite institutions: Milton Academy, Harvard, and Oxford), he occupied a position in the emerging global economic and class system that enabled him to accumulate still more—for example, the "scraps" of languages he tells his sister he will "pick up" at the office and, presumably, put to use later on.

This chapter argues that two experiences, Eliot's career as a London banker and his migration from Saint Louis to the metropolitan crossroads of London, were the catalysts for his modernist attempt to nurture the idea of a global culture. As the cultural goods flowed through London, he attempted to order and transpose them into a single textual space, *The Waste Land,* a work we might now see as the foundation myth of the global village. Yet though Eliot policed the different voices of the metropolis in order to forge a tentative sense of community, many subsequent readers have read the poem as a cacophonous babel of irreconcilable scraps. I recall that my first reading of the poem as an undergraduate was, to say the least, a very confusing and disorienting experience. Having been told in advance that this was "great literature," I subsequently rummaged through the anthology to make sure I had read the right poem. I suspect that I am not the only undergraduate to have had this initial reading experience of this century's most

celebrated poem. Only now can I see that my feelings of disorientation, not unlike those of a naive newcomer to the Big City, have been
shared by a substantial number of the poem's readers and critics.

Indeed, I had unknowingly stumbled on one of the most important
questions in the critical debate surrounding the poem: Does it have a
single speaker or many?[2] In this critical debate, we can see the central
tensions of both modernism and postmodernism: Is the new aesthetic
beautiful or ugly? Is it utopian or dystopian? Is this art a well-wrought
urn or history's ash can? Can it be grasped sensibly and rationally or is
modernity best figured as a tale told by an idiot? Is our multicultural
world to be one of harmony or dissonance? Will it be increasingly
homogenous and boring (as in Orwell's *1984*) or excitingly carnivalesque? In other words, what kind of community is articulated by
The Waste Land? Does it even articulate community?

Since Eliot's Western currency was strongest, financially and culturally,
in a world market, he converted or Westernized non-Western cultural
currency, as we can see when he assimilates the Buddhist Fire Sermon
to Augustine's *Confessions*. Yet such a conversion, as we saw most point-
edly in *The Sign of Four*, is a two-way street. In Eliot's juxtaposition of
the Fire Sermon with Augustine, the Western text does not so much
subsume the Eastern as it is simply conjoined to it. In his note to line
309, Eliot wrote: "The collocation of these two representatives of eastern and western asceticism, as the culmination of this part of the poem,
is not an accident." It is this poetic method, "collocation" of carefully
selected scraps of historical and cultural traditions, not the incoherent
juxtaposition or random scraps, that rules *The Waste Land*. Michael
Levenson argues that this is

> the way the poem works: it collocates in order to culminate. It offers us
> fragments of consciousness, "various presentations to various view-
> points," which overlap, interlock, "melting into" one another to form
> emergent wholes. The poem is not, as it is common to say, built upon
> the juxtaposition of fragments; it is built out of their interpenetration.
> Fragments of the Buddha and Augustine combine to make a new liter-
> ary reality which is neither the Buddha nor Augustine but which in-
> cludes them both.[3]

In the financial realm, one can see the same thing happening in the
process of foreign exchange, where one value is converted as it "melts
into" another, creating a new monetary reality. International finance

capital is built upon the interpenetration of different regimes of economic value, and though this process can seem mysterious and spooky, it happens in real sites like Lloyd's Bank. Eliot's poem is, then, one that could best be written by a poet with his fingers literally on the pulse of international media, capital, and cultural flows. But it is also a poem written by someone whose own life story is caught up in these economic and historical currents. As discussed later in the chapter, the Saint Louis–born Eliot migrated to Boston and later London. Although he was moving in a direction opposite to the contemporary "tides" of migrants from Europe to the United States, Eliot was part of that mobilization of peoples that thinkers from Georg Lukács to Raymond Williams to Salman Rushdie have articulated as a central preoccupation of modernity; indeed, it is perhaps the most important social transformation in our century. People, as well as commodities and capital, were becoming increasingly international and cosmopolitan as cultural identity, like currency, became less fixed and more variable.

Thus, in thinking about Eliot's cultural production, it is important to consider not only the position of cultural power from which he writes as a London banker, but also his journey from the dynamic margins of European imperialism on the U.S. frontier to its very center. Eliot was not, at least in the first instance, an elite British insider. Instead, it would be more accurate to think of him as an immigrant exile who was missionary and convert—a migrant professional. Like Henry James before him, Eliot idealized London as an originary ur-WASP culture. One reason, among others, he left his native United States in 1914 was to escape the rapid changes of modernity, especially the massive immigration and the urban nightmare depicted by Upton Sinclair in (and as) *The Jungle* (1906).

Of course, what Eliot found in London was not an Eden of noble Englishmen but the urban jungle of degenerate city "savages" that we saw in the writings of Booth and London. The turn-of-the-century English capital, like Chicago, New York, and Boston, was an anarchic culture of different voices—working-class and Irish, upper-class and Greek, Roman Catholic, Protestant, Jewish. It was a world of poetry, newspaper headlines, financial jargon, and the music of the opera and dance hall. And Eliot loved it all. In order to thread a path through this metropolitan Babel, later in his career Eliot would shape a poetic theory whose keywords are *tradition* and *depersonalization*. In part, these theories are his attempts to deny modernity, to remain uncontaminated and simple, and to hew back the jungle and clear a space for his dream London. At the same time, they are also his attempts to embrace modernity, to revel in the complexity of metropolitan life, and to lose himself ("depersonalize") in the urban jungle. In *The Waste Land* (1922), Eliot depicts the metropolis as he experienced it—as a banker, poet, reader, lecturer, amateur anthropologist, and, most significantly, a seeker after roots. The city he describes is a linguistic and cultural Babel, an urban jungle, and both the heart and frontier of empire. This view of Eliot as a cultural outsider, when juxtaposed with the context of his daily experience as a reader and writer in the offices of financial power, is richly suggestive for thinking about his literary output and his relationship to his roots, rootlessness, empire, and the metropolis, as well as his place in an emergent modernist global culture.

The significance of Eliot's banking career for *The Waste Land* has been paid scant attention in the critical commentary.[4] Typically, Eliot's day job is discussed in negative terms, as obstructing his more important work as a poet, essayist, and literary editor. Quite simply, Lloyd's Bank is usually blamed for robbing the world of great poetry. This view was originally and most extensively propagated by Eliot's friend and collaborator Ezra Pound. In June 1920, Pound wrote to John Quinn about Eliot's bank work: "No use blinking the fact that it is a crime against literature to let him waste eight hours vitality per diem in that bank." He continues, "The boy hasn't got my constitution, certain sorts of prolific outpourings can't (thank god) be expected of him. It is a question of saving three or four books like his volume of poems from remaining in the limbo of not getting written."[5]

In writing about Eliot, Pound offers a number of terms that are key themes in Eliot's poem: *saving, waste, constitution,* and *vitality*. Interestingly, Pound's emphases recall Dr. Watson's anxieties that Holmes's cocaine habit will damage his constitution and drain him of those great powers with which he is endowed. Just as Holmes's habit is a crime against those people whom his work could potentially assist, Eliot's bank work is a "crime against literature." Although Pound's bankerly diction could suggest that these words are written in jest, throughout Eliot's tenure at the bank, Pound and others schemed behind Eliot's back to raise money (a ransom?) to free him in the name of literature. Yet it would be several years before Eliot would give up banking and devote himself full time to literary pursuits.

Why? For one thing, both Eliot and his English wife enjoyed the fairly high standard of living made possible by the banker's income. It provided Eliot with a sense of financial stability; it was the "money" that, another friend and canonical modernist, Virginia Woolf, said was essential if one wanted to write.[6] In addition, the job provided routine and discipline, according Eliot's day the ritual structure that he always cherished. But beside these more obvious pragmatic concerns, Eliot had a flair for the work and was, as we saw above in the letter to his sister, intellectually passionate about it. Pound never understood this. When Eliot finally gave up banking for literature in 1925, he left for a career as an editor-publisher at Faber & Gwyer. There is some suggestion that he obtained this position not because of his considerable literary abilities, but because of his financial and administrative experience.[7] Perhaps it was these nonliterary domains that made that position attractive from Eliot's vantage.

Although it is typically discussed as a drain on his poetic talents, Eliot's work at the bank actually propped up his aesthetic pursuits in a more direct way than those already described. We can see this at both thematic and formal levels. Eliot joined the Colonial and Foreign Department of Lloyd's Bank in March 1917. According to one biographer, Peter Ackroyd, Eliot's "first job [at the bank] was to tabulate and interpret the balance sheets so that their development could be charted."[8] In an expanded sense, this financial work of collection and interpretation required and honed the judicious reading and research skills of the future editor and quintessential scholarly poet. In addition, this was adventurous surveillance work, more than what one might typically think of as banker's work. Instead, we might think of Eliot as an intelligence agent engaged in a Kiplingesque Great Game, a plainclothes policeman who, like Kim, serves the empire by gathering knowledge, evaluating it, and providing information to his superiors. Eliot was, after all, a Kipling fanatic. In his last years, he would spend evenings reading sections of *Kim* to his second wife. It is interesting to ponder Kim in the context of *The Waste Land*. Kipling's picaresque novel follows Kim on his travels around India as he gathers information for the colonial police. The son of an Irish officer in India, Kim is chosen for this work because of his command of disguise and facility with languages. Like Eliot's epic, the novel treats issues of translation, costuming, acting, the accumulation of information, and imperial police work. But unlike Kim, Eliot never had to leave his office—information came to him at the center of a web.

Because of his abilities and exemption from military service, Eliot moved up the bank hierarchy very quickly. Many who would have gained promotions before him were fighting and dying in the Great War on the Continent. Valerie Eliot reports that, by 1920, his "salary had risen to five hundred pounds" (precisely the sum in Woolf's legacy), "he had been put in charge of settling all the pre-War debts between the Bank and the Germans," and "he was kept busy 'trying to elucidate knotty points in that appalling document the Peace Treaty.'"[9] It is a critical commonplace that *The Waste Land* records Eliot's experience of cultural fragmentation and tentatively attempts to reconstruct the bits and pieces of a shattered European culture into a unified text. It is less well-known that Eliot was also engaged, more directly, in a financial attempt to unify Europe and prevent further financial and political instability and chaos. As both poet and banker, he was a piece-keeper and a peacekeeper.

In 1923, Eliot was "placed in charge of the Foreign Office Information Bureau," where part of his job "consisted in compiling a sheet of extracts each day from the foreign press" and composing "a monthly commentary on foreign exchange movements."[10] When I. A. Richards once visited Eliot at the bank, he found him in a basement office, "stooping, very like a dark bird in a feeder, over a big table covered with all sorts and sizes of foreign correspondence."[11] Like Conrad's assistant commissioner of police, Eliot spent his days in a London office, surrounded by a vast litter of paper that had come to his worktable from all corners of the globe. Hovering over his "foreign correspondence," Eliot is figured as a bird of prey, like Dickens's Gaffer Hexam in the opening scene of *Our Mutual Friend,* or a fisherman (a Fisher King?) who peers into the financial and media streams, fishes out what is valuable, and throws out the small-fry. In this sense, he is also a cultural regulator, like Sherlock Holmes (whose adventures Eliot read fanatically).[12] Although Eliot's exposure to the ends of empire is mediated by the newspapers and exchange reports he reads, evaluates, and edits, he wields a great degree of power in deciding upon and composing the information that gets passed on to his superiors at the bank.

At Lloyd's Bank, then, the world comes together and Eliot is the one responsible for composing the text. He cuts and pastes *(collocates)* information from all over the world in order to compose a single world text —the daily "sheet of extracts" from the foreign press. As opposed to the unifying narrative of a summary or report, the technique used by

Eliot in this composition is the modernist one of pastiche or collage. Like both the newspapers from which his scraps are culled and the worktable described by Richards, the visual presentation of the juxtaposed bits and pieces of his final text probably resembled surrealist art.

This "cut-and-paste" method is precisely the one used by Eliot in composing *The Waste Land*.[13] As Edmund Wilson points out, the poem interweaves seven different languages and fragments that allude to "thirty-five different writers" and "several popular songs."[14] Like the "sheet of extracts," the bank itself, in its function as a repository, offers Eliot a metaphor for the poem's form and content. Just as the bank shores up savings against future financial ruin, Eliot's poem shores up fragments against future cultural ruin and devastation like that caused by the recent war and modern crisis of meaning. Writing in the war's aftermath, Eliot the cultural banker is trying to cut losses by collecting and reassembling the fragments of a culture that have yet to be destroyed or emptied of meaning. Indeed, *The Waste Land* actually invests in Eastern and primitive cultures as a way to safeguard against future devastation and decay in Europe. To construct another analogy with *Our Mutual Friend*, the poet of *The Waste Land* is like Mr. Venus, who rearticulates skeletons from fragments that flow into his London rag-and-bone shop from the outposts of empire. Eliot also restitches a cultural garment from the torn shreds of many cultures. That garment resembles nothing so much as the one worn by Conrad's Harlequin, who resembles nothing so much as the multicolored map of a partitioned Africa.[15] Situated at the heart of global cultural and capital flows, the banker sought to produce a "world" poem.

Eliot's professional and poetic compositions partake of, and reform, large imaginary structures borrowed from other late-Victorian texts as diverse as *Our Mutual Friend*, Mayhew's *London Labour and the London Poor*, Frazer's *The Golden Bough*, and Conrad's *Heart of Darkness*. Eliot's original title for the poem, "He Do the Police in Different Voices," is an allusion to Sloppy, a character in *Our Mutual Friend*. In his "Notes on 'The Waste Land,'" Eliot writes, "[T]o another work of anthropology I am indebted in general, one which has influenced our generation profoundly; I mean *The Golden Bough*; I have used especially the two volumes *Adonis, Attis, Osiris.*" As to Conrad, the original epigraph, as indicated in the facsimile of drafts of the poem, was Marlow's famous meditation on Kurtz: "Did he live his life again in every detail of desire, temptation, and surrender during that supreme moment of complete knowledge? He cried in a whisper at some image, at some vision,—he cried out twice, a cry that was no more than a breath—'The horror! the horror!'" Of the remaining writer listed above, Mayhew, I have to say I have no knowledge that Eliot was familiar with him; however, I mention him here because he strikes me as a pertinent synthesis of Frazer and Dickens, an urban ethnographer that anticipates Eliot's chronicle of "high" and, especially, "low" London. These texts and structures, along with his work as a collocator at the bank, crystalized and catalyzed Eliot's sense of London as an urban jungle in need of heroic representation.

Michael Levenson has written about Eliot's interest in and debts to the discipline of anthropology: "Eliot's pursuit of the historical sense culminated naturally in the anthropological search for origins. . . . It is that modern discipline which offers the broadest view and which through its 'comparative method' hopes to bring pattern into the heterogeneity of human culture. It thus provides a framework for the modern mind; it is a prosthesis for the dissociated sensibility." Levenson goes on to demonstrate how Eliot complexly weaves together different historical artifacts—the biblical story of Christ and the disciples at Emmaeus, the Grail Knight's sojourn in the Chapel Perilous, and the hooded armies of the Russian Revolution—because "each new parallel represents an implied challenge to any enclosed body of beliefs and each forcibly obliges us to enlarge our notion of the cultural tradition."[16]

Although Eliot's seemingly endless parade of analogies, like Frazer's before him, might look like cultural relativism, it is instead an attempt to construct a vision of a more inclusive culture, one whose historical depth and spatial reach challenge parochial Eurocentrism. But, and this is crucial, it is in fact a rather concentrated sensibility, one nurtured by the paradoxically infinite locality of metropolitan London and Lloyd's Bank, that is the condition of possibility for the more expansive sense of culture articulated by *The Waste Land*.

Like Levenson, Marc Manganaro has argued that we read *The Waste Land* as structurally modeled on the Victorian anthropology of Frazer, demonstrating that his influence on the poem goes much deeper than content such as Fisher King myths. I like Manganaro's analogy, and I want to extend it: the poet of *The Waste Land* is like the armchair anthropologist Frazer, who produces a narrative by cutting and pasting accounts from a wide variety of sources in order to weave a global text.

In this sense, anthropology and financial analysis are kindred activities. Both the armchair anthropologist and the banker (at least, the kind of banker Eliot was) have a metropolitan relationship to information, envisioning themselves as invisible hands or facilitators who compile neutral collages. In 1924, Eliot praised the form and scientific ambition of Frazer's work. For Eliot, the most positive quality in Frazer's work was "the absence of speculation" that was heroically achieved through "a conscious and deliberate scrupulousness" and that "will not fail to have a profound effect upon the literature of the future."[17]

Borrowing Frazer's own rhetoric, Eliot noted that Frazer's work is of more lasting value than Freud's "because it is a statement of fact which is not involved in the maintenance or fall of any theory of the author's." Because facts have a lasting value, they were, for Eliot, a better risk-free investment than theories, positions in critical debates, or, for that matter, intellectual "speculation." Theories may come and go, rise or fall in the intellectual marketplace, but facts remain ever the same. Facts were the gold, theories only paper money. This is why Eliot valued Frazer's approach. Eliot wanted to be a disinterested collector or gatherer and self-consciously aimed for this separation of fact and theory in *The Waste Land*. In this realm of facts, the individual author is as inconsequential as the shred of platinum in Eliot's famous metaphor for poetic creation.

Of course, what Eliot and Frazer leave out in their vision of the polyvocal objective text is the issue of agency, the work of collecting, selecting, classifying, arranging, and composing. When we accept their version of the objectivity of the anthropological compendium or the modernist collection, we stop thinking about who picked the stories for *The Golden Bough* and who chose the fragments that *The Waste Land* shores together as dissociated consciousness. Who decides which myths and what kind of arrangement would represent a universalized primitive society? Frazer. Who decides which voices to do and in what order? Eliot (and Pound). Or, to return to the metaphorics of banking, who decides in which projects to invest and divest, which economies are stable or unstable, what has value, what is dross? The banker (whom we should see as a producer, not simply a conserver, of value). If, as I am suggesting, the anthropological text and modernist poem are to be seen as cultural banks, then we need to remember that there are bankers who set up procedures and structures from which they profit.

Another important generative influence on Eliot's vision of London as an urban jungle was Conrad. In the preceding chapter, I discussed how Conrad's vision of Africa as a "heart of darkness" structured his later depiction of London as a place of darkness in his autobiographical writing and in *The Secret Agent*. Eliot's vision of London is also structured by Conrad's vision. The original epigraph for *The Waste Land* came from *Heart of Darkness;* some critics, notably Grover Smith, argue that the poem's persona can be read as an urban Kurtz.[18] Although the Conrad reference was excised from the poem's final version, the lush, impenetrable, brooding jungles of Conrad were clearly on Eliot's mind as he began composing the poem. This parallel has been noted by Robert Crawford, who notes that "in *Heart of Darkness,* Marlow is one who had deviated from the routine life of a city clerk into the life of the African jungle, but Eliot, though he can set the jungle of India against his City, tends to use not so much the jungle but the desert as the counter to the city in *The Waste Land*."[19] At first, Crawford's subordination of the jungle seems right. Eliot's depiction of London as an arid "waste land" is very different from the tangled jungles of Doyle, London, Booth, and Conrad. *The Waste Land* is filled with images of the desert, the void, and emptiness: "stony rubbish," "dry stone," "red rock," "cracked earth," "stony places," and "mountains of rock." This pattern of images suggests a landscape that is the opposite of a lush, verdant jungle. Yet the poem also contains a corresponding amount of rampant vegetable imagery.

I disagree with Crawford's subordination of the jungle in the finished poem, especially given its importance in the poem's final section, "What the Thunder Said":

> Ganga was sunken, and the limp leaves
> Waited for rain, while the black clouds
> Gathered far distant, over Himavant.
> The jungle crouched, humped in silence.
> Then spoke the thunder . . . (lines 396–400)

Eliot's interest in *The Waste Land* is not in finding the appropriate landscape, but in showing how his London is an overlapping or conflation of landscapes that include the desert, but also the jungles of India and Africa. Ultimately, he is placing these (at least) four locales—London, the desert, Africa, and India—alongside each other as facts, from which a pattern might then emerge. Eliot's juxtaposition of lush vegetation and arid plain re-fuses a contradiction in the etymology of the word *jungle.* In 1922, *jungle* was still a relatively new word in the English language. Like so many of the other things discussed in this book, it, too, was imported into the language via a colonial encounter. According to *The Oxford English Dictionary,* it entered the language in 1776 via Hindi and Sanskrit through the work of the East India Company. In Hindi, *jangal* or *jungul* literally means "waste or uncultivated ground." The first reference found by the compilers of the *OED* reads, "Land waste for Five Years . . . is called Jungle." Following this definition, Eliot's title figure—waste land—is a straight translation of the Hindi. With later English usage, the word changed in meaning to signify "land overgrown with underwood, long grass, and tangled vegetation." An 1813 citation reads, "the banks were covered with thick jungle down to the very brink of the water." In the subsequent history of the word, the English version increasingly refers to "a wild tangled mass" or "place of bewildering complexity."

As an adept linguist and student of Eastern mysticism, Eliot was most likely aware of this ambiguity in the word's meanings. His version of the urban jungle exploits this ambiguity by juxtaposing both visions: desert and mass of tangled vegetation. For him, these two meanings are not so very different than they first appear. For the cognitive experience of the desert as an empty "waste land" turns out to be qualitatively the same as that of the "tangled mass" of bewildering complexity. Both defy signification. As a symbol of august nature, the desert functions much like the jungle in the modern imagination. Again both defy signification. Thus Eliot's text also resembles other Anglo-American modernist texts such as T. E. Lawrence's *The Seven Pillars of Wisdom,* Zane Grey's *The Riders of the Purple Sage,* and D. H. Lawrence's tales of Mexico and the American Southwest.[20] The emptiness of uncultivated nature and the overstimulation of the metropolis both lead to a kind of blankness, emptiness, and numbness.[21] As a guiding metaphor for urban experience, the "jungle" reveals the extent to which English culture has been transformed through imperial and colonial encounters; it has become overgrown with meanings and, at the same time, emptied of any one stable meaning. Both culturally and professionally, Eliot felt invaded most deeply at the level of language and culture; he writes *The Waste Land* as a "wild tangled mass" or site of "bewildering complexity" that mimics the montage of his early-twentieth-century metropolitan experience.

We saw in the 1813 citation from the *OED* that early usage associates, not accidentally, the words *jungle* and *bank.* The earliest versions of the jungle were produced by explorers and traders who scanned the dense riverbanks, not unlike Conrad's Marlow, from the vantage point of their passing boats. This is a view we get, in kaleidoscope fashion, in "The Fire Sermon," the third part of the poem. (This view overlaps with other views we get in the poem where a figure is seated on a bank of the Thames, fishing or simply gazing at the water.) Here, Eliot takes us along the Thames: "Down Greenwich reach / Past the Isle of Dogs" (lines 275–76); "By Richmond I raised my knees / Supine on the floor of a narrow canoe" (lines 294–95); and "On Margate Sands" (line 300). As we saw in the preceding chapter, Conrad depicts London as a jungle (in *The Mirror of the Sea*) from the vantage point of someone on a ship traveling up the Thames for the first time. For him, the jungle is a riverbank. Similarly in *The Waste Land,* the only use of the word *bank* refers to a bank of the Thames: "A rat crept softly through the vegetation / Dragging its slimy belly on the bank / While I was fishing in the dull canal" (lines 187–89).

In conceiving of himself as the poet of this jungle, Eliot also invokes the Victorian naturalist Darwin, who describes a tangled jungle bank in the last paragraph of *The Origin of Species:* "It is interesting to contemplate a tangled bank, clothed with many plants of many kinds, with birds singing on the bushes, with various insects flitting about, and with worms crawling through the damp earth, and to reflect that these elaborately constructed forms, so different from each other, and dependent in so complex a manner, have all been produced by laws acting around us."[22] Darwin uses the metaphor of a bank as synecdoche for nature and for the jungle. It is a place teeming with life, a diversity of clothing, songs, movements, and species, so "different," yet so "dependent." In order to represent these "elaborately constructed forms" that comprise the jungle bank, the naturalist Darwin must break it down and describe the different voices at play here: birds, insects, plants. For Darwin, there is pleasure in the contemplation of the bank, both in losing oneself in its complexity and in mastering the chaos through an act of narrative composition.

Like the chaotic Conradian and Darwinian jungles, Eliot's urban jungle is immense. In an attempt to capture its physical size and describe the myriad species it contained, Eliot's early drafts of *The Waste Land* were extensive—much longer than the final 433-line version. In a sheer quantitative sense, the early drafts demonstrate Eliot's urge to collect and gather together as many pieces as possible. In doing so, the drafts of the poem resemble long, nineteenth-century works like those by Mayhew, Darwin, and Frazer. They rhetorically communicate a will to a nearly infinite inclusiveness—nothing is to be discarded because the poem-bank, like the London it is meant to represent, resemble, textually reassemble, and conserve, should be a home for all. Darwin's *The Origin of Species* is, by his own admission, only an "Abstract" of a much larger book that he never wrote. In 1859, Darwin became aware that Alfred Wallace was about to publish his one account of "the natural history of the Malay archipelago" and that he had "arrived at almost exactly the same general conclusions that I have on the origin of species." He hoped, later, to publish "in detail all the facts, with the references, on which my conclusions have been grounded."[23]

Likewise, with Frazer, during the thirty years it took him to complete *The Golden Bough,* the text became for him a Frankenstein's monster. Frazer writes,

[T]he primary aim of this book is to explain the remarkable rule which regulated the succession to the priesthood of Diana at Aricia. When I first set myself to solve the problem thirty years ago, I thought the solution could be propounded very briefly, but I soon found that to render it probable or even intelligible it was necessary to discuss more general questions, some of which had hardly been broached before. In successive editions the discussion of these and kindred topics has occupied more and more space, the enquiry has branched out in more and more directions, until the two volumes of the original work have expanded into twelve.

Frazer uses an organic metaphor of the text "branch[ing] out in more and more directions." Unlike Darwin, who is forced to abstract, Frazer is an incompetent literary gardener; his text resembles the plant in *Little Shop of Horrors* that starts off as a potted exotic curiosity before feeding, growing, spreading, and expanding into an all-encompassing and all-consuming jungle. Who, we might ask, is controlling whom? Eliot's original manuscripts for *The Waste Land* mimic not only Frazer's *The Golden Bough,* but also Dickens's *Our Mutual Friend.* Typical editions of the Dickens work are approximately eight hundred pages in length.

As we have seen, *Our Mutual Friend* also supplied Eliot with the original title for the poem, "He Do the Police in Different Voices." I concur with those critics who believe it also supplied the conception of a single speaker for the poem who mimics a variety or medley of voices. The phrase refers to a character in the novel who reads aloud police reports from the daily newspapers. Betty Higdon announces, "Sloppy is a beautiful reader of an newspaper. He do the police in different voices." In the history of the poem's evolution, Sloppy predates Tiresias as a figure for the narrator. But behind both figures lurks Eliot, who was himself, according to his employers at Lloyd's Bank, a "beautiful reader" of newspapers written in a variety of voices. But while Sloppy and Dickens might have been important generative influences on the poem, they disappear from the final version. Why?

One typical answer is Ezra Pound. At Eliot's invitation, Pound pared the poem and transformed it into a much more compact work. Indeed, prior to Pound, it was not much of a work as much as it was a more limitless and open-ended text. I believe that Pound sensed that poetry could offer a new experience, similar to that of reading Frazer, Dickens, and Mayhew, but without the time-consuming trudge through the impenetrable textual jungles of several volumes and hundreds, or thousands, of pages. Perhaps we can still uncover traces of the encyclopedic form in Eliot's division of the poem into five sections, or units, that suggest chapters, or volumes, or acts of a play. This is one explanation why the reference to *Our Mutual Friend* drops out of sight in the final poem. Pound's editing taught Eliot that, while Sloppy's form might have been appropriate for Dickens to tell London's story in the 1860s, it had become a much too sloppy way for Eliot to tell London's story in 1922.

For Pound and, by extension, Eliot, the modernist collector must be more selective than the urbanist one. Pound helped Eliot capture the experience of the urban jungle through techniques of close juxtaposition, compactness, sharp transition, linguistic disjuncture, historical overlap, disorder, and anarchy—the "tangled bank" of modern urban experience in which both time and space seem to have contracted. Eliot's completed poem demonstrates that the ethnographic or urban compendium of a Frazer or Dickens could now be experienced in a much shorter period of time. In this sense *The Waste Land*'s relationship to Frazer and Dickens is a dialectical one. *The Waste Land* offers the reader a compact experience of chaotic difference; in fact, the compactness heightens the experience of difference by creating abrupt transitions and syntheses. Compactness is what readers new to the poem experience as shock. Everything, and there are lots of things here, come at the reader in a manner that is too fast to process. New fragments are experienced without context other than that of the preceding fragments. There is no time to linger, reflect, or make sense of what is happening. The poem rushes readers along with fast-paced rhythms and the repeated urgent exhortation of the publican: "HURRY UP PLEASE IT'S TIME."

While this answer is persuasive, it is contradicted by one important fact. Grover Smith has pointed out that we cannot credit Pound with excising Dickens's title because the facsimile of Eliot's manuscripts indicate that Pound drew no lines through "He Do the Police in Different Voices." And Pound was, to say the least, immodest with his editorial ink. Apparently, Eliot himself excised the old title and renamed the poem. So, once again, we ask, Why?

Michael Levenson has supplied an answer to the question of Eliot's revisions that, among other things, allows us to maintain a sense of Eliot as the primary author and not a complacent slave to Pound's mastery:

> It is worth noticing a distinctive pattern in a number of Eliot's revisions of *The Waste Land*. He removed the original epigraph from *Heart of Darkness* in favor of the existing one from the *Satyricon*. For the heading of the second section, he replaced the Jamesian "In the Cage" with "A Game of Chess" derived from Middleton. He changed the poem's title from Dickens' "He Do the Police in Different Voices" to the present title with its allusion to pre-Christian nature cults. . . . In each instance, a more recent reference has given way to a reference more remote: Conrad to Petronius, James to Middleton, Dickens to a vegetation ritual.[24]

In referring to Eliot's penchant for the remote, Levenson emphasizes historical remoteness. Yet, alongside Eliot's moving back into literary history, I would also want to emphasize how the final version of the poem, almost systematically, abandons things English for a wider geographical scope of referents. While it is not to be contested that Dickens's evocation of the 1860s offers a metropolis profoundly shaped by imperialism, by the 1920s it could cast a wider constitutive net—wider in terms of both historical depth and geographic reach. If Eliot sought inspiration in the polyphony of Sloppy, a character emblematic of mid-Victorian London, he in effect out-Dickensed Dickens by writing a poem in which the sense of global mutuality was more all-encompassing.

Eliot's poem is richly overcrowded with "ethnographic moments" offering the reader not simply an experience of metropolitan difference, but also an objective correlative for urban overcrowding. He describes mating habits, records the leisure activities and domestic lives of the lower- and upper-classes—from the bedroom to the pub to the parks

—notes the demeanors and pathways people take to and from work, catches different class dialects and languages, records snippets of conversation and popular song. If Forster's Edwardian dictum "always connect" was still close to Dickens, then Eliot's more modest modernist programmatic is simply "always collect." Like the speaker in "The Fire Sermon," there is a part of Eliot that sees, not patter, but one who "can connect nothing with nothing" (301–2). On the other hand, Eliot also gives voice to the man in "A Game of Chess" who can remember and implicitly connect Shakespearean quotation ("Those are pearls that were his eyes" [line 125]) with Shakespearean popular culture ("O O O O that Shakespeherian Rag—" [128]). Formally then, *The Golden Bough* is to the jungles of the colonies what *The Waste Land* is to the metropolitan jungle. Or to conceive this differently, *Our Mutual Friend* is to the Victorian metropolis what Eliot's poem is to the modernist one. *The Waste Land*'s method combines the anthropological practices of ethnographic writing with the Frazer-like project of quotation, allusion, and comparative anthropology.

I have argued that Eliot implicitly conceives of the poet as a disinterested collector, a banker, an ethnographer, and a detached supercultural observer. These notions resonate with his statements about poetic creation and the "depersonalization of art" in his essay "Tradition and the Individual Talent." For Eliot, the artist-analyst should be an outsider (like an explorer) who remains impervious to the milieu (the urban jungle) to which he seeks to give form. He describes poetic creation with the scientific analogy of a chemical reaction.

> I therefore invite you to consider, as suggestive analogy, the action which takes place when a bit of finely filiated platinum is introduced into a chamber containing oxygen and sulphur dioxide. . . . The analogy was that of a catalyst. When the two gases previously mentioned are mixed in the presence of a filament of platinum, they form sulphurous acid. This combination takes place only if the platinum is present; nevertheless the newly formed acid contains no trace of platinum, and the platinum itself remains unchanged. The mind of the poet is the shred of platinum. It may partly or exclusively operate upon the experience of the man himself; but, the more perfect the artist, the more completely separate in him will be the man who suffers and the mind which creates; the more perfectly will the mind digest and transmute the passions which are its material.[25]

In the presence of the fragment of metal, the separate gases combine, react, and form a new chemical substance within the chamber, a structure or container like *The Waste Land,* in which different fragments coalesce to form a new poem. Those structures, chamber and poem, also resemble a financial institution—a bank. Investors deposit their savings in a bank; those values mystically circulate, mix, and mingle; and new value is created in the from of interest. Under ideal circumstances, platinum, bankers, and poets catalyze new acids, profits and interest, and poetry. These processes are dialectically conservative and creative.

This scientific theory of creation goes hand in hand with Eliot's theory of the "de-personalized" artist-catalyst. The poet, so he argues, should not have any agenda or deep commitment beyond conserving the past in order to ensure future stability. Eliot conceives of the poet as a shard of platinum that catalyzes, yet remains unchanged or unconverted by its encounter. The most perfect artist is the one who remains most cold, passionless, and metal-like—one who separates emotion and feeling from the passively creative intellect. Eliot's vision of the poet is like Holmes's definition of the consulting detective as an "automaton" or "calculating machine." For Holmes, a client is not a person but "a mere unit, a factor in a problem."[26]

This inclusion of the client as a "factor" should alert us to one factor that Eliot's analogy obscures. In Holmes's world, clients come to him. In Eliot's, the members of the tradition can hardly come knocking at the doors of a housebound filament; rather, there is someone who introduces the symbolic gases into the chamber and that person is the poet, or at least another aspect of the poet's persona, the scholar-gatherer. Perhaps Holmes's cocaine scenario would be a better frame of reference for Eliot's chemical reaction. The poet is the injector and the injected, the agent of the needle and the body, the scientist and the chamber itself. The detective and poet, who are both intellectual laborers like a banker, must remain steady, solid, confident, and unruffled. Not accidentally, the cold metallic qualities Eliot desires for the artist (his nighttime persona) are often those associated with the cool, calm, and collected banker (his daytime persona) whose greatest fear is the panic in which things fall apart.

Platinum is an especially apt metaphor for Eliot's willful paradoxical detachment from and immersion in the metropolitan crucible of London. The poetic self must remain an outsider while, at the same time, surrendering to something outside of itself. It must "conform" not just to the chaos in which it finds itself, but to the "ideal order" or "the mind of Europe" or "to the mind of his own country—a mind which he learns in time to be much more important than his own private mind." Over time, through immersion in London and the traditions that cross paths there, the poet will melt into that mind and exchange individuality for immortality. Eliot argues that "the emotion of art is impersonal" and the "poet cannot reach this impersonality without surrendering himself to the work to be done." He calls for a denial of self, personality, and emotion that is both detachment from one's self and a surrender to the greater cultural entity that was there before the poet. The poet must "conform" to it in order to join it and belong. For Eliot, these qualities are not just part of an aesthetic theory, but a mentality that grows out of his own outsider-immigrant experience: the poet is like an immigrant. In Eliot's case, the poet *is* an immigrant. In order to assimilate to the tradition, the poet, like the immigrant, must suppress what came before—the more personal and less essential identity. He must police those voices that threaten to drown out those voices he now wishes to do. "Poetry is not a turning loose of emotion, but an escape from emotion; it is not the expression of personality but an escape from personality."[27] This version of poetry is, like immigration, founded on a desire to "escape" an old self and become someone new.

Yet, this exchange of identities is not simply a matter of trading places or masks. For Eliot, this "someone new" is defined by his relationship with Tradition and his imaginary kinship with an invented family of poets that reaches back in time and out in space. Eliot's theory is not simply an immigrant aesthetic, but also, more broadly conceived, a "corporate" one. In "The Politics of the We," Marianna Torgovnick explains how "Eliot identifies with the great names of the past as one in an immortal but expandable line of descent."[28] Like Dante before him, Eliot "positions himself within a 'we' that effaces particularities and affirms identification with a larger body whose common features are relatively bloodless—consisting mostly of maleness, European origin, and education in literary and philosophical traditions." I would challenge only the Europeanness of this equation, for Eliot is, as we see in the African, Buddhist, and Indian references, reaching out to a more global sense of corporate self than would have been available to Dante.

Later, Eliot would discover what many immigrants learn: that such self-denial and depersonalization threatens to undercut any sense of belonging for oneself. Rather than surrendering the self in order to gain a place within an adopted community, the act of depersonalization renders one placeless, as a fragmented or hybrid self who is anchored in multiple sites. As we saw in Conrad's Italian restaurant scene, Eliot's assimilation is not an act of *re*personalization but *de*personalization; he does not seek a new "personality" but the transcendence of ("escape" from) individuality altogether by covering more terrain and constructing an identity in relation to multiple voices, traditions, and histories. Thus, we get the depersonalized persona that unifies *The Waste Land*. Like Henry James, Henry Adams, and James Joyce, Eliot desires to be a citizen of the world. Like the persona of the poem, he is and wants to be a wanderer. Wandering is quite different from disembodied floating. For the persona and poet of *The Waste Land* do not escape tradition so much as they wish to expand by visiting and inhabiting a grander one. Eliot is not one who wishes to cut off his roots; he wants to put down more of them. His provocative question, "What are the roots that clutch . . . ?" (19) once again obscures the process, casting the wanderer in the waste land as the passive object of roots rather than the active seeker after roots to clutch. In the context of this assumed passivity, it is apt once again to introduce the paranoid aspect of *The Sign of Four*, which imagines Londoners as the objects of cannibalism rather than voracious imperialists. Tradition in Eliot's waste land is a ghost, a resurrected body, clutching at the poet, rather than a corpse the scholar actively seeks to dig up.

Eliot's sense of personal location was always ambiguous. Like Joyce's Stephen Dedalus, he felt himself to be a stranger in his own home and a "resident alien."

> Although he referred to Americans as "us" in a letter to John Quinn, he was also in the same year [1918] referring to the English as "we." In one letter . . . he described his unhappiness at the fact that he no longer had any real connection or sympathy with Americans, and yet in the *Egoist* itself he also described the density and stupidity of the English environment, an awareness compounded by his sense of the spiritual degeneration of English life. That sense never left him, and his attitude is one of pervasive ambiguity: he was never completely at home anywhere and, even after he adopted British citizenship, he would sometimes sign himself "metoikos," the Greek for "resident alien." He cultivated such distance and detachment as if by not belonging, or wholly participating, something of himself was preserved—something secret and inviolable which he could nourish.[29]

Eliot never felt either American or English. Steve Ellis attacks the cliché that Eliot became "more English than the English": "The fact is that the years of Eliot's greatest concern with English institutions and contexts in his writing—which we can agree are 1925–45—coincide with his keenest interest in a Latin tradition that, in readers like Virgil and Dante, represents a universality that all national concerns must be related to."[30] Ellis wants to argue, instead, that Eliot is actually "less English than the English." I agree with Ellis's position that Eliot sought to cultivate a European or more universal identity rather than an English one. I would, however argue, that this identity was not specific to Eliot, can best be labeled a metropolitan one, and is in evidence before 1925. This distinction is not insignificant since it accounts for Eliot's earlier career as exemplified by *The Waste Land,* which certainly bears traces of a keen interest in both Dante and Virgil. Further, it extends Eliot's "concern with English institutions" back to include his career at Lloyd's Bank, an institution that is quintessentially English and yet, through its global reach, is ambiguously not-English.

Eliot's signature—"metoikos" or "resident alien"—signifies his cultivation of the detachment of the resident alien and an attachment to a home from which he feels exiled: a fraternity of culturally elite speakers of Greek. (There must have been an unusually high concentration of public school men familiar with classical Greek at Lloyd's Bank.) By extension, we can read the Greek epigraph to the final version of *The Waste Land* as Eliot's attempt to phone home. By naming himself "metoikos" or "resident alien," Eliot fashions a self that enables him to straddle inside and outside, both sides of the border. In his essay "Metoikos in London," Harvey Gross note that "At Athens the *métoikos* was legally allowed to live in the *polis* but excluded from enjoying civil rights. Eliot doubtless was using the pseudonym with characteristic self-irony; by 1945 [when Eliot refers to himself as "metoikos" in print] he had lived in England and been a resident of London for thirty years." Eliot's long-term residence indicates that he was a "resident alien" not because the British lacked hospitality, but rather because of his will to remain apart and separate from any narrow category of national identity. Eliot's use of the name is not, as Gross suggests, "doubtless" self-irony, but a revealing moment of self-denomination. Eliot's sense of a "true home" is connected to something that he called Tradition, a tradition that is larger than any existing national one. Gross also suggests another compelling way to view "metoikos," connected to Eliot's views of Jews. He shows that "[i]t was Charles Maurras who established the modern fortunes of the word *métèque*. Maurras, a programmatic and unregenerate anti-Semite, spoke derisively of Jews as the *métèques* of the modern *polis*. Eliot was aware of Maurras' hatreds and his concept of the *métèque;* Marraus' career and views had deep, and in some ways unfortunate, effects on Eliot. . . . For Eliot to name himself *metoikos* in 1945, to identify himself with the despised aliens excoriated in the pages of Maurras' journal *L'Action Française,* reveals Eliot's lingering sense of isolation."[31] This self-naming act reveals not only a "lingering sense of isolation," but also a moment in which Eliot, a known anti-Semite, actually identifies with the Jews.

Perhaps his most famous statement of anti-Semitism came in a 1933 address to an audience at the University of Virginia: "Yet I think the chance for the re-establishing of a native culture are perhaps better here than in New England. You are farther away from New York; you have been less industrialized and less invaded by foreign races. . . . The population should be homogeneous; where two or more cultures exist in the same place they are likely to be either fiercely self-conscious or both to become adulterate. What is still more important is unity of religious background; and reasons of race and religion combine to make any large number of free-thinking Jews undesirable."[32] As my argument has tried to suggest, this Eliot, an Eliot interested in the "re-establishing of a native culture," has a very different concern than the poet of *The Waste Land,* who seeks to avoid the privileging of any particular native tradition. It would be tempting, albeit wrong, simply to suggest that, sometime between 1922 and 1933, Eliot does an about-face in the direction of anti-Semitism. Eliot's anti-Semitic portraits are in the poetry very early: Bleistein and Rachel née Rabinovich both appeared in *Poems 1920,* two years before *The Waste Land.*

If there is, then, a consistent strain of anti-Semitism that can be traced throughout the career, what are we to make of his 1945 moment of self-identification? I suggest that we should not jettison the charge of anti-Semitism against Eliot, but that we need to rethink how that prejudice is, by extension, an act of self-loathing. He loathed outsiders and wanderers; yet, at the same time, he knew that he was one. This wandering self, one that he allowed free play and serious attention in *The Waste Land,* is a deep-seated aspect of Eliot that, at times, he vigorously denied and repressed. This self-identification of Eliot with the Jews is strengthened by his career as a banker, a stereotypically Jewish profession. In this context, it is also interesting to speculate on the prevalence of nine-teenth- and twentieth-century anti-Semitism and its relationship to the increasing instability of liquid capital, and the fact that, as a culture of immigrants, exiles, and highly mobile workers, many citizens of our world are now wanderers or modern nomads. In order to discover the full significance of Eliot's sense of himself as a "resident alien," its con-nection to his immigrant experience, and his ongoing concerns about his own relationship to borders and homelands, we need to further examine Eliot's biography before returning, by way of conclusion, to the topic of Eliot's fascination with foreign money.

This book began its account of the development of the urban jungle with a story linking the American West and metropolitan London—Holmes and the Range. That link now appears once again: "The Range" of Conan Doyle's imagination was the place of Eliot's birth; metropol-itan London was his adopted home and the place of his death. Eliot was born in Saint Louis, Missouri, in 1888. In his writing on London as a "waste land," there is always an echo of his ancestors' frontier experi-ence. Eliot's story begins on several different frontiers. In 1928, he wrote to a friend,

> Some day I want to write an essay about the point of view of an Amer-ican who wasn't an American, because he was born in the South and went to school in New England as a small boy with a nigger drawl, but who wasn't a southerner in the South because his people were north-erners in a border state and looked down on all southerners and Virgin-ians, and who so was never anything anywhere and who therefore felt himself to be more a Frenchman than an American and more an English-man than a Frenchman and yet felt that the USA up to a hundred years ago was a family extension.[33]

Eliot's American (himself) is a collection of persons fundamentally split at the root. His fashioned identity of "resident alien" dates back to his childhood, deriving from the loneliness he experienced at the junc-ture of several borders. He is neither a Northerner, because he was born in the South, nor a Southerner, because "his people were north-erners." They have taught him to "look down on all southerners," which, by virtue of his birthplace, is the same as looking down on him-self. As a North-South hybrid, he is on the border between white and black—white-skinned with a black voice ("a nigger drawl"). Furthermore, his home on the banks of the Mississippi places him on the dividing line between East and West.[34] Eliot grew up in a city founded by the French and retaining much of that character in the 1880s. Finally, and perhaps most importantly, he is on another (temporal) border between the old America of his ancestors and the new America of an industrial future.

The Eliots, an old American family, went west to Saint Louis in the 1830s, as missionaries. Eliot's grandfather was a Unitarian minister with a degree from the Harvard Divinity School. He went West "in order to establish that faith in the frontier wilderness." In the then largely French Catholic town, he established his own church and helped found three schools, Washington University, a poor fund, and a sanitary commission. Although Eliot never knew his grandfather directly, the evidence of his work surrounded him as a boy. In the youth of Eliot's father, Henry Ware Eliot, Saint Louis was "still a 'frontier town' between white and Indian Americans, close to that border with the savage and primitive that was to be one of his son's preoccupations. As a boy, Henry Ware Eliot would follow the troops of Indians to their camping places and there taunt them with renditions of their own 'war whoops'; they would endure it as long as they could, and then they would turn and 'make a dash' at him and his companions."[35]

While Saint Louis was no longer a town bordering close-by Indian encampments during Eliot's youth, it had been a frontier in recent history, and this fact was an important part of the consciousness of his parents' generation. As Robert Crawford discusses, that presence was more physical than the memories of family legend. Saint Louis was filled with several burial mounds, whose origin and fate were "a subject of discussion in Eliot's boyhood. Their physical presence, making the savage past a resolute part of the urban present, was still felt. . . . The presence of such remains would seem a good reason for Eliot's Wild West beginning specifically at Forest Park on the western, genteel side of town, and it demonstrates how physically, in the poet's earliest environment, city and savage were inextricably bound together."[36] Eliot's family was an important part of the American pioneer movement that brought "civilization" into "savage" lands.

By the 1880s when Eliot was born, Saint Louis had lost its place on the geographic frontier. However, it was emerging as another kind of border place, located on the boundary between the agrarian America of the nineteenth century and the industrial America of the twentieth.

Ackroyd suggests that the famous yellow fog in Eliot's first great poem "The Love Song of J. Alfred Prufrock" is "the fog that blew from the factory chimneys across the Mississippi—drab, an exhalation of urban squalor."[37] Eliot, the urban poet, grew up "amid dereliction and rapid decay." Though in later life he would describe the urban landscape as a barren "waste land," he was always curiously attracted to it, as one is to scenes of childhood. As an adolescent, Eliot "derived a strange pleasure from walking through the alleys and the slums." I argue that Eliot's "strange pleasure" is of the same quality that drew his countryman Jack London to London's East End "Abyss." It is also of that same quality that drew another American, Upton Sinclair, to write his 1906 novel of the Chicago slums, *The Jungle*. All three writers give us vivid pictures of the urban jungle as a place of horror. But at the same time, they also seem to derive a perverse pleasure from raking in the industrial muck, an ooze that melts into the primal. In the Saint Louis of his youth, Eliot lived an intense contradiction between the world of his ancestors— a missionary world where "civilization" meets "savagery"—and the world of his future—an industrial world where "civilization" reverts to "barbarism."

While America underwent a rapid industrial transformation in Eliot's youth, it also underwent two other transformations. First, it became increasingly urban. Second, in order to meet the growing demand for factory labor, it became increasingly diverse.[38] Marcus Klein argues that the American exiles who powerfully shaped "high" modernism— Henry James, Ezra Pound, Gertrude Stein, Ernest Hemingway, F. Scott Fitzgerald, T. S. Eliot, and others—saw themselves as a "dispossessed social aristocracy."[39] Most of them were born in the 1880s, the Age of Robber Barons, and came of age during the Age of the Muckrakers. I argue that we can see their flight to Europe as a return to origins in two senses. First, they fled to those western European cultures—particularly France and England—that they thought constituted a "true" American stock that was becoming polluted. If people in northern and western Europe feared an invasion by people from the south or the east, then turn-of-the-century America was the place where that fear was realized. In cities like New York, Chicago, Saint Louis, and Boston, Europe came together. Secondly, the modernist "exiles" fled an increasingly heterogeneous culture to one that they imagined to be purer and more homogeneous.

Of course, as I have argued throughout the book, Eliot's flight to an idealized London was doomed to frustration by the urban jungle he discovered. London had also been transformed by immigration from Ireland and eastern Europe and the migration of dispossessed agricultural labor into the cities. Eliot comes to London from a fear of foreigners only to find there his urban nightmare writ large.

Finding an urban jungle in the land of his origins, he responded by becoming a missionary like his grandfather. Eliot sought to resurrect the textual London of his dreams. As a self-fashioned "resident alien," he kept himself apart. He worked to convert the British by reverting to the past and challenging them with his version of their Tradition, one firmly wedded to the Continent. Like those Old Testament prophets whom he pasted into "The Burial of the Dead" in the opening section of *The Waste Land* (Ezekiel, the Ecclesiastes poet), he proclaims to the English that their tradition has become fragmented and lost through neglect, but that he has come to help them recollect it. For Eliot, Tradition is like a Lost City that he hopes to discover as a lever for social critique—the Real City that became Unreal when the jungle enveloped it. In some sense, it is like those Lost White Civilizations that English adventurers sought in the Victorian romances of Doyle, Haggard, Kipling, and others—a report, a rumor, a myth, a dream to which Eliot clings with the steadfast zeal of religious belief.

Eliot wants to reclaim Tradition from the urban jungle that has swallowed it up. This "real" city is a version of how things were and would be still if history, change, invasion, democracy, and immigration had not mucked things up. For him, that real city is the (textual) Home from which he feels exiled. Like so many other exile-explorers of the urban jungle, Eliot sees himself as like Dante. Critics comment that Eliot admired Dante because he saw him as the poet of a medieval mind that was unified. What they tend to ignore is that Dante's Florence has much in common with Eliot's London. In its day, it was a very cosmopolitan place, a center of learning, a crossroads on the Italian peninsula, and, not least, an important center of finance and banking.[40]

While the American Eliot, inspired by fears of foreign invasion, fled to London, in doing so he became one of those immigrant invaders, a "metoikos," from outside the polis. Perhaps it was himself that he feared most deeply, a self that was not "pure" but a hybridized collection of many selves. At the end of *The Waste Land,* the speaker questions whether he should begin setting his own lands (his own selves) in order. This is Eliot's question and task, as well.

Today, *The Waste Land* remains an important poem not because it tells an ahistorical story, nor even because it tells the universal story of "modern man," but because it records an immigrant experience of metropolitan culture that has become increasingly common as the twentieth century progresses. Eliot is an early example of those "radically new types of human beings" whom Salman Rushdie, a later twentieth-century London immigrant, has described as the result of "mass migrations"—"people in whose deepest selves strange fusions occur, unprecedented unions between what they were and where they find themselves."[41] Like Rushdie, Eliot came from a frontier place of "strange fusions" to live in a "frontier" city of "strange fusions" where he worked, as a banker and poet, composing texts of "strange fusions." Like Sherlock Holmes, he polices the urban jungle that exists both around him and within his deepest self. For he was himself a collection of strangers. As a poet, he attempted to order the chaos and transform the disparate tribes of the urban jungle into a polis, the Greek city-state that was Eliot's figure for the well-wrought poem and home. Thus, "He Do The Police In Different Voices" is Eliot's attempt to control not only the voices he hears in the streets, or cuts and pastes in the Lloyd's Bank foreign office, but also those that comprise the tangled jungle bank of his own metropolitan persona.

NOTES

1. AN IRRITATION TO METAPHOR

1. Raban, *Soft City*, 93.
2. Williams, *Country and the City*, 13–34.
3. Doyle, *A Study in Scarlet*, in *Sherlock Holmes: Complete* 4.
4. The application of scientific laws to cultural processes was most evident in the work of Herbert Spencer. Spencer believed that evolution occurs "everywhere after the same manner" and that part of this process included a turn to "devolution" in which integrated systems fall apart (*First Principles*, 558–59). Spencer's ideas were especially important to novelists like George Eliot, Thomas Hardy, and Joseph Conrad and reflect a widespread fear that cultural decline and decadence, while understandable, are unavoidable.

5. I borrow the term *imaginative geography* from Edward Said's *Orientalism*, but, in a more general sense, I wish to align my literary critical intervention with that of *critical geography*, or the recent work of scholars across disciplines that has begun to examine how our sense of space and place are socially constructed.

6. This geographical transformation exists alongside and, to a degree, is the result of the Darwinian revolution in the natural sciences. In 1859, Darwin articulates the biological dilemma: "When we attempt to estimate the amount of structural difference between the domestic races of the same species, we are soon involved in doubt, from not knowing whether they have descended from one or several parent species" (*Origin*, 15). While Darwin "[does] not think it possible to come to any definite conclusion," his work certainly provided much evidence for the view of mankind as one vast "family" (16). In the years following Darwin, it became very difficult to argue for the radical separation of races based upon independent acts of creation. For a good introduction to ideas about race in the nineteenth century, see Bolt, *Victorian Attitudes to Race*, particularly her discussion of monogenesis and polygenesis (9–12).

7. In referring to the more traditional "literature of imperialism," I have in mind authors such as Stevenson, Kipling, Haggard, and Conrad and texts that are set in the traditional distant locales of the exotic. Such literature is what we typically think of when we hear the term *literature of imperialism,* and is what has been studied in important texts by Martin Green *(Dreams of Adventure)* and Patrick Brantlinger *(Rule of Darkness)*. One of my tasks is to expand our notion of what constitutes the literature of imperialism to include, at the very least, narratives focused *on* or *in* London, a task I share with recent scholars such as Thomas Richards, Anne McClintock, Stephen Arata, John MacKenzie, and the Edward Said of *Culture and Imperialism*.

8. Showalter, *Sexual Anarchy*, 79; Gilbert and Gubar read Haggard's *She* in *No Man's Land*, 2:3–46. For their argument on gender and modernism, see chapter 3, "Tradition and the Female Talent," *No Man's Land*, 1:125–62.

9. Harkness, *In Darkest London*, 3–4. Harkness's description of the urban street scene is not unique. The following passage from the periodical *Chemist and Druggist*, written two decades earlier, illustrates many of the same themes as the one from *In Darkest London:*

> That which probably distinguishes London from every other city in the world is the utter absence of any special character. . . . London . . . would be very imperfectly described if we simply called it an English city. The observant wanderer through its streets finds its features change like the scenes in a kaleidoscope as he moves from quarter to quarter. French-row, Spanish-row, Italian-row are here and there; indeed little Continental cities are almost to be found within the metropolitan area; the day is not far distant when Germany may give up asking the interminable question as to where is its Fatherland, and decide for London. Ireland is here, and loves to crowd in our dirtiest slums; and if by chance an interstice does occur anywhere, a Jew or Scotchman instantly fills it. A fashionable suburb in the West is known as Asia Minor, from the favour it has won in the eyes of the English nabobs who have returned from the East; but Asia Minor *vera* is in the neighbourhood of the docks. Every ruler in the world, not utterly savage, has some subjects in London, and the remarkable thing about it is that in so small a degree, as a rule, is the individuality or the nationality of these immigrants affected by residence here. Some say London is a home for no one, surely no city is such a home for all. If ever a word had an extended meaning, *home* has in London. Much more is known of the worst of these homes now, than was known twenty years ago; but acres of houses still remain a *terra incognita*. ("Opium Smoking in Bluegate Fields," 259)

10. Much attention has been paid in recent years to the imprecision of using the term *oriental* and the violence done to the unique cultures whose identities have been collapsed under this rubric. While this has been an important issue, it has prompted me to think about the inaccuracies promulgated by a term like *London*. It has been, to say the least, a vexing problem to base a study on imaginative approaches to a site that is itself a fiction. To the degree that I can, I attempt to be as local as possible in talking about the specific sites of metropolitan imperial encounters. To generalize about London has seemed irresponsibly abstract. Yet it also seems important to recognize that London (like "the Orient"), as a totalizing construct, is an important referential category—however imprecise it may be—in the imaginative geography of Victorians and others. I suppose that the problem of "London" is about being an outsider or insider. For those who live there, the sense of the whole seems less pragmatically crucial than a geography that offers greater differentiations. For those less familiar with London, the whole seems more important, more evocative, than the details.

11. As Colin Holmes points out, "British experience of 'strangers' through the immigration and settlement of racial and ethnic groups has received far less atten-

tion than imperial and colonial contact" (*Immigrants and Minorities,* 13). The experience of immigration in Britain certainly does not match that paid to the issue by students of U.S. history and culture; one certainly would not make the claim that London was transformed by immigration to the degree that New York, Boston, or Chicago was.

Nevertheless, Holmes does supply some striking numbers for Britain. The most significant immigrant group in late-nineteenth-century Britain was the Irish, who came primarily in the 1840s and 1860s. However, the number of Irish immigrants in Britain was never very stable because, unlike Irish immigrants to the United States, those in Britain continually moved back and forth between England and Ireland. From the 1880s onward, there was a large influx of Russian Poles, most of whom were Jewish. In 1901, there were 53,537 Russian Poles living in London, 80 percent of whom were concentrated in the East End borough of Stepney (Holmes, *John Bull's Island,* 26). By 1911, there were 20,389 Italians living in England and Wales and 1,871 Chinese (30–32). There are no specific numbers for African and Afro-Caribbean immigrants at this early date, all of whom would have been lumped together in the census category of "British colonies and dependencies." In 1910, the community of Indian students numbered between 1,000 and 2,000 (34). One of the most famous Indian immigrants was Gandhi, who studied law in London between 1887 and 1890 (35).

12. See Fishman, *East End 1888,* 131–76.

13. It could, however, be argued that Harkness's novel and its categorizing narrator does transform the streetscape into an organized spectacle for her readers, a vicarious exhibition to be consumed in the home. Alongside this, it should be noted that, despite its pretensions to organization, the crowds who visited the Great Exhibition of 1851 did not always behave in the prescribed fashion.

14. I refer here to Wordsworth's sonnet "Composed Upon Westminster Bridge" (*William Wordsworth: Selected Poetry,* 199).

15. Harkness, *In Darkest London,* 275; the best introduction to the Victorian obsession with urban sanitation is Wohl, *Endangered Lives.*

16. I will return to a fuller discussion of the metropolitan politics of food in chapter 6, where I discuss Conrad's depiction of an Italian restaurant in *The Secret Agent.*

17. For more on the widespread metropolitan skepticism about the theatricality of poverty, see Audrey Jaffe, "Detecting the Beggar"; Doyle's story was published in 1891.

18. Harkness, *In Darkest London,* 148.

19. This whole emphasis on authenticity is a denial of history, as Conrad suggests in a passage in the opening pages of *Heart of Darkness:*

But darkness was here yesterday. Imagine the feelings of a commander of a fine—what d'ye call'em?—trireme in the Mediterranean, ordered suddenly to the north; run overland across the Gauls in a hurry; put in charge of one of these craft the legionaries—a wonderful lot of handy men they must have been too—used to build, apparently by the hundred, in a month or two, if we may believe what we read. Imagine him here—the very end of the world, a sea the colour of lead, a sky the colour of smoke, a kind of ship about as rigid as a concertina—and going up this river with stores, or orders, or what you like. Sand-banks, marshes, forests, savages,—precious little to eat fit for a civilized man, nothing but Thames water to drink. (30)

20. Pratt, *Imperial Eyes*, 6.

21. In a recent edition of *Harvard Design Magazine* devoted to "Popular Places," William Saunders describes the way in which cultural studies tends to take two approaches to mass culture: elitism and populism. "Populists believe that most people have few illusions; elitists believe they have many." I agree with Saunders's assessment that the truth probably lies somewhere in the middle. "'Ordinary' people visiting popular places often are aware of attempts to manipulate them; yet very few people are capable of sustained perceptiveness and autonomy in a culture saturated by advertising and mass media" (Saunders, "From the Editor").

22. Wordsworth, *Selected Poetry*, 222–25.

23. Ibid.

24. Mayhew, *London Labour*, 1.

25. McClintock, *Imperial Leather*, 33. In charting McClintock's discussion of the transformation or evolution from scientific to commodity racism, I think it important to keep in mind that we are talking about relative emphasis and not strict periodization. Obviously, as we can see in a landmark work like George Stocking's *Victorian Anthropology*, the populist ethnological spectacle and its importance for commodity culture happen alongside the work of more scientific practices like those of Edward Tylor or Alfred Marshall.

26. Arthur Conan Doyle's Sherlock Holmes stories span the remainder of his life: the first, the novella *A Study in Scarlet*, was published in 1887; the last was published in 1927. In referring to the years 1886–96 as the "moment" of Holmes, I refer to these years as the crucial ones in which we see the genesis of Holmes and his moment of greatest popularity. (As I will discuss below, there was a significant hiatus in the writing between 1893 and 1902.)

27. In chapter 6, I discuss at greater length Benjamin's classic essay "The Work of Art in the Age of Mechanical Reproduction" as a way to read turn-of-the-century instantiations of urban ethnic cultures. Besides McClintock's work on soap, I have also benefited from Rachel Bowlby's discussion of cigarette marketing and Wilde's *Dorian Gray* (see *Shopping with Freud*, 7–24) and Thomas Richards's work on marketing empire in *The Commodity Culture of Victorian England* (especially chapter 3, "Marketing Darkest Africa," 119–67).

28. Likewise, as Nancy Metz has shown, it is true that Dickens, at moments as early as *Sketches by Boz* (1837) and as late as *Little Dorrit* (1855–56), identified with the charismatic Egyptian explorer Giovanni Belzoni ("*Little Dorrit*'s London"). However, that connection seems much more episodic than Booth's close identification with Stanley.

29. I would not go so far as to say that *The Secret Agent*, because of its setting, is the most urban of Conrad's texts. Conrad, though the central figure in the classical literature of British imperialism, is throughout his corpus writing the city. I argue that just as the writer of historical fiction is always writing (about) the

present, so too is the writer of exotic fiction always talking about the *here* of the writing.

30. Bongie writes that Conrad, "faced with the complete dissolution of exotic horizons . . . envisions a world given entirely, and hopelessly, over to modernity" (Bongie, *Exotic Memories*, 18). Yet Conrad, argues Bongie, can "choose not to abandon this empty project but rather to re-inscribe [himself] within what [he] know[s] to be no more (yet no less) than a dream" (20).

2. HOLMES AND THE RANGE

1. Some notable exceptions to the relative critical ignorance of the Holmes tales include Audrey Jaffe, "Detecting the Beggar," and Rosemary Hennesy and Rajeswari Mohan, "The Construction of Woman in Three Popular Texts of Empire."

2. Leavis, *Great Tradition*, 210.

3. For Elaine Showalter, "the revival of 'romance' in the 1880s was a men's literary revolution intended to reclaim the kingdom of the English novel for male writers, male readers, and men's stories" (*Sexual Anarchy*, 79).

4. All references to *A Study in Scarlet* are cited parenthetically in the text by page number of *Sherlock Holmes: Complete.*

5. A typical response is that of T. S. Eliot, who, in 1929, writes that "Sherlock Holmes reminds us always of the pleasant externals of nineteenth-century London. I believe he may continue to do so even for those who cannot remember the nineteenth-century; . . . I remember the hansom cabs, the queer bowlers, Holmes's fore-and-aft cap, Holmes in a frock coat after breakfast . . . in the Sherlock Holmes stories, the late nineteenth century is always romantic, always nostalgic" (Eliot, "Books of the Quarter," 553). For one of the preeminent Anglo-American modernists, Holmes's "cesspool" London has already vanished and is already "nostalgic" and "pleasant." Eliot, because he needs a pretty, "romantic" picture against which, as poet, he can measure his own disgust for the "wasteland" of modernity, like most twentieth-century readers ignores the fact that Doyle's late-Victorian London is a violent "cesspool."

6. For more on Doyle's debt to these predecessors, see the seminal work of Haycraft, *Murder for Pleasure*, 1–62. Haycraft establishes the "great tradition" of detective fiction, beginning with Poe and Gaboriau and Doyle, with a minor detour through Wilkie Collins and Dickens. Similar genealogies are set forth in the best critical biographies of Doyle: Nordon, *Conan Doyle*, 212–22, and Jaffe, *Arthur Conan Doyle*, 32–33. Critics also see an influence in Doyle's medical-school teacher, Dr. Joseph Bell. I do not mean to displace any of these influential models, but to add an ignored, but crucial, influence to the discussion.

7. In his autobiography, Doyle traces his childhood literary beginnings: "My tastes were boylike enough, for Mayne Reid was my favourite author, and his "Scalp Hunters" my favourite book. I wrote a little book and illustrated it myself in early days. There was a man in it and there was a tiger who amalgamated shortly after they met" (*Memories and Adventures*, 7). Doyle traces his artistic career to the reading and writing of stories involving Native Americans and the "amalgamation"

of man and beast. In Sherlock Holmes, who is frequently compared to a tiger, we can see strong traces of Doyle's earliest literary creation.

8. Holmes's cocaine use in *The Sign of Four* is the subject of the following chapter.

9. Doyle's proto-Western tale of the Mormons is a plot borrowed largely from Stevenson's "The Story of the Destroying Angel" in *The Dynamiter* (1885). I call these proto-Westerns because, in the 1880s, the Western had not yet fully developed as a genre. Most critics see Owen Wister's *The Virginian* (1902) as the first classical Western (see Tompkins, *West of Everything*, 131–55).

10. Doyle's narrative keeps separate two landscapes—the urban "cesspool" and the "Great Alkali Plain" of the desert—which Eliot will superimpose in *The Waste Land*. Although it would be inaccurate to label *A Study in Scarlet* as modernist, its juxtaposition of the urban and the primitive is part of an emerging modernist aesthetic.

11. For an account of historical attitudes toward the Mormons, see Larson, *"Americanization" of Utah*. Larson places the dominant public uproar over polygamy alongside the less explicit resentment of U.S. and British business interests over the Mormon monopoly on commerce in the territory, and within the context of struggles over sovereignty between the federal government and territorial leadership in the Civil War era.

12. A later, more popular attack on Mormon vigilantism, polygamy, and ruthless economic greed is Zane Grey's canonical Western *Riders of the Purple Sage* (1912).

13. In September 1857, a party of California-bound pioneers was slaughtered near Mountain Meadows in Washington County, Utah, in what became known as the Mountain Meadows Massacre. According to contemporary accounts, the pioneers, attacked by a group of Indians, held out for three days. Promised safe passage by John Lee, a Mormon elder, they left their wagon barricades, only to be attacked by whites and Indians under Lee's command.

The "massacre" occurred against the backdrop of congressional debates about whether to suspend the governor, Brigham Young, and send a delegation of federal troops to the territory. The Mormons vowed to resist this intrusion on their sovereignty. According to Larson, President Buchanan, a Democrat and champion of popular sovereignty, had to bend to the opposition of the emerging Republican Party, whose party platform decried the "twin relics of barbarism": slavery and polygamy. Senator Stephen Douglass, a Democrat, tried to divert attention away from the Republicans' outrage about polygamy and focus attention on other outrages. "He denounced the Mormons as alien and disloyal, bound by oaths and penalties to sustain the authority of Brigham Young and engaged in forming secret alliances with Indian tribes to rob and murder loyal Americans and enemies of the Saints" (Larson, *"Americanization" of Utah*, 22).

14. Ibid., 38.

15. Ibid., 41.

16. My comments on Doyle's use of stereotypes is indebted to Jane Tompkins's reading of Cooper's *The Last of the Mohicans*. Tompkins notes that "What has been overlooked in the effort to protect Cooper from the charge that he relies

too much on formula and stereotypes are the formulas and stereotypes themselves" (Tompkins, *Sensational Designs*, 100). In "The Country of the Saints" and in nearly all the other Holmes stories, Doyle displays what Tompkins calls "an obsessive preoccupation with systems of classification" (105). Both Cooper and Doyle, his close literary descendant, write fiction that is "a meditation on kinds . . . an attempt to calculate exactly how much violation or mixing of its fundamental categories a society can bear" (106). Doyle wrote several historical novels (of the chivalric *Ivanhoe* variety) at the same time he was producing Holmes fiction. Two of them, *Micah Clarke* (1889) and *The Refugees* (1893), were set in the era of the 1688 revolution and can be seen as bicentennial meditations on a moment of important national definition. Doyle always considered this work more important than the Holmes tales. However, these two different kinds of literary production were part of the same project of constructing or representing a national identity.

17. My seemingly easy collapse of differences here, between the Native American and Middle Eastern, is not unproblematic. However, as the following passage from Burton indicates, there is a tendency among many Victorian writers to essentialize the variety of differences manifested by a range of foreigners.

18. Burton, *City of the Saints,* ix, 1, 3, 524.

19. Estleman, introduction, xiii.

20. Jaffe, *Arthur Conan Doyle,* 36.

21. Anonymous reviewer in the *Graphic,* quoted in Baring-Gould, *The Annotated Sherlock Holmes,* 12–13.

22. The suggestion that the formal split is naive failure is contradicted by the evidence of the later tales. A split will return in the next Holmes story, *The Sign of Four* (1890), and in a much later novella, *The Valley of Fear* (1912). The slicker Holmes narratives develop not out of any artistic maturity, but rather from the literary marketplace's demand for the short stories Doyle published in *Strand Magazine.* Although the historical digressions are more obvious in the longer novellas, even the formulaic short stories usually transport the reader historically and geographically. The primary difference between novella and short story is that the longer explanation of motive increases our sympathy for the criminal. In the short stories, we focus more on the contemporary fact of a crime, which, disconnected from any elaborate discussion of social cause, appears to be irrational or the effect of some supernatural, metaphysical evil.

23. Jaffe, *Arthur Conan Doyle,* 36.

24. As Stephen Knight reminds us, "Holmes was a hero shaped for a particular class in a particular time and place, but like many other heroes he has survived out of context as a figure of heroism" (Knight, *Form and Ideology,* 103). I know of no critical account that has attempted to chart changes in Holmes, Watson, or the fictional landscape of London over the course of his thirty-five-year career. Of course, there may be no significant changes to uncover, which would, of itself, be interesting in light of the social changes that catalyzed other writers of the modernist era.

25. Nordon, *Conan Doyle,* 227.

26. Lukács, *The Historical Novel,* 17.

27. Ibid., 47.

28. In the light of Lukács's work on the novel as a site that narrativizes histor-ical clashes, Doyle's novella displays how that history unfolds in geographical space. That is, its heroes are embodiments not just of moments of capitalist devel-opments, but of specific places as well.

In calling attention to the importance of geography here, I wish to join Edward Soja in challenging "an overdeveloped historical contextualization of social life and social theory that actively submerges and peripheralizes the geographical or spatial imagination" (Soja, *Postmodern Geographies*, 15).

29. The link between the detective and the Native American tracker outlasts Holmes in the history of the detective genre. Its centrality survives in one of the best-selling contemporary mystery writers, Tony Hillerman. Set in the American Southwest (which geographically is not too far from Doyle's Utah), Hillerman's plots star two Navaho policemen who have a Holmes-like ability to read tracks. Jim Chee and Joe Leaphorn, like Holmes, combine primitive and modern tech-nologies and knowledge. Both have been brought up in Navaho culture but also have university degrees in anthropology from state universities. Their identity is a hybrid of Anglo and Navaho, traditional and modern, oral and literate, academic and common sense. Footprints and tire treads often hold the key to Hillerman's mysteries. Produced by a writer steeped in the Anglo-American detective tradi-tion, the literary lineage of Hillerman's detectives can be traced back to Holmes, and signals how, in the postmodern era, the heroes of detective fiction have come full circle back to the supposed bearer of "primitive" knowledge. That is, Hiller-man's fictions invoke and partake of a tradition—shaped by Doyle and Holmes—whose origins, I argue, extend back through Cooper's frontiersman to the Native Americans who were Cooper's models.

30. Doyle, "The Boscombe Valley Mystery," in *Sherlock Holmes: Complete*, 281.

31. Doyle, *Memories and Adventures*, 7.

32. Although Holmes and Hope both are figured as hounds, Holmes is of a more civilized variety—the domesticated "foxhound" of sport; Hope is of a less-tamed variety—the bloodhound who tracks enemies, fugitives, and meat. The two kinds of hounds demonstrate a kinship between the two heroes, yet also a difference in terms of the relative degree of their savagery and their class associa-tions.

33. Although John Wayne was not an available model for Doyle, the writer would have had in mind characters like the English adventurers in narratives like *King Solomon's Mines*. In the "imperial romance," exoticism, masculinity, violence, and nature are always closely related. For Doyle's readers, Hope would be a repre-sentative of such a tradition, a character whose tragic flaw is that he leaves the frontier.

34. Another important tension here is that between the Anglo Holmes and the American Hope. At the end of the nineteenth century, the balance of trade between the two nations was shifting to favor the United States, and Britons were becoming increasingly nervous about U.S. investment and involvement in British economic life. On this level, Holmes's victory over Hope gives his British reader-ship a compensatory fantasy for anxieties about American invasions and their own national destiny. While Doyle was an advocate of Anglo-American reconcil-

iation and refederation, he also saw the British as the benevolently dominant partner in the relationship.

35. Foucault, *Discipline and Punish*, 73.

36. According to Stephen Knight, the *Strand Magazine,* a publication that had only recently been founded, "had a bourgeois, middle-brow, content and a satisfying modern format." It "was widely distributed through railway bookstalls to catch the commuting white-collar market" (Knight, *Form and Ideology*, 70). Holmes was the perfect hero for this white-collar market. An intellectual laborer like them, he was, however, also an independent amateur. Holmes thus provided a fantastic model of unalienated labor to the bureaucrats whose brainwork was increasingly standardized drudgery performed as a service for their employer-superiors.

37. In fact, over the course of Holmes's career, we never see him testify in "official" court, although he occasionally presides over a mock court of his own creation. This absence is not simply Doyle's attempt to keep his hero away from the institutions of punishment. The tales and their hero—although they serve "the Law"—often stand in a curious relation to it. The law's official representatives are bumblers. When opposed to Hope's hot-blooded vengeance, Holmes represents the cold-blooded rule of law. Yet he always exists outside of social norms and organizations: he appears as bachelor, drug addict, consulting detective. Like Hope, he often does take justice into his own hands, winking at crimes he finds excusable. While in this first case he is in dialectical conflict to Hope, in later cases he will be more Hope-like in relation to the cold-blooded liberalism of the law.

38. Turner, *The Frontier in American History*, 1.

39. The etymologically rich name *Sherlock Holmes* appears in the *OED* next to the entry for *sheriff.* Nordon argues that the original name of Doyle's hero—Sherrinford Holmes—expressed Doyle's desire to link his detective to his own Irish origins. When *Sherrinford* becomes *Sherlock,* all that Doyle retains is the *Sher.*

Sheriff (shire + reeve) was a pre-Norman office that is retained to the present. The sheriff functions as the royal representative in a shire (county). Holmes is not only the guardian of the "home"—he who ensures "sure locked" homes—but also the shire-lock, or regulator, responsible for keeping the lock on the shire of the metropolis. He decides who stays and who goes.

40. According to Pierre Nordon, the Doyle family resembles "most Irish Catholic families; their history had been punctuated by wars, insurrections, looting, destruction and religious persecution, including the long martyrdom inflicted on them by the enforcement of the penal laws against the Catholic landed gentry" (Nordon, *Conan Doyle,* 4).

41. Nordon notes that "Pius IX's decision to create an archbishopric and twelve bishoprics in England was treated as a provocative act by a section of the newspapers and public. Some of the reactions to it took a violent form—procession, broken windows, the looting of Catholic churches—and *Punch* stood in the front rank of the opposition as champion of the Protestant cause" (Nordon, *Conan Doyle,* 13). Anti-Catholic sentiments were especially high in the 1850s, not only because of the pope's intervention but also because of fears directed at the large

population of Irish immigrants who went to England in the wake of famines in
the 1840s.

42. Jaffe, *Arthur Conan Doyle,* 18–19.

43. "J. Habakkuk Jephson's Statement," in *Captain of the Polestar.*

44. Jaffe, *Arthur Conan Doyle,* 22.

45. In "The Dancing Men" and *The Valley of Fear.* There may also be an implicit
reference to the Irish as dupes (in "The Red Headed League") and beggars (in "The
Man with the Twisted Lip"), if we assume that red hair has to signify Irishness.

46. Cecil Eby notes that although "Doyle argued for mobilization of all citizens
capable of bearing arms into a national militia responsible for home defense," the
British public was averse to a policy that looked like "conscription." However, at a
local level, Doyle "organized a private rifle company in his village of Hindhead
and paid the cost of rifles and targets from his own pocket." Years later, at the
outbreak of World War I, Doyle would take credit for founding "the Civilian Reserve,
a paramilitary force consisting of those too old, or too feeble, to fight, which
would protect the coast from German invaders" (Eby, *The Road to Armageddon,*
184–85).

47. In a subsequent short story, "The Adventure of the Empty House," Holmes
tells Watson that after faking his death at Reichenback Fall, he spent three years
wandering the world.

> I travelled for two years in Tibet, therefore, and amused myself by visiting
> Lhassa, and spending some days with the head lama. You may have read of
> the remarkable explorations of a Norwegian named Sigerson, but I am sure
> that it never occurred to you that you were receiving news of your friend. I
> then passed through Persia, looked in at Mecca, and paid a short but inter-
> esting visit to the Khalifa at Khartoum, the results of which I have commu-
> nicated to the Foreign Office. Returning to France, I spent some months in
> a research into the coal-tar derivatives, which I conducted in a laboratory at
> Montpellier, in the south of France. (Doyle, "Empty House," 670–71)

48. For information on "foreign feuds" in late-Victorian London, see the work
of W. J. Fishman, including *East End Jewish Radicals, 1875–1914; The Insurrectionists;*
and *East End 1888.*

3. THE ROMANCE OF INVASION

1. Doyle, *The Sign of Four,* in *Sherlock Holmes: Complete,* 107. All further references to the text are cited parenthetically by page number.

2. The recent Granada adaptations of Holmes include a fine version of *The
Sign of Four.* Its one glaring fault is a total omission of the framing cocaine plot, a
narrative device that I argue is central to understanding the text's cultural work.

3. On Holmes's cocaine habit, see Jack Tracy, *Subcutaneously.* Tracy reports
that "cocaine, in fact, is a vegetable alkaloid . . . the principal active ingredient in
the South American coca plant." Though "brought to Europe by the Spanish early

in the sixteenth century," it "was not chemically isolated until at least 1844. Its commercial manufacture was begun in 1862, and in 1883 its medical applications first came to light when a Bavarian army doctor discovered its usefulness as an anti-fatigue agent" (18).

4. There is another important link to the title in the phonetic association between "sign of four" and signs of the fore(ign). My discussion of the invasion theme works with both kinds of invasion, those from the outside and those from the past.

5. *The Sign of Four* is also the centerpiece of John Thomspon's chapter "The Adventurous Detective" (*Fiction, Crime, and Empire*, 60–79).

6. In referring to the events in India in 1857, one faces a difficult choice. One's options include terms like *Indian Mutiny, Sepoy Rebellion, Indian Uprising*. As in all situations of naming, there is no politically neutral or objective choice. Despite its colonialist resonances, I have chosen to use *Mutiny*, not out of any solidarity with British colonialism but because that is the term used by the authors dealt with in this study.

7. As Franco Moretti points out, Holmes's work for work's sake is analogous to the fin de siècle movement of art for art's sake: "[H]e sacrifices his individuality to his work: his endless series of disguises, sleepless nights, and inability to eat during an investigation are all metaphors for this. . . . This voluntary repression of the self is at one with Holmes's (and every other classic detective's) dilettantism. Dilettantism is not superficiality, but work done for the pleasure of work: 'To the man who loves art for its own sake . . . it is frequently in its least important and lowliest manifestations that the keenest pleasure is to be derived'" (Moretti, *Signs Taken for Wonders*, 142). In my reading, Holmes's disgust for dull routine and his craving for satisfactory brainwork bring together the critical projects of a number of Victorian cultural critics, including Marx, Ruskin, Morris, and Wilde.

8. In this novella, we can see the confluence of the Holmes phenomenon and the rapid increase of suburbanization in late-Victorian London. "In the history of the middle-class residential suburb, the late nineteenth century railroad suburb represents the classic form, the era in which suburbia most closely approached the bourgeois monument and bourgeois utopia. It exemplified the central meaning and contradiction of suburbia: a natural world of greenery and family life that appeared to be wholly separate from the great city yet was in fact wholly dependent upon it" (Fishman, *Bourgeois Utopias*, 134). As Fishman points out, the development of suburbia was sponsored by the expanding network of metropolitan commuter rail companies that carried the passengers who bought the *Strand* at the stations and read Holmes stories on their way back to their suburban retreats. These three phenomena—Holmes, suburbia, and the metropolitan railways—are inextricable. After killing off Holmes in 1893, Doyle wrote a novelistic send-up of suburbia, *Beyond the City* (1894).

9. Or out of Wilde's *The Picture of Dorian Gray*. Sholto's sanctum is remarkably similar to Lord Henry's library, where we see Dorian reclining in a "luxurious arm-chair" at the beginning of chapter 4. In the character of Thaddeus Sholto, the presence of Oscar Wilde is one that haunts Doyle's text (published 1890). Interestingly, at an 1889 dinner meeting where the American editor of *Lippincott's Monthly*

Magazine commissioned Doyle to write *The Sign of Four,* the other guest was Oscar Wilde, whose commission that evening became *The Picture of Dorian Gray* (see Ackroyd's introduction to Wilde, *Dorian Gray*).

10. I am indebted to Vaneeta Palecanda for insight on the importance of Doyle's choice of Pondicherry.

11. The maps from Bacon's atlas (of four-inch and nine-inch scale) were reproduced in facsimile by Ralph Hyde as *The A to Z of Victorian London.* In looking at the neighborhood chosen by Doyle, I have relied on the newer four-inch maps (Hyde, *A to Z,* 109). According to Hyde, "the 'Four Inch' maps are especially useful in showing the villages around London as they were shortly before being engulfed by the metropolis. Many of the suburban branch railways that triggered off their drastic development are already shown in position" (vii). Doyle certainly knew his London well enough not to have needed an atlas; yet, there was a good one recently available to him, and my research indicates that it is quite faithful to Doyle's cartographic imagination. For example, in "The Man with the Twisted Lip" (1891), Doyle and Watson visit a suburban villa named "The Cedars" in Lee. Bacon's map indicates a villa of precisely that name near Lee (70).

12. Richards, *Commodity Culture of Victorian England,* 17.

13. In the official catalog, we read:

> Nobody, however, who has paid any attention to the particular features of our present era, will doubt for a moment that we are living at a period of most wonderful transition, which tends rapidly to the accomplishment of that great end to which, indeed, all history points—the realization of the unity of mankind. Not a unity which breaks down the limits, and levels the peculiar characteristics of the different nations of the earth, but rather a unity the result and product of those very national varieties and antagonistic qualities. The distances which separated the different nations and parts of the globe are gradually vanishing before the achievements of modern invention, and we can traverse them with incredible ease; the languages of all nations are known, and their acquirements placed within the reach of everybody; thought is communicated with rapidity and even by the power of lightning. (Prince Albert, quoted in the introduction to the *Official Descriptive and Illustrated Catalogue for the Great Exhibition,* 3)

14. According to Hobhouse,

> the age was so obsessed with "steam intellect" and "railway intelligence," with Stephenson's bridges and Brunel's broad gauges, with all the perpetual improvement and invention that was revolutionizing the heavy industries, that agriculture had been relegated to the back of the picture. The country had survived the repeal of the Corn Laws, contrary to its own prediction: and with that settled, the country was easily forgotten. The Exhibition in fact was so far a wholly urban enterprise, a positive triumph of coal and iron over corn and cattle. Protection was dying, and it seemed that it could never live again. But it was still capable of a pretty vigorous protest. (*1851 and the Crystal Place,* 19)

15. Doyle's account of the Andaman Islanders closely resembles that offered by the first Englishman to visit the islands, Frederic Mouat, who was sent there to explore their suitability for a convict settlement to imprison the participants in the 1857 Mutiny. Like Holmes's text, Mouat's records that "the inhabitants of the Andamans have always been considered one of the most savage races on the face of the earth, whom civilization has yet found it impossible to tame, or even almost to approach." From Mouat, *The Andaman Islanders*, 3–4. Mouat's text was originally published in 1863 as *Adventures and Researches Among the Andaman Islanders*. The Andaman Islanders were a hot topic of discussion in ethnological circles from the 1860s onward; many other possible sources are listed in the bibliography of David Tomas's article "Tools of the Trade," in Stocking, *Colonial Situations*, 75–108.

16. Defoe, *Robinson Crusoe*, 163.

17. According to Eby, between 1871 and 1914 "English writers of popular fiction —that is to say, fiction prepared for wide circulation to a mass audience—churned out more than sixty narratives describing invasion (or attempted invasion) of their sceptred isle" (*Road to Armageddon*, 11). However, Eby's count does not even begin to do justice to the hold of "invasion narratives" on the late-Victorian reading public. Eby consciously omits those "narratives treating actual invasions of the historical past" (such as Hardy's *The Trumpet-Major*, set amid the fear of a Napoleonic invasion of Britain) and treats only "fictive pieces professing to describe a future war." Eby's tally is also limited by his narrow concern with fictions prophesizing invasions by nations such as Germany, France, Japan, and the United States; these narratives were overtly propagandistic, the "productions of what might be termed a professional cadre of writers housed within the military or naval establishment of Great Britain" (25). Although Eby does include Wells's Martians (*The War of the Worlds*), he ignores other fantastic invaders such as Stoker's *Dracula*, Haggard's African Queen Ayesha (*She*), and Doyle's countless aliens. It is my belief that these latter narratives, comprising a genre that Patrick Brantlinger calls the "imperial gothic," had an equally strong hold on the public imagination and were more crucial to late-Victorian formulations of national identity. See Brantlinger, *Rule of Darkness* (227–53) and Schmitt, *Alien Nation* (135–55).

18. Surrey and Kent are also, significantly, precisely those counties proximate to London that were prime sites of late-Victorian suburbanization.

19. Holmes's surveillance of the East End docks suggest important instances of geographical and historical context. In terms of location, it was these docks that functioned as the main entrepôt for the empire's trade with London, not to mention the rest of the nation. Historically, the novella comes close on the heels of the Ripper murders in late 1887 and the dockers' strike in 1888. Tonga's murder of the suburban Sholto inverts one popular myth about Jack the Ripper; namely, that he was a middle-class gentleman preying upon East End female victims. Tonga and Small might also be read as allegorical figures for the labor unrest of the late-1880s. While both of these events are historically relevant, what seems more important to keep in mind is the general middle-class fear of the East End in 1890—the anxieties that it will not or cannot be geographically contained. Holmes can go east, but more importantly and fearfully, the East (Tonga and Small) can go west and south to the Upper Norwood suburb.

20. McClintock, *Imperial Leather*, 33.

21. Knight, *Form and Ideology*, 70.

22. Kiralfy's influence on the exhibition genre was considerable. In Greenhalgh's view:

> Kiralfy's rise to pre-eminence in Britain meant several things for the exhibition genre. It meant empire would be a constant source of subject-matter for events and that the tableau-vivant format would be in regular use. Under his influence, international exhibitions in Britain changed emphasis, the educational and philanthropic flavours of the earlier South Kensington shows being decisively replaced by those of theatre and fairground. Kiralfy did not seek particularly to educate or improve his audience so much as entertain and propandise them with his special effects. Many sections in his exhibitions were virtual replicas of the extravaganzas he had staged in the first part of his career. Once he had realised its potential, the native village as an idea came to suit him perfectly as a dramatic medium to express his imperial beliefs through. (*Ephemeral Vistas*, 91)

23. Machray, *The Night Side of London*, 129.

24. For a fine account of Kiralfy's career and the Empire of India Exhibition, see Brendan Gregory, "Staging British India."

25. Kiralfy, *Empire of India Exhibition Catalogue*, 9.

26. Ibid., 9.

27. As my remarks here indicate, my reading of imperial culture is like that of John MacKenzie, who sees "orientalism" more as a complicated critique of industrial modernity within Britain than a discourse about the domination of the colonized. See MacKenzie, *Orientalism*, 21–39.

28. *Colonial and Indian Exhibition, Special Catalogue*, iv–v.

29. Gregory, "Staging British India," 164.

30. Kiralfy, *Empire of India Exhibition Catalogue*, 375–76.

31. *Colonial and Indian Exhibition Catalogue*, iv.

4. COLONIZING THE URBAN JUNGLE

1. General William Booth, *In Darkest England and the Way Out*, 6. All further references to Booth's *In Darkest England* will be cited parenthetically in the text. Booth's language here mimics that of George Sims in "How the Poor Live" (1883). Sims writes, "I propose to record the result of a journey into a region which lies at our own doors—into a dark continent that is within easy walking distance of the General Post Office. This continent will, I hope, be found as interesting as any of those newly-explored lands which engage the attention of the Royal Geographic Society—the wild races who inhabit it will, I trust, gain public sympathy as easily as those savage tribes for whose benefit the missionary Societies never cease to appeal for funds" (65–66).

2. Jones, *Outcast London*, 13–14.

3. Greenwood's most famous account of terra incognita was his career-launching "A Night in the Workhouse," published in January 1866 in the *Pall Mall*

Gazette, edited by his brother Frederick. In this work, Greenwood ventured incognito to spend a night in the Lambeth Workhouse. His "discoveries" became a matter of public scandal and debate about his journalistic methods. In addition to publishing other works on the world of the London lower classes such as *The True History of a Little Ragamuffin* (c.1865), *The Seven Curses of London* (1869), and *Low Life Deeps and an Account of The Strange Fish To Be Found There* (1876), Greenwood was also the author of imperial adventure fiction for boys such as *The Adventures of Reuben Davidger, Seventeen Years and Four Months Captive Among the Dyaks of Borneo.* For more on Greenwood, see Keating, *Working Classes in Victorian Fiction,* 38–40.

4. See chapter 1, n. 10.

5. This figuration of an urban area as imperial space is what Anne McClintock calls the creation of "anachronistic space." "In the industrial metropolis . . . the evocation of an anachronistic space (the invention of the archaic) became central to the discourse of racial science and the urban surveillance of women and the working class" (*Imperial Leather,* 40–42). This "invention of the archaic" and its instantiation in a seemingly real locale functioned to constitute its obverse, the "invention of the modern."

6. Here and throughout this chapter I will refer to General Booth as the author of *In Darkest England.* However, Booth had a ghostwriter, the sensational journalist W. T. Stead. The latter was well known in this period for his editorship of the *Pall Mall Gazette* in the 1880s and as the central figure in the so-called Maiden Tribute of Modern Babylon scandal (child prostitution) in 1885. General Booth's son Bramwell stood trial with Stead because the Salvation Army was involved in Stead's "Maiden Tribute" endeavors. For a history of the scandal, see Walkowitz, *City of Dreadful Delight,* 81–120.

7. For more on the Stanley expedition, see Richard Hall, *Stanley,* 286–330.

8. It is unclear whether Booth or Stead was responsible for the Darkest England discourse. Booth's most sympathetic biographer, Harold Begbie, asserts that the book would have been surer of literary "immortality had it been written from the first page to the last in the vigorous, direct, unpolished, but wonderfully dynamic vernacular of William Booth. It is quite possible to see where Booth breaks in upon the well-ordered and elaborate sentences with a stroke of his own, and excellent as Mr. Stead's work may be, those strokes in the midst of it are like a door blowing suddenly open, or like a human voice shouting great news above the murmur of bees. It is as if a sermon by Bossuet contained every now and then an exclamation by Bunyan" (Begbie, *Life of William Booth,* 93). Those familiar with Stead's sensationalist rhetoric might find it hard to believe that anyone, even Booth, could rival it. Whether this is the voice of Booth, Stead, or an amalgam of the two, the important point is that the "darkest England" plan sold, and Booth became an "urban Stanley" whether self-cast or not.

9. Sandall, *History of the Salvation Army,* 75.

10. Stanley's feminized description of the "inner womb of the true tropical forest" pre-dates Conrad's depiction of the savage African woman as an embodiment of the African landscape: "She was savage and superb, wild-eyed and magnificent; there was something ominous and stately in her deliberate progress. And

in the hush that had fallen suddenly upon the whole sorrowful land, the immense wilderness, the colossal body of the fecund and mysterious life seemed to look at her, pensive, as though it had been looking at the image of its own tenebrous and passionate soul" (*Heart of Darkness,* 101). For more on this passage see Torgovnick, *Gone Primitive,* 154–57. For more on masculine fantasies that portray heroic endeavor as an encounter with a feminized landscape, see McClintock's reading of Haggard's *King Solomon's Mines* (*Imperial Leather,* 1–9, 24–30) and Theweleit, "Floods, Bodies, History," in *Male Fantasies,* volume 1, chapter 2.

11. Stedman Jones, quoted in Jukes, *A Shout in the Street,* 9.

12. Quoted in Jukes, 16. For a fine history of street-clearance schemes in Victorian London, see Winter, *London's Teeming Streets.*

13. Booth's metaphor of the city as "a tangle of monotonous undergrowth" remains with us late in the twentieth century. In the early 1990s, a Bush administration plan to revive inner cities in the United States was called the "Weed and Seed" program. This label simultaneously obscures human agency by rendering a social environment as natural and dehumanizes those people who are to be "weeded" out. Booth's language of pecking at the surface also demonstrates how even his own elaborate solution is intended to deal with, not underlying economic and social structures, but symptoms, such as alcoholism, prostitution, and lack of church attendance.

14. Discussed more fully in the next chapter.

15. Doyle, *The Sign of Four,* 122.

16. Later in this book, in my chapters on Jack London, Conrad, and Eliot, we will see that hell as depicted by Dante is crucial to the aesthetic representation and moral evaluation of the urban jungle. The importance of Dante to the modernist imagination is detailed in Pike, *Passage through Hell.*

17. Booth's invocation of Dante is only the most prominent of analogies linking his project to the Victorian fascination with medieval Christianity. At other moments, he calls for "more crusades" (164) and a "slum crusade" (166). He also compares himself to Saint Francis and his followers to an order of saints: "All the great towns in both the Old World and the New have their slums, in which huddle together, in festering and verminous filth, men, women, and children. They correspond to the lepers who thronged the lazar houses of the Middle Ages. As in those days St. Francis of Assisi and the heroic band of saints who gathered under his orders were wont to go and lodge with the lepers at the city gates, so the devoted souls who have enlisted in the Salvation Army take up their quarters in the heart of the worst slums" (166).

18. Booth's invocation of devils and hell recalls how Sherlock Holmes, in *The Sign of Four,* initially read Tonga's invasion as "hellish."

19. Inglis suggests that, in 1890, Booth turns his attention from spirituality to the problem of poverty in a manner unprecedented for him. He credits this largely to the growing influence of Frank Smith, a commissioner in Booth's army who was put in charge of the "American command," where he was influenced by Henry George and Ben Tillet. "Smith turned the screw farther towards social reform. It was he who organized the first labour bureau and the first factory. Where the slum officers were giving relief to the workless, Smith began to offer them work.

The title allowed for his new command—the Social Reform Wing—shows the extent of Booth's conversion to his methods" (Inglis, *Churches and the Working Classes*, 202).

20. Here, it is worth noting that Booth imagines the poor not as the victim to be saved but as the enemy "army" to be vanquished.

21. Search, *Happy Warriors*, 4.

22. Catherine Booth is quoted in Inglis, *Churches and the Working Classes*, 176.

23. See note 6.

24. Begbie, *Life of William Booth*, 139.

25. Sandall, *The History of the Salvation Army*, 79–81.

26. Jay, *Life in Darkest London*, 141.

27. Ausubel, "General Booth's Scheme of Social Salvation," 521.

28. These letters were then compiled and published as a book, *Social Diseases*.

29. Huxley, *Social Diseases*, 58.

30. Ibid., 57–61.

31. Haggard, *Regeneration*, 7–8.

32. Begbie, *Life of William Booth*, 2:40.

33. Ibid.; quoted at 2:55.

34. According to Tolen, "After the change in name, its members sought to appropriate the signs and practices of a military order. They soon began wearing secondhand British Army uniforms of various styles and periods. Later, custom-made uniforms were designed to invest the bodies of members with the signs of a military order in a more standardized manner. 'General' Booth founded an order of 'Articles of War' that all Salvation Army members were to sign, and a military hierarchy was replicated in a ranking system of lieutenants, commissioners, captains, and cadets" (Tolen, "Colonizing and Transforming the Criminal Tribesman," 114). In clothing his converted followers in these military trappings, Booth anticipates and, perhaps, influences the strategy of uniforming urban youth adopted by the Boys Brigades and, later, Baden-Powell's Boy Scouts. See Rosenthal, *Character Factory*. Booth's original use of British army uniforms demonstrates how, for him at least, his urban Christian mission was closely tied to a nationalist vision. According to Inglis, "the rules and regulations of the British army, [Booth] once remarked, had helped him more than all the constitutions of the churches; and he kept a copy of them by his bed" (Inglis, *Churches and the Working Classes*, 182).

35. Begbie, *Life of William Booth*, 2:129.

36. Booth's plan for a return to village life is published a decade before Ebenezer Howard's landmark *The Garden Cities of To-morrow* (1902), which many urban historians cite as the birth of modern town planning. While not recognized as a formal work of planning, Booth's manifesto resembles Howard's project and, like it, is a reaction to urban overcrowding and suburban sprawl.

37. Inglis argues that it was Stead who suggested the Oversea Colony to Booth. In a letter, Stead writes that he has "got the Salvation Army not only for Social Reform but also for Imperial Unity. I have written to Rhodes about it and we stand on the eve of great things" (Quoted in Inglis, *Churches and the Working Classes*, 203).

38. At the conclusion of Harkness's *In Darkest London,* the title character is sent by the Army to work in Australia.

39. Tolen, "Colonizing and Transforming the Criminal Tribesman," 114.

40. From a letter of 27 August 1886, published in F. Booth-Tucker, *Muktifauj,* xvi.

41. Ibid.; quoted at xvi–xvii.

42. Bramwell Booth, quoted in Sandall, *History of the Salvation* Army, 80–81.

43. Although it is not my main concern here, it is worth noting that the metaphorical linkage of East Enders and colonial others works both ways. I have concentrated on how Booth sees the East End as a jungle and East Enders as savages. The reversal of this paradigm is examined by Tolen in "Colonizing and Transforming the Criminal Tribesman." As indicated by her title, Tolen argues that the Salvation Army's work in India helped produce the notion of an Indian "criminal caste" by appropriating urban rhetoric about crime and applying it to Indian laborers. Thus, the metaphorical counterpart of the urban savage is the "criminal tribesman."

5. WRITING LONDON

1. Jack London, *The People of the Abyss,* vii. All further quotations from this work will be cited parenthetically in the text.

2. A series of fictional sketches published in *Strand Magazine* during 1894 and then as a book.

3. For more on Crane, see Trachtenberg, "Experiments in Another Country."

4. An urban missionary who responded to General Booth in print cited the importance of residency among the poor, arguing that before one could convert the natives, one had to convert the self to their point of view: "Residence amongst the people is the key to the whole question. If I had not gone at once amongst men to live, and, if necessary, to die, I might as well not have undertaken my task at all. The role of the professional philanthropist, who lives at the West and writes of the East, was by no means what I strove after or desired. Indeed, in such matters no words can avail: work and life alone can do anything" (Reverend A. Osborne Jay, *Life in Darkest London,* 19). Unlike Booth, who emphasizes action and reform, Jay stresses participation and the pursuit of knowledge as ends in themselves.

5. In using *participant-observation* as a term to discuss London's work, I am not bothered by the fact that his work predates Malinowski's. James Clifford has argued for the influence of Conrad, a more precise contemporary of *The People of the Abyss,* on Malinowski (*Predicament,* 92–113). It is not unreasonable to believe that Conrad was also an influence on London or, even more likely, that Conrad and London both engaged in practices of wider discursive relevance to the subsequent work of Malinowski.

6. Clifford and Marcus, *Writing Culture,* 13.

7. In stating that this discourse is "new" or foreign to the city, I do not wish to forget that imperialist discourses are typically Western and, perhaps, metropolitan inventions. Institutionally, discourses on colonial others have their basis in Western subjectivities and are produced in sites such as the Royal Geographical Society.

8. Pratt, "Fieldwork in Common Places," 31–32.

9. London's account suggests that friends and others were of little help and that he had to go it alone. James Lundquist, however, suggests that London received a great deal of assistance: "[H]e was assisted in his introduction to the East End by British Marxists (members of the Social Democratic Federation), who apparently found lodgings for him in the Flower and Dean Street area made famous by Jack the Ripper. The federation also provided the official reports that London later cited in documenting the conditions he had observed" (Lundquist, *Jack London*, 53).

10. Torgovnick, *Gone Primitive*, 18.

11. London's dressing down closely resembles this self-description in the first paragraph of Greenwood's "A Night in the Workhouse" (1866):

> From that door emerged a sly and ruffianly figure, marked with every sign of squalor. He was dressed in what had once been a snuff-brown coat, but which had faded to the hue of bricks imperfectly baked. It was not strictly a ragged coat, though it had lost its cuffs—a bereavement which obliged the wearer's arms to project through the sleeves two long inelegant inches. The coat altogether was too small, and was only made to meet over the chest by means of a bit of twine. This wretched garment was surmounted by a 'bird's eye' pocket-handkerchief of cotton, wisped about the throat hangman fashion; above all was a battered billy-cock hat, with a dissolute drooping brim. Between the neckerchief and the lowring brim of the hat appeared part of a face, unshaven, and not scrupulously clean. The man's hands were plunged into his pockets, and he shuffled hastily along in boots which were the boots of a tramp indifferent to miry ways. ("A Night in the Workhouse," 34)

12. This passage echoes Engels's dedication "To the Working Classes of Great Britain" at the beginning of *The Condition of the Working Class*:

> I wanted more than a mere *abstract* knowledge of my subject, I wanted to see you in your own homes, to observe you in your everyday life, to chat with you on your condition and grievances, to witness your struggles against the social and political power of your oppressors. I have done so: I forsook the company and the dinner-parties, the port wine and champagne of the middle classes, and devoted my leisure hours almost exclusively to the intercourse with plain Working Men; I am both glad and proud of having done so. Glad, because thus I was induced to spend many a happy hour in obtaining a knowledge of the realities of life—many an hour, which else would have been wasted in fashionable talk and tiresome etiquette. (Engels, 9)

London's goal is Engels's goal, but London believes his incognito will get him even closer to "the realities of life" and substantial "intercourse with plain Working Men."

13. Lundquist, *Jack London*, 53.

14. Jack London's cleansing bath reverses Greenwood's baptism into casual life. For Greenwood, the plunge into "a liquid so disgustingly like weak mutton broth" was his passage into poverty ("A Night in the Workhouse," 36).

15. London escapes the squalor of the East End and travels imaginatively to the American West just as Doyle had done with his Utah plot in *A Study in Scarlet*.

16. Quoted by Peluso, "Gazing at Royalty," 55. Peluso's argument that London's narrative be read primarily in the context of evolving relations between Britain and the United States resembles the argument about London's American self-fashioning I make later in this chapter.

17. Quoted by Labor in *Jack London*, 92. Labor's account of *The People of the Abyss* uncritically accepts London's project in terms that the author himself has set. In Labor's description, London heroically "disappeared into the black heart of the East End" and "emerged a month later from the jungle" with manuscript in hand. Labor admires his subject to such a degree that he often calls the writer by his first name: "Jack said," "Jack's compassion was so profound," and so forth. In qualifying Labor's reading, I want to read London's heroism and compassion alongside his rush to flee the East End he depicts as a metaphysical "hellhole."

18. According to Lundquist, "two-thirds" of the photos are London's (*Jack London*, 53). I have been unable to discover who took the rest of the photographs, but the mere presence of another undercuts London's claim to a strictly solitary individualist adventure.

19. This is yet another instance in which London's account closely resembles Greenwood. In "A Night in the Workhouse," Greenwood writes evocatively of "Kay," in a passage with overtly homoerotic resonance: "He was a very remark-able-looking lad, and his appearance pleased me much; Short as his hair was cropped, it still looked soft and silky; he had large blue eyes set wide apart, and a mouth that would have been faultless but for its great width; and his voice was as soft and sweet as any woman's. Lightly as a woman, too, he picked his way over the stones towards the place where the beds lay" (Greenwood, 41).

20. Lundquist, *Jack London*, 53.

6. WHERE DOES THE EAST END?

1. Galsworthy, *In Chancery*, 28.

2. Hampson, "Topographical Mysteries," 168–69.

3. Meyers, *Joseph Conrad*, 230.

4. Hampson, 174. To Hampson's list, I would also add *The Mirror of the Sea*, 106–21.

5. Martin Ray has another explanation for the limited London landscape of *The Secret Agent*: "There are some thirty roads and buildings identified by name, but this is very much a tourist's view of London: the Houses of Parliament, Picca-dilly, the Strand, Whitehall, Victoria Station. This makes an interesting contrast to Conrad's only other novel located, to any substantial degree, in London; *Chance* portrays industrial and residential districts such as Dalston, Tower Hamlets, Beth-nal Green and Limehouse" (197). This is a "tourist's view" only if we ignore the touristic tradition of writing about the East End. I must disagree with Ray's sug-gestion that the novel "does not betray any profound intimacy with the capital" and assert that it does, but not with those locales central to previous writing on the urban jungle (Ray, "The Landscape of *The Secret Agent*," 197).

6. Fleishman, *Conrad's Politics*, 187.

7. Ibid., 212.

8. "Which Is the Most Interesting Street in London?" 314, 321, 316–17.

9. Quoted in Summers, *Soho*, 158.

10. "In the Slums of Soho."

11. Good histories of Soho include Summers, *Soho*; Tames, *Soho Past*; Clergy of St. Anne's, *Two Centuries of Soho*; and, Mort, *Cultures of Consumption*.

12. "Soho of Today."

13. Summers, *Soho*, 176, 157.

14. In his study of the literature of British imperialism, Abdul JanMohammed has named this dualist tendency "manichean aesthetics." It is no less prevalent in writing about the urban jungle.

15. Thiriat, "The Continent in London."

16. Tames refers to documentation that should be read as even more implausible than Cardwell's tally: "A survey of ethnic minorities in Soho in the 1890s estimated that they totalled 4,295. Of these, the largest groups were the Germans (1,070), French (901), Italians (652), and Poles. There were also substantial numbers of Swiss (258), Russians (232), Belgians (174), Swedes (127), Austrians (107), Dutch (88), and Americans (81). There were a few Spaniards (29), Hungarians (27), and Danes (26), but scarcely any Turks (9) or Greeks (7). And although there were four each of Portuguese, Rumanians, and (undifferentiated) 'Africans,' and even two Persians and a solitary Serb—there was not one single Chinese" (*Soho Past*, 41).

17. Thiriat, "The Continent in London."

18. Late-Victorian London was abuzz with working-class discontent, both organized and anarchic. Along with the Fabians, there were several marches by workers from the East End to West End destinations such as Trafalgar Square and Hyde Park from the late-1880s onward. See, for example, Fishman, *East End 1888*, 266–302, and Stedman Jones, *Outcast London*, 281–321. In focusing on anarchy, Conrad exaggerates the importance of the most extreme brand of discontents and undervalues the organization and discipline of groups like the trade unions. In this context, we might also consider that Conrad writes *The Secret Agent* in 1906–7, at a moment when the Liberals have come back into power after a twenty-year period of Tory hegemony (Webb, *Modern England*, 428). This twenty-year Conservative reign is, perhaps not accidentally, framed by the mid-1880s, a period of organized worker unrest and the setting for *The Secret Agent*, and the mid-1900s, the date of *The Secret Agent*'s composition and publication.

19. Besant's preface to Clergy of St. Anne's, *Two Centuries of Soho*, vii.

20. Baedekker, *London and its Environs* (1905).

21. For Morrison, interest in London is typically in a vanishing London. In 1895, he was encouraged to write a novel on the old Nichol in Shoreditch. The resulting text, *A Child of the Jago* (1896), was published when "the Old Nichol had all but ceased to exist;" it was pulled down to make way for a new "L.C.C. [London County Council] housing estate." See Keating, introduction to *A Child of the Jago*, 33.

22. P. J. Keating argues that

the one image, which, if hardly "new," is used in a new way at the turn of the century, is of the working classes and the poor as inhabiting an "abyss" at the edge of society. An element of class fear, whether from contagious diseases or revolution, is never entirely absent from the work of earlier social explorers, but the repeated use of the word "abyss" marks a real change of attitude. . . . An abyss still conveys enough sense of distance to be attractive to the social explorer, but it carries with it an eeriness which replaces the more exotic associations of travel. You don't journey *to* an abyss: you descend or fall into it. It is all very well claiming that a Dark Continent lies at one's doorstep but that metaphorically is more welcome than a gaping hole. And what may walk out of an African rain forest is one thing, what *climbs* out of an abyss is quite another. Its use also implies a change in class relationships with the explorer peering over the edge at, or climbing down to, the massed poor below. (*Into Unknown England,* 20–21)

23. See Reeder, introduction to *Charles Booth's Descriptive Map.*

24. See Masterman, "The Social Abyss," *Contemporary Review* 81 (1902): 23–35.

25. Quoted in *Daily Express.*

26. Many commentators have noted that embassies (for example, the one visited by Verloc) are legally territories of the nations who occupy them. Ray notes that "the political geography of the city is just as subject to these ruptures and disjunctures, to the point where one can say that most of chapter 2 of *The Secret Agent* is set in Imperial Russia," (Ray, "The Landscape of *The Secret Agent,*" 206). Thus, in a very real sense, Verloc heads west here to visit a vaguely defined "Eastern" country.

27. Like the East End, Soho is a dubious candidate for a locus of containment because it has no fixed geographic identity. There is, for instance, no administrative borough or district called Soho and no official sense of where to mark its boundaries. Though in general, we might see it as bounded by Regent Street (west), Oxford Street (north), Charing Cross Road (east), and Shaftesbury Avenue (south), all of these boundaries are inexact and fluid with one significant exception: there seems to be nearly universal agreement that Regent Street rigidly marks Soho's western border.

28. Its separateness had been orchestrated in the early nineteenth century by John Nash, whose "purpose" in designing the grand Regent Street had explicitly been to separate radically and improve the value of "all the streets occupied by the higher classes," the new bourgeois developments in Mayfair from "all those bad streets" to the East; that is of a decaying Soho that had been the haven of fashionable London in the eighteenth century (Crook, "Metropolitan Improvements," 90).

29. Conrad, *Heart of Darkness,* 29, 30–31, 27.

30. "Conrad's inauguration of proleptic ironies and paradoxes is here [*Heart of Darkness*] superbly assured, fluent and dexterous. His method is to interlink and confuse stereotypical dichotomies of contrasting kinds. Thus, London is depicted as both a source of light and a devourer of light; both a source of greatness and a sender of destruction" (Watts, "Conrad and the Myth of the Monstrous Town," 24). For another account of Conrad's propensity to invoke concepts and values and to expose them as "hollow," see chapters 1, 2, and 5 in Bongie, *Exotic Memories.*

31. Conrad, *The Mirror of the Sea,* 107–8.

32. Ibid., 112.

33. *The Secret Agent*, xii. All further page references to the text are cited parenthetically.

34. Watts, "Conrad and the Myth of the Monstrous Town," 27.

35. Harpham, "Abroad by Only a Fiction," 88.

36. "Conrad's account of the start of his writing career, in *A Personal Record*, includes the statement that he had 'explored the mazes of streets east and west in solitary leisurely walks without chart and compass'" (Hampson, "Topographical Mysteries," 171).

37. Tames, *Soho Past*, 44–45.

38. During the period Conrad wrote the novel, the Conrads were first in Montpellier on the southern coast of France; they then lodged in Galsworthy's London apartment in Kensington, and subsequently returned to Montpellier. The visits to France were for health reasons. See Meyers, *Joseph Conrad*, 230–31.

39. *Heart of Darkness*, 97.

40. The letter was written 5 January 1907. Quoted in Gurko, *Joseph Conrad*, 161.

41. Ibid., 162.

42. While I do not disagree with a critical tradition that sees the horrific Verloc domestic drama as a working out of Conrad's own domestic woes, the assistant commissioner of police who goes into Soho, has his adventure, and returns to civilization to report on it seems to be an even more powerful writerly analogue. The assistant commissioner can leave Soho as easily as he enters; Verloc, in more ways than one, is stuck there.

43. *Heart of Darkness*, 50.

44. Doyle, "The Adventure of the Empty House," in *Sherlock Holmes: Complete*, 670.

45. Cynical, that is, as a version of idolatry or hollow platonism. The classical Conradian version of this is Marlow's sermon in *Heart of Darkness*: "The conquest of the earth, which mostly means the taking it away from those who have a different complexion or slightly flatter noses than ourselves, is not a pretty thing when you look into it too much. What redeems it is the idea only. An idea at the back of it; not a sentimental pretence but an idea; and an unselfish belief in the idea— something you can set up, and bow down before, and offer a sacrifice to" (50–51).

46. This Conradian example of species descent echoes other writers' descriptions of street life. In an 1891 essay, Arthur Morrison described the East End as "an evil growth of slums which hide human creeping things" (Morrison, "A Street," quoted by Keating, introduction to *A Child of the Jago*, 21) and we have already heard Inspector MacKay designate Greek Street, Soho, as home to "the vilest reptiles in London."

47. Woolf, "Street Haunting," 155, 165–66.

48. For a full account of Kiralfy's Empire of India Exhibition, see Gregory, "Staging British India," 163.

49. For lengthier discussions of these events, see the following: on exhibitions, Richards, *Commodity Culture of Victorian England;* on department stores, Walkowitz, *City of Dreadful Delight* (45–50); on imperial spectacle and ritual, Shephard, "Showbiz

Imperialism," and Cannadine, "The Context, Performance, and Meaning of Ritual"; and on imperial theater, Bratton, *Acts of Supremacy*. My discussion of Conrad's Italian restaurant is an attempt to view ethnic restaurants as another important series of sites where we can study metropolitan imperial encounters.

50. For more on the Victorian fascination with Renaissance Italy, see Fraser, *The Victorians in Renaissance Italy*.

51. From unpublished work by Paul Walker Clarke, quoted with author's permission.

52. Newnham-Davis, *Dinners and Diners*, ix.

53. Baedekker, *London and Its Environs* (1905).

54. Benjamin, "Work of Art," 220.

55. David Harvey, *Consciousness and the Urban Experience*, 11.

56. Booth, *In Darkest England*, 18.

57. Benjamin, "Work of Art," 220.

58. French, if we believe such reports on white slavery as those offered by General Booth, or Stead's "Maiden Tribute of Modern Babylon."

59. Geertz, "Notes on the Balinese Cockfight," 424.

60. This distance between Conrad, on the one hand, and the assistant commissioner and Woolf, on the other, is also the gulf that separates, according to Paul Armstrong, the Conradian dystopia of the "ultimate groundlessness" of our commitments from the Rortian liberal utopia in which the citizens are all "ironists," able and happy to "combine commitment with a sense of their contingency and ultimate groundlessness." See Armstrong, "The Politics of Irony," 85.

7. "WHAT ARE THE ROOTS THAT CLUTCH?"

1. Eliot to Charlotte Eliot, 21 March 1917, in *The Letters of T. S. Eliot*, ed. Valerie Eliot, 165–66.

2. In his book on the poem, Calvin Bedient takes as part of his title Eliot's original title "He Do the Police in Different Voices." Bedient is trying to answer what he sees as the poem's major critical issue—"that of the existence or nonexistence of a single protagonist; of the nature or purpose of the apparent medley of voices" (ix). Bedient argues "for the view that all the voices in the poem are the performances of a single protagonist," appropriating Bakhtin's notion of heteroglossia and his work with genre theory (ix–x). I find Bakhtin's work very helpful in elucidating the poem, especially if we think about the poem's speaker as the metropolis itself or a metropolitan persona.

3. Levenson, *Genealogy of Modernism*, 190.

4. One notable exception is Andrew Ross, who discusses Eliot's banking career in "*The Waste Land* and the Fantasy of Interpretation." Unlike my approach, Ross's psychoanalytic method uses banking metaphors to describe the poem's relationship to Eliot's own symbolic economy.

5. Quoted in Valerie Eliot's introduction to *The Waste Land: A Facsimile*, xviii.

6. Reading Eliot's career as a banker alongside Woolf's preoccupation with money in works such as *A Room of One's Own* and *Three Guineas* suggests the need for a study on the pivotal connection between money and modernism. Though

Woolf is not my topic here, I do want to note that the £500-a-year legacy she credits with allowing her to write fiction was received from an aunt who lived most of her life in India. Perhaps it is not too much to say that colonial capital underwrote her literary production. I would also note that, along with Woolf, the most influential intellectual of the Bloomsbury Group was an economist—John Maynard Keynes.

7. "F. V. Morley, indeed, suggests that in 1925 the newly established Faber and Gwyer offered him a job less for any opinion they had of his writings, than for his banking experience" (Maxwell, "He Do the Police in Different Voices," 170).

8. Ackroyd, *T. S. Eliot,* 77.

9. Valerie Eliot, introduction to *The Waste Land: A Facsimile,* xviii.

10. Ackroyd, *T. S. Eliot,* 132.

11. Ibid.; quoted at 100.

12. Ackroyd reports that Eliot habitually impressed new acquaintances with his ability to quote "long passages of Sherlock Holmes from memory" (ibid., 167).

13. I realize that there is a chronological problem: Eliot did not assume his responsibilities as head of the Lloyd's Bank Foreign Office Information Bureau until 1923, a year after *The Waste Land* appeared; however, I would argue that this compositional activity surrounded him in prior years at the bank as he worked in the Information Department. Eliot actually composed most of the poem while he was away from the bank. "In September 1921 he suffered a 'nervous breakdown' and went off to Lausanne." In December, he writes his brother with the news "I am very much better and not miserable here—at least there are people of many nationalities, which I always like. . . . I am certainly well enough to be working on a poem!" (quoted in Gross, "Metoikos in London," 148). While he composed away from the bank, it was the bank experience and compositional style from which he appropriated the aesthetic form that gave shape to his experiences of the international spa-asylum and the metropolis in the poem he was working on.

14. Wilson, *Axel's Castle,* 109.

15. "His clothes had been made of some stuff that was brown holland probably, but it was covered with patches all over, with bright patches , blue, red, and yellow—patches on the back, patches on the front, patches on the elbows, on knees; coloured binding around his jacket, scarlet edging at the bottom of his trousers; and the sunshine made him look extremely gay and wonderfully neat withal, because you could see how beautifully all this patching had been done" (Conrad, *Heart of Darkness,* 90).

16. Levenson, *Genealogy of Modernism,* 195–96, 203.

17. From "A Prediction," quoted in Manganaro, *"The Tangled Bank* Revisited," 107.

18. Smith, "The Making of *The Waste Land,*" 135.

19. Crawford, *Savage and the City,* 24.

20. For more on this convergence, see Tompkins, *West of Everything,* and Torgovnick, *Gone Primitive,* 191.

21. In "The Metropolis and Mental Life," Georg Simmel discusses how the metropolis fosters "an incapacity . . . to react to new sensations with the appropriate energy." Simmel's name for this specifically metropolitan form of consciousness

is the "blasé attitude": "There is perhaps no psychic phenomenon which has so unconditionally reserved to the metropolis as the blasé attitude. The blasé attitude results first from the rapidly changing and closely compressed contrasting stimulation of the nerves" (51).

22. Darwin, *Origin*, 395. Manganaro's essay called my attention to Stanley Hyman's *The Tangled Bank*, which takes its title from this Darwinian passage.

23. Darwin, *Origin*, 3–4.

24. Levenson, *Genealogy of Modernism*, 203.

25. Eliot, "Tradition and the Individual Talent," 40–41.

26. Doyle, *The Sign of Four*, 117.

27. Eliot, "Tradition and the Individual Talent," 39, 44, 43.

28. Torgovnick, "The Politics of the We," 47.

29. Ackroyd, *T. S. Eliot*, 88.

30. Ellis, *The English Eliot*, 1.

31. Gross, "Metoikos in London," 143–44.

32. Quoted in Klein, *Foreigners*, 15.

33. Quoted (ibid., at 16) from Herbert Read's, "T. S. Eliot—A Memoir."

34. "It is London, 'the spirit of the place,' which might be named the 'hero' of *The Waste Land*, just as Eliot named the Mississippi River the hero of *Huckleberry Finn*" (Gross, "Metoikos in London," 151). Both Saint Louis by the Mississippi and London by the Thames are border spaces—the borderlands of his youth and adulthood. If we look at Eliot's biography as a story of three places—Mississippi boyhood, New England coming-of-age, London maturity—then *The Waste Land* becomes a modernist rewrite of another Twain classic, *A Connecticut Yankee in King Arthur's Court*.

35. Ackroyd, *T. S. Eliot*, 16, 19.

36. Crawford, *Savage and the City*, 14.

37. Ackroyd, *T. S. Eliot*, 23.

38. During the 1880s, the New Immigration began, comprised of immigrants from southern and eastern Europe: Sicilians, Greeks, Slavs, and Polish-Russian Jews. The population of U.S. cities expanded by 50 percent during the decade and, until 1930, continued to expand exponentially at a rate of 30 to 40 percent per decade. In 1916, after Eliot had left for Europe, the great migration of African-Americans to northern cities had begun (Klein, *Foreigners*, 16). As Klein notes, by 1922 and the publication of *The Waste Land*, well over half of the population of the United States was located in the cities (12–13). This was the increasingly plural and polyethnic America from which Eliot had fled to Europe just prior to World War I.

39. Ibid., 11.

40. For more on the Eliot-Dante connection, see Schwarz, *Broken Images*, 22–30.

41. Rushdie, "The Location of Brazil," 124–25.

BIBLIOGRAPHY

Ackroyd, Peter. *T. S. Eliot: A Life*. New York: Simon & Schuster, 1984.

Arata, Stephen. "The Occidental Tourist: Dracula and the Anxiety of Reverse Colonization." *Victorian Studies* 33, no. 4 (summer 1990): 621–45.

Armstrong, Paul. "The Politics of Irony in Reading Conrad." *Conradiana* 26, nos. 2–3 (1994): 85–101.

Ausubel, Herman. "General Booth's Scheme of Social Salvation." *American Historical Review* 56, no. 3 (1951): 519–25.

Baedekker. *London and Its Environs* (1905).

Baring-Gould, William. *The Annotated Sherlock Holmes*. Vol. 1. New York: Potter, 1967.

Bedient, Calvin. *He Do the Police in Different Voices: The Waste Land and Its Protagonist*. Chicago: Univ. of Chicago Press, 1986.

Begbie, Harold. *Life of William Booth: The Founder of the Salvation Army*. 2 vols. London: Macmillan, 1920.

Benjamin, Walter. "The Work of Art in the Age of Mechanical Reproduction." In *Illuminations*. New York: Schocken, 1969.

Bolt, Christine. *Victorian Attitudes toward Race*. London: Routledge, 1971.

Bongie, Chris. *Exotic Memories: Literature, Colonialism, and the Fin de Siècle*. Stanford: Stanford Univ. Press, 1991.

Booth, William. *In Darkest England and the Way Out*. London: International Headquarters of the Salvation Army, 1890.

Booth-Tucker, Frederick. *Muktifauj, or Forty Years with the Salvation Army in India and Ceylon*. London: Marshall Bros., 1929.

Bowlby, Rachel. *Just Looking: Consumer Culture in Dreiser, Gissing, and Zola*. New York: Methuen, 1985.

———. *Shopping with Freud*. London: Routledge, 1993.

Brantlinger, Patrick. *Rule of Darkness: British Literature and Imperialism, 1830–1914*. Ithaca: Cornell Univ. Press, 1988.

Burton, Richard. *The City of the Saints and Across the Rocky Mountains to California*. London: Longmans, 1861.

Cannadine, David. "The Context, Performance, and Meaning of Ritual: The British Monarchy and the 'Invention of Tradition,' c. 1820–1977." In *The Invention of Tradition*, ed. Eric Hobsbawm and Terence Ranger. Cambridge: Cambridge Univ. Press, 1983.

Clergy of St. Anne's, The. *Two Centuries of Soho: Its Institutions, Firms and Amusements*. Preface by Walter Besant. London: Truslove & Hanson, 1898.

Clifford, James. *The Predicament of Culture: Twentieth-Century Ethnography, Literature, and Art*. Cambridge: Harvard Univ. Press, 1988.

Clifford, James, and George Marcus. *Writing Culture: The Poetics and Politics of Ethnography.* Berkeley: Univ. of California Press, 1986.

Colonial and Indian Exhibition, Special Catalogue. London: William Clowes, 1886.

Conrad, Joseph. *Chance: A Tale in Two Parts.* Garden City, NY: Doubleday, 1921.

———. *Heart of Darkness.* Harmondsworth, U.K.: Penguin, 1983.

———. *The Mirror of the Sea.* Garden City, NY: Doubleday, 1921.

———. *The Secret Agent.* Garden City, NY: Doubleday, 1921.

Cooper, James Fenimore. *The Last of the Mohicans.* New York: Dodd, Mead, 1951.

Crawford, Robert. *The Savage and the City in the Work of T. S. Eliot.* Oxford: Clarendon, 1987.

Crook, J. Mordaunt. "Metropolitan Improvements: John Nash and the Picturesque." In *London: World City, 1800–1840.* Ed. Celina Fox. New Haven: Yale Univ. Press, 1992.

Daily Express (6 May 1910).

Darwin, Charles. *The Origin of Species.* Oxford: Oxford Univ. Press, 1996.

Defoe, Daniel. *Robinson Crusoe.* London: Penguin, 1965.

Dickens, Charles. *Bleak House.* New York: New American Library, 1964.

———. *Little Dorrit.* Oxford: Clarendon, 1979.

———. *Our Mutual Friend.* Harmondsworth, U.K.: Penguin, 1971.

———. *Sketches by Boz and Other Early Papers, 1833–39.* London: Dent, 1994.

Doyle, Arthur Conan. *Beyond the City.* Chicago: Tennyson Neely, 1894.

———. "J. Habakkuk Jephson's Statement." In *The Captain of the Polestar.* London: Longmans, 1904.

———. *Memories and Adventures.* Boston: Little, Brown, 1924.

———. *Micah Clarke.* London: Murray, 1925.

———. *The Refugees: A Tale of Two Continents.* London: Murray, 1925.

———. *Sherlock Holmes: The Complete Novels and Stories.* Vol. 1. Ed. Loren Estleman. New York: Bantam, 1986.

Eby, Cecil. *The Road to Armageddon: The Martial Spirit in English Popular Literature, 1870–1914.* Durham, NC: Duke Univ. Press, 1987.

Eliot, T. S. "Books of the Quarter." *Criterion* 8, no. 32 (1929): 552–56.

———. *The Letters of T. S. Eliot.* Ed. Valerie Eliot. San Diego: Harcourt, Brace, Jovanovich, 1988.

———. "A Prediction in Regard to Three English Authors." *Vanity Fair,* Feb. 1924, 29.

———. "Tradition and the Individual Talent." In *Selected Prose of T. S. Eliot.* Ed. Frank Kermode. New York: Harcourt, Brace, Jovanovich, 1975.

———. *The Waste Land: A Facsimile and Transcript of the Original Drafts.* Ed. Valerie Eliot. New York: Harcourt, Brace, Jovanovich, 1971.

Eliot, Valerie. Introduction to *The Waste Land: A Facsimile and Transcript of the Original Drafts,* ed. Valerie Eliot. New York: Harcourt, Brace, Jovanovich, 1971.

Ellis, Steve. *The English Eliot: Design, Language, and Landscape in Four Quartets.* London: Routledge, 1991.

Engels, Friedrich. *The Condition of the Working Classes in England in 1844.* Oxford: Oxford Univ. Press, 1993.

Estleman, Loren. Introduction to *Sherlock Holmes: The Complete Novels and Stories,* by Arthur Conan Doyle.

Fishman, Robert. *Bourgeois Utopias: The Rise and Fall of Suburbia*. New York: Basic Books, 1987.

Fishman, William. *East End 1888: A Year in a London Borough among the Labouring Poor*. London: Duckworth, 1988.

———. *East End Jewish Radicals, 1875–1914*. London: Duckworth, 1975.

———. *The Insurrectionists*. London: Methuen, 1970.

Fleishman, Avrom. *Conrad's Politics: Community and Anarchy in the Fiction of Joseph Conrad*. Baltimore: Johns Hopkins Univ. Press, 1967.

Forster, E. M. *A Passage to India*. London: Harcourt, Brace, Jovanovich, 1984.

Foucault, Michel. *Discipline and Punish: The Birth of the Prison*. Trans. Alan Sheridan. New York: Vintage, 1979.

Fraser, Hilary. *The Victorians in Renaissance Italy*. Oxford: Blackwell, 1992.

Galsworthy, John. *In Chancery*. New York: Scribner's, 1920.

Geertz, Clifford. "Deep Play: Notes on the Balinese Cockfight." In *The Interpretation of Cultures: Selected Essays*. New York: Basic Books, 1973.

Gilbert, Sandra, and Susan Gubar. *No Man's Land: The Place of the Woman Writer in the Twentieth Century*. Vols. 1 and 2. New Haven: Yale Univ. Press, 1988.

Gissing, George. *The Nether World*. Oxford: Oxford Univ. Press, 1992.

Green, Martin. *Dreams of Adventure, Deeds of Empire*. New York: Basic Books, 1979.

Greenhalgh, Paul. *Ephemeral Vistas: The Expositions Universelles, Great Exhibitions, and World's Fairs, 1851–1939*. New York: St. Martin's, 1988.

Greenwood, James. *The Adventures of Reuben Davidger, Seventeen Years and Four Months Captive among the Dyaks of Borneo*. London: Warne, 1860–69.

———. *Low Life Deeps and an Account of the Strange Fish to be Found There*. London: Chatto & Windus, 1881.

———. "A Night in the Workhouse." In *Into Unknown England*, ed. P. J. Keating. Manchester: Manchester Univ. Press, 1976. 33–54.

———. *The Seven Curses of London*. Boston: Fields, Osgood, 1869.

———. *The True History of a Little Ragamuffin*. London: Ward, Lock, Bowden, 1892.

Gregory, Brendan. "Staging British India." In *Acts of Supremacy: The British Empire and the Stage, 1790–1930*, ed. J. S. Bratton. New York: St. Martin's, 1991.

Grey, Zane. *Riders of the Purple Sage*. New York: Simon & Schuster, 1980.

Gross, Harvey. "Metoikos in London." *Mosaic* 6, no. 1 (1972): 143–55.

Gurko, Leo. *Joseph Conrad: Giant in Exile*. New York: Macmillan, 1962.

Haggard, H. Rider. *King Solomon's Mines*. New York: Dutton, 1963.

———. *Regeneration: Being an Account of the Social Work of the Salvation Army in Great Britain*. London: Longmans, 1910.

———. *She: A History of Adventure*. London: Longmans, 1887.

Hall, Richard. *Stanley: An Adventurer Explored*. Boston: Houghton Mifflin, 1975.

Hampson, Robert. "Topographical Mysteries: Conrad and London." In *Conrad's Cities: Essays for Hans van Marle*, ed. Gene M. Moore. Amsterdam: Rodopi, 1992.

Hardy, Thomas. *The Trumpet-Major*. Harmondsworth, U.K.: Penguin, 1984.

Harkness, Margaret [John Law]. *In Darkest London: A New and Popular Edition of Captain Lobe, A Story of the Salvation Army*. London: William Reeves, 1891.

Harpham, Geoffrey. "Abroad by Only a Fiction: Creation, Irony, and Necessity in Conrad's *The Secret Agent.*" *Representations* 37 (winter 1992): 79–103.

Harvey, David. *Consciousness and the Urban Experience: Studies in the History and Theory of Capitalist Urbanization.* Baltimore: Johns Hopkins Univ. Press, 1985.

Haycraft, Howard. *Murder for Pleasure.* New York: Appleton, 1941.

Hennessy, Rosemary and Rajeswari Mohan. "The Construction of Woman in Three Popular Texts of Empire: Towards a Critique of Materialist Feminism." *Textual Practice* 3, no. 3 (1989): 323–59.

Hobhouse, Christopher. *1851 and the Crystal Palace.* New York: Dutton, 1937.

Holmes, Colin. *John Bull's Island: Immigration and British Society, 1871–1971.* Basingstoke: Macmillan, 1988.

———. *Immigrants and Minorities in British Society.* London: Allen & Unwin, 1978.

Howard, Ebenezer. *Garden Cities of To-morrow.* London: Faber & Faber, 1946.

Huxley, T. H. *Social Diseases and Worse Remedies: Letters to "The Times" on Mr. Booth's Scheme.* London: Macmillan, 1891.

Hyde, Ralph. *The A to Z of Victorian London.* Lympne Castle, Kent, U.K.: Margary, 1987.

Hyman, Stanley. *The Tangled Bank.* New York: Atheneum, 1962.

"In the Slums of Soho." *Cassell's Saturday Journal* (8 August 1900): 992.

Inglis, Kenneth. *Churches and the Working Classes in Victorian England.* London: Routledge, 1963.

Jaffe, Audrey. "Detecting the Beggar: Arthur Conan Doyle, Henry Mayhew, and 'The Man with the Twisted Lip.'" *Representations* 31 (summer 1990): 96–117.

Jaffe, Jacqueline. *Arthur Conan Doyle.* Boston: Twayne, 1987.

JanMohamed, Abdul. *Manichean Aesthetics: The Politics of Literature in Colonial Africa.* Amherst: Univ. of Massachusetts Press, 1983.

Jay, A. Osborne. *Life in Darkest London: A Hint to General Booth.* London: Webster & Cable, 1891.

Jones, Gareth Stedman. *Outcast London: A Study in the Relationship between Classes in Victorian Society.* Oxford: Clarendon, 1971.

Jukes, Peter. *A Shout in the Street: An Excursion into the Modern City.* Berkeley: Univ. of California Press, 1991.

Keating, P. J. *Into Unknown England, 1866–1913: Selections from the Social Explorers.* Manchester: Manchester Univ. Press, 1976.

———. Introduction to *A Child of the Jago,* by Arthur Morrison. London: MacGibbon & Kee, 1969.

———. *The Working Classes in Victorian Fiction.* New York: Barnes & Noble, 1971.

Kiralfy, Imre. Introduction to *Empire of India Exhibition Catalogue.* London: Keliher, 1895.

Klein, Marcus. *Foreigners: The Making of American Literature, 1900–1940.* Chicago: Univ. of Chicago Press, 1981.

Knight, Stephen. *Form and Ideology in Crime Fiction.* London: Macmillan, 1980.

Labor, Earle. *Jack London.* New York: Twayne, 1974.

Larson, Gustave. *The "Americanization" of Utah for Statehood.* San Marino, CA: Huntington Library Papers, 1971.

Leavis, F. R. *The Great Tradition: George Eliot, Henry James, Joseph Conrad.* New York: New York Univ. Press, 1963.

Levenson, Michael. *A Genealogy of Modernism: A Study of English Literary Doctrine, 1908–1922.* Cambridge: Cambridge Univ. Press, 1984.

London, Jack. *The People of the Abyss.* London: Macmillan, 1903.

Lukács, Georg. *The Historical Novel.* Trans. Hannah and Stanley Mitchell. Lincoln: Univ. of Nebraska Press, 1983.

Lundquist, James. *Jack London: Adventures, Ideas, Fictions.* New York: Ungar, 1987.

Machray, Robert. *The Night Side of London.* Edinburgh: Paul Harris, 1894.

MacKenzie, John M. *Orientalism: History, Theory, and the Arts.* New York: St. Martin's, 1995.

Manganaro, Marc. "*The Tangled Bank* Revisited: Anthropological Authority in Frazer's *The Golden Bough.*" *Yale Journal of Criticism* 3, no.1 (1989): 107–27.

Masterman, Charles. "The Social Abyss." *Contemporary Review* 81 (1902): 23–35.

Maxwell, D. E. S. "'He Do the Police in Different Voices.'" *Mosaic* 6, no. 1 (1972): 167–80.

Mayhew, Henry. *London Labour and the London Poor.* Vol. 1. New York: Dover, 1968.

McClintock, Anne. *Imperial Leather: Race, Gender and Sexuality in the Colonial Contest.* New York: Routledge, 1995.

Metz, Nancy. "*Little Dorrit's* London: Babylon Revisited." *Victorian Studies* 33, no. 3 (1990): 465–86.

Meyers, Jeffrey. *Joseph Conrad: A Biography.* New York: Scribner's, 1991.

Mort, Frank. *Cultures of Consumption: Masculinities and Social Space in Late Twentieth-Century Britain.* London: Routledge, 1996.

Moretti, Franco. *Signs Taken for Wonders: Essays in the Sociology of Literary Forms.* London: Verso, 1983.

Morrison, Arthur. *A Child of the Jago.* Chicago: Academy Chicago, 1995.

Mouat, Frederic. *The Andaman Islanders.* Delhi: Mittal, 1979.

Newnham-Davis, Nathaniel. *Dinners and Diners: Where and How to Dine in London.* London: Grant Richards, 1901.

Nordon, Pierre. *Conan Doyle.* Trans. John Murray. New York: Holt, 1967.

Official Descriptive and Illustrated Catalogue of the Great Exhibition, 1851. London: Spicer Bros., 1851.

"Opium Smoking in Bluegate Fields." *Chemist and Druggist* 11 (1870): 259–61.

Peluso, Robert. "Gazing at Royalty: Jack London's *The People of the Abyss* and the Emergence of American Imperialism." In *Rereading Jack London,* ed. Leonard Cassuto and Jeanne Campbell Reesman. Stanford: Stanford Univ. Press, 1996.

Pike, David. *Passage through Hell: Modernist Descents, Medieval Underworlds.* Ithaca: Cornell Univ. Press, 1997.

Pratt, Mary Louise. "Fieldwork in Common Places." In Clifford and Marcus, *Writing Culture.*

———. *Imperial Eyes: Travel Writing and Transculturation.* New York: Routledge, 1992.

Raban, Jonathan. *Soft City.* London: Hamilton, 1974.

Ray, Martin. "The Landscape of *The Secret Agent.*" In *Conrad's Cities: Essays for Hans van Marle,* ed. Gene M. Moore. Amsterdam: Rodopi, 1992.

Reeder, D. A. Introduction to *Charles Booth's Descriptive Map of London Poverty 1889.* London: London Topographical Society, 1984.

Richards, Thomas. *The Commodity Culture of Victorian England: Advertising and Spectacle, 1851–1914.* Stanford: Stanford Univ. Press, 1990.

Rosenthal, Michael. *The Character Factory: Baden-Powell and the Origins of the Boy Scout Movement.* New York: Pantheon, 1986.

Ross, Andrew. "*The Waste Land* and the Fantasy of Interpretation." *Representations* 8 (fall 1984): 134–58.

Rushdie, Salman. "The Location of *Brazil.*" In *Imaginary Homelands: Essays and Criticism, 1981–1991.* London: Granta, 1991.

———. *The Satanic Verses.* New York: Viking, 1988.

Said, Edward. *Culture and Imperialism.* New York: Vintage, 1993.

———. *Orientalism.* New York: Pantheon, 1978.

Sandall, Robert. *The History of the Salvation Army.* Vol. 3: *1883–1953.* London: Nelson, 1955.

Saunders, William. "From the Editor." *Harvard Design Magazine* (winter/spring 1998): 2.

Schmitt, Cannon. *Alien Nation: Nineteenth-Century Gothic Fictions and English Nationality.* Philadelphia: Univ. of Pennsylvania Press, 1997.

Schwarz, Robert. *Broken Images: A Study of The Waste Land.* Lewisburg: Bucknell Univ. Press, 1988.

Scott, Walter. *Ivanhoe.* New York: New American Library, 1962.

Search, Pamela. *Happy Warriors: The Story of the Social Work of the Salvation Army.* London: Arco, 1956.

Shephard, Ben. "Showbiz Imperialism: The Case of Peter Lobengula." *Imperialism and Popular Culture.* Ed. John M. MacKenzie. Manchester: Manchester Univ. Press, 1986.

Showalter, Elaine. *Sexual Anarchy: Gender and Culture at the Fin de Siècle.* New York: Viking, 1990.

Simmel, Georg. "The Metropolis and Mental Life." In *Classic Essays on the Culture of Cities,* ed. Richard Sennett. New York: Appleton, 1969. 47–60.

Sims, George. "How the Poor Live." In *Into Unknown England, 1866–1913: Selections from the Social Explorers,* ed. P. J. Keating. Manchester: Manchester Univ. Press, 1976. 65–73.

Sinclair, Upton. *The Jungle.* New York: New American Library, 1990.

Smith, Grover. "The Making of *The Waste Land.*" *Mosaic* 6, no. 1 (1972): 127–41.

"Soho of Today, The: A Chat with the Rev. J. H. Cardwell." *Westminster Observer* (24 January 1903).

Soja, Edward. *Postmodern Geographies: The Reassertion of Space in Critical Social Theory.* London: Verso, 1989.

Spencer, Herbert. *First Principles.* New York: Appleton, 1896.

Stevenson, Robert Louis. *More New Arabian Nights: The Dynamiter.* New York: Scribner's, 1895.

Stocking, George W., Jr. *Victorian Anthropology.* New York: Free Press, 1987.

Stoker, Bram. *Dracula.* London: Penguin, 1979.

Summers, Judith. *Soho: A History of London's Most Colourful Neighbourhood.* London: Bloomsbury, 1989.

Tames, Richard. *Soho Past.* London: Historical, 1994.

Theweleit, Klaus. *Male Fantasies.* Vol. 1. Trans. Stephen Conway. Minneapolis: Univ. of Minnesota Press, 1987.

Thiriat, Paul. "The Continent in London." *Sphere* (29 Oct. 1906).

Thompson, John. *Fiction, Crime, and Empire: Clues to Modernity and Postmodernism.* Urbana: Univ. of Illinois Press, 1993.

Tolen, Rachel. "Colonizing and Transforming the Criminal Tribesman: The Salvation Army in British India." *American Ethnologist* 18, no.1 (1991): 106–25.

Tomas, David. "Tools of the Trade: The Production of Ethnographic Observations on the Andaman Islands, 1858–1922." In *Colonial Situations: Essays on the Contextualization of Ethnographic Knowledge,* ed. George W. Stocking Jr. Madison: Univ. of Wisconsin Press, 1991. 75–108.

Tompkins, Jane. *Sensational Designs: The Cultural Work of American Fiction, 1790–1860.* New York: Oxford Univ. Press, 1985.

———. *West of Everything: The Inner Life of Westerns.* New York: Oxford Univ. Press, 1992.

Torgovnick, Marianna. *Gone Primitive: Savage Intellects, Modern Lives.* Chicago: Univ. of Chicago Press, 1990.

———. "The Politics of the We." *South Atlantic Quarterly* 91, no. 1 (1992): 43–64.

Trachtenberg, Alan. "Experiments in Another Country: Stephen Crane's City Sketches." In *American Realism: New Essays,* ed. Eric J. Sundquist. Baltimore: Johns Hopkins Univ. Press, 1982. 138–54.

Tracy, Jack. *Subcutaneously, My Dear Watson: Sherlock Holmes and the Cocaine Habit.* Bloomington: Rock, 1978.

Turner, Frederick Jackson. *The Frontier in American History.* New York: Holt, 1920.

Twain, Mark. *A Connecticut Yankee in King Arthur's Court.* New York: Oxford Univ. Press, 1996.

Walkowitz, Judith. *City of Dreadful Delight: Narratives of Sexual Danger in Late-Victorian London.* Chicago: Univ. of Chicago Press, 1992.

Watts, Cedric. "Conrad and the Myth of the Monstrous Town." In *Conrad's Cities: Essays for Hans van Marl,* ed. Gene M. Moore. Amsterdam: Rodopi, 1992.

Wells, H. G. *The War of the Worlds.* New York: New American Library, 1986.

"Which Is the Most Interesting Street in London?" *Strand Magazine* 34 (1907): 314–22.

Wilde, Oscar. *The Picture of Dorian Gray.* Ed. Peter Ackroyd. Harmondsworth, U.K.: Penguin, 1985.

Williams, Raymond. *The Country and the City.* New York: Oxford Univ. Press, 1973.

Wilson, Edmund. *Axel's Castle: A Study in the Imaginative Literature of 1870–1930.* New York: Scribner's, 1969.

Winter, James. *London's Teeming Streets: 1830–1914.* London: Routledge, 1993.

Wister, Owen. *The Virginian.* New York: New American Library, 1979.

Wohl, Anthony. *Endangered Lives: Public Health in Victorian Britain.* Cambridge: Harvard Univ. Press, 1983.

Woolf, Virginia. *A Room of One's Own.* New York: Harcourt, Brace, Jovanovich, 1991.

———. "Street Haunting." In *Collected Essays,* vol. 4. New York: Harcourt, Brace, Jovanovich, 1967. 155–66.

———. *Three Guineas.* New York: Harcourt, Brace, Jovanovich, 1966.

INDEX

Ackroyd, Peter, 192
Adams, Henry, 187
Adorno, Theodor, 157
advertising, 17
aesthetes and aestheticism, 21, 56, 59–61
alcoholism, 92
alienation, 9
allegory, 54–55, 67, 70
"anachronistic space," 209 n. 5
anarchism and anarchy, 134, 137, 139, 142,
  153, 156, 162–63
Andaman Islands, 55, 56, 66–67, 68, 69, 71,
  207 n. 15
Anglo-Saxonism, 9, 23, 32–33, 127, 129–32
anthropology, 66–67, 73, 130, 172, 175–77,
  184
anti-Semitism, 25, 189
Arabian Nights, 60, 91
Arata, Stephen, 195 n. 7
Armstrong, Paul, 218 n. 60
"art for art's sake," 205 n. 7
Augustine, 170
Ausubel, Herman, 81, 95
authenticity, 12–13, 24, 155–59, 161,
  163–66

babel/Babel, 26, 138, 139, 147–48, 169,
  171, 172
Bacon, G. W., 63
Baden-Powell, Robert, 50, 211 n. 34
Baedekker, 139, 159
Bakhtin, Mikhail, 26, 218 n. 2
banking, 25, 168–75, 177, 185, 193, 218 n.
  6, 219 n. 13
Barnum, P. T., 75
Bedient, Calvin, 218 n. 2
Begbie, Harold, 97, 209 n. 8
Belloc, Hilaire, 146
Belzoni, Giovanni, 198 n. 28
Benjamin, Walter, 17, 24, 158–63, 165, 198
  n. 27
Besant, Walter, 139

Bishop of Kensington, 141
Blake, William, 14, 150
Boer War, 19, 50, 104, 129
Bolt, Christine, 195 n. 6
Bongie, Chris, 25, 198 n. 28
Booth, Bramwell, 209 n. 6
Booth, Catherine, 91, 97
Booth, Charles, 95, 140–41
Booth, Emma, 101
Booth, General William, 4, 5, 18, 21–22,
  23, 79–103, 104, 106, 133, 149, 160, 161,
  168, 171, 178, 198 n. 28, 212 n. 4; In
  Darkest England, 4, 21–22, 79–103, 143
Booth-Tucker, Frederick de LaTour, 101
Bosanquet, Bernard, 95
Bowlby, Rachel, 16, 198 n. 27
Braddon, Mary Elizabeth, 5
Brantlinger, Patrick, 70, 195 n. 7, 207 n. 17
Buddhist Fire Sermon, 170
Bunyan, John, 86
Burton, Richard Francis, 35, 201 n. 17

cannibalism, 20, 55–57, 62–73, 86, 123, 187
Cardwell, Rev., 136–39
Carlyle, Thomas, 95
Cassell's Saturday Journal, 136
Catholicism, 46–50, 166, 203 nn. 40, 41
centers and peripheries, notions of, 1, 29
Chemist and Druggist, 196 n. 9
Chesterton, G. K., 146
Chinatown, 76
Clarke, Paul Walker, 157, 159
classification, 6, 16, 34, 87–88, 122, 151, 197
  n. 13, 200–201 n. 16
Clifford, James, 106, 212 n. 5
clothing, 8, 101, 113–15, 211 n. 34, 213 n.
  11, 219 n. 15
cocaine, 20, 53–64, 204–5 n. 3
Cold War, 92
Coleridge, Samuel Taylor, 121
Collins, Wilkie, 5, 199 n. 6
Colonial and Indian Exhibition, 74, 77–78

229

commodity culture, 16–18, 20, 24, 26, 55, 61, 63, 68, 72–74, 78, 159–63, 198 n. 25
"commodity racism," 17, 74, 198 n. 25
commuters, 74, 203 n. 36, 205 n. 8
Conrad, Joseph, 14, 15, 16, 23–25, 27, 47, 84, 103, 132, 183, 195 nn. 4, 7, 198 n. 28, 210 n. 16, 212 n. 5; *Heart of Darkness*, 1, 24, 65, 92, 102, 108, 123, 126, 142–44, 146, 156, 164, 175, 177, 180, 197 n. 19, 209–10 n. 10, 216 n. 30, 219 n. 15; *Lord Jim*, 24, 156; *The Mirror of the Sea*, 143–44; *Nostromo*, 27, 144; "An Outpost of Progress," 57; *The Secret Agent*, 23–26, 27, 133–67, 177, 187, 198 n. 28
consumption. *See* commodity culture
contact zones, 12
Cook, Thomas & Son, 108–9
Cooper, James Fenimore, 19, 30, 41, 43, 45, 47, 96, 97, 200–201 n. 16, 202 n. 29
Corn Laws, 64, 206 n. 14
cosmopolitanism, 5, 137–39, 141–42, 171
Crane, Stephen, 22, 105
Crawford, Robert, 178, 191
crime fiction, 19, 27
critical geography, 195 n. 5, 202 n. 28
crowds, 6, 14–15, 101, 112–15, 197 n. 13
Crusoe, Robinson (character), 67
Crystal Palace. *See* Great Exhibition of 1851
cuisine, 158–59
cultural studies, 18–19

Dante, 86, 108, 150, 151, 186, 188, 193, 210 n. 16
Darwin, Charles, 10, 108, 126, 151, 180, 181, 195 n. 6
Davies, W. H., 146
decadence, 20, 56, 59–62, 195 n. 4
degeneration, 20, 54, 59–62, 67, 79, 124–26, 130, 172, 195 n. 4
DeQuincey, Thomas, 14
depersonalization, 26, 171, 184–85, 187
detective fiction, 19, 29, 31, 36–38, 42, 199 n. 6, 201 n. 22
dialectics, 41, 44, 45
Dickens, Charles, 14, 46, 51, 56, 70, 80, 102, 146, 184, 198 n. 28, 199 nn. 6, 7, 202 n. 29; *Bleak House*, 15, 16, 21, 145; *Our Mutual Friend*, 145, 174, 175, 176, 181–83

Disraeli, Benjamin, 8, 140
domesticity, 53, 66, 72, 145
Doyle, Arthur Conan, 2, 6, 14, 16, 17, 19, 20, 22, 25, 27–78, 79, 80, 96, 103, 104, 142, 156, 178, 199 n. 6; *The Hound of the Baskervilles*, 50–51; "J. Habakkuk Jephson's Statement," 47–48, 51, 66, 124; *The Sign of Four*, 3, 20–21, 23, 52, 53–74, 86, 87, 118, 161, 163, 187, 193, 200 n. 8, 201 n. 22; *A Study in Scarlet*, 2, 11, 19, 20, 27–46, 49, 51, 53, 93, 198 n. 26, 214 n. 15
Doyle, Charles, 47
Doyle, Dicky, 46
drugs, 20, 53–73, 200 n. 8. *See also* cocaine

Eby, Cecil, 204 n. 46, 207 n. 17
Eliot, George, 195 n. 4
Eliot, Henry Ware, 191
Eliot, T. S., 15, 25–26, 59, 121, 122, 168–94, 199 n. 3, 200 n. 10, 210 n. 16; *The Waste Land*, 15, 25, 130, 149, 167, 168–94
Ellis, Steve, 188
Empire of India Exhibition, 74–78, 154
Engels, Friedrich, 8, 14, 21, 80, 105, 213 n. 12
Estleman, Loren, 36–37
ethnic minorities, 137, 215 n. 16
ethnographic self-fashioning, 104, 107, 120, 126–32
ethnography, 8, 22, 104–21, 183–84
Eurocentrism, 176
evolution, 69–70, 130, 151, 195 nn. 4, 6
exhibitions, 6, 17, 26, 74–78, 154, 197 n. 13, 198 n. 25, 208 n. 22

Faber & Gwyer, 173
Fabians, 215 n. 18
feminization, 3, 60–61, 84, 86, 209 n. 10
Fenians, 49
Fishman, Robert, 205 n. 8
Fitzgerald, F. Scott, 192
Fleishman, Avrom, 134
"focused gathering," 164
Ford, Ford Maddox, 146
Forster, E. M., 56, 155, 184
Foucault, 17; power-knowledge, 17, 44
Fourier, Charles, 98
Frazer, James, 65, 175, 176, 177, 181, 182, 184
French Revolution, 124

Freud, Sigmund, 49, 112–13
Futurism, 121

Gaboriau, Emile, 19, 29, 30, 199 n. 6
Galsworthy, John, 25, 133, 134, 137, 146, 147, 166–67
Gandhi, Mohandas, 197 n. 11
Gaskell, Elizabeth, 8
Geertz, Clifford, 164
George, Henry, 210 n. 19
Gilbert, Sandra, 3
Gissing, George, 10, 145, 147, 151
globalization, 1, 16, 17, 26, 55, 65–66, 159, 168–69, 172, 206 n. 13
Goffman, Erving, 164
Gordon, General, 81
Great Exhibition of 1851, 6, 63, 197 n. 13, 206 nn. 13, 14
Great War, the, 174
Green, Martin, 195 n. 7
Greenhalgh, Paul, 208 n. 22
Greenwood, James, 14, 80, 105, 128, 208–9 n. 3, 213 nn. 11, 14, 214 n. 19
Grey, Zane, 179
Gross, Harvey, 188
Gubar, Susan, 3
Gurko, Leo, 148

"H. B.," 46
Haggard, H. Rider, 3, 19, 28, 30, 50, 93, 95–96, 103, 142, 156, 193, 105 n. 7, 202 n. 33, 207 n. 77
Hampson, Robert, 133–34
Hardy, Thomas, 195 n. 4, 207 n. 17
Harkness, Margaret, 2, 4–14, 15, 93, 133, 197 n. 13
Harpham, Geoffrey Galt, 145
Harvey, David, 159, 160
Haussman, Baron von, 85
Haycraft, Howard, 199 n. 6
Hegel, G. W. F., 40, 41
Hemingway, Ernest, 3, 192
Hillerman, Tony, 202 n. 29
historical materialism, 16
historical novel, 19, 30, 38, 40, 45, 49–50, 198 n. 28, 201 n. 22, 202 n. 28
Hobson, J. A., 16
Holmes, Colin, 197–98 n. 11
Holmes, Sherlock (character), 2, 13, 15, 17, 24, 26, 79, 118, 134, 148, 149, 161, 165,

168, 172, 174, 185, 190, 194, 199 n. 3, 219 n. 12
Home Mission Movement, 97
homosexual panic, 123
Horkheimer, Max, 157
Howard, Ebenezer, 211 n. 36
Huxley, T. H., 95, 97, 98, 102, 105
hybrid and hybridity, 6, 12–13, 87, 148, 167, 187, 190, 193–94

imaginative geography, 2–3, 80, 142, 195 n. 5, 196 n. 9
immigrants and immigration, 5, 8, 9, 18, 25, 131, 138, 147, 165, 186, 190, 192–94, 196 n. 9, 197 n. 11, 220 n. 38
"imperial gothic," 207 n. 17
Indian Mutiny (1857), 20, 56, 63, 70–71, 205 n. 6, 207 n. 15
industrial revolution, 96, 191–92
invasion, 20–21, 29, 53–78, 179, 202 n. 34, 207 n. 17

Jack the Ripper, 123, 207 n. 19, 213 n. 9
Jaffe, Jacqueline, 37, 47
James, Henry, 25, 171, 183, 187, 192
Jay, A. Osborne, 94, 212 n. 4
Jews and Jewishness, 9, 135, 189
Jones, Gareth Stedman, 79–80, 85
Joyce, James, 150, 187

Keating, P. J., 215–16 n. 22
Kelly-Wischnewetsky, Florence, 105
Keynes, John Maynard, 219 n. 6
Kipling, Rudyard, 50, 173, 193, 195 n. 7
Kiralfy, Imre, 74–78, 154, 208 n. 22
Klein, Marcus, 25, 192
Knight, Stephen, 201 n. 24, 202 n. 36

Labor, Earle, 130
Lang, Andrew, 28, 50
Larson, Gustave, 33, 200 nn. 11, 13
Law, John. *See* Harkness, Margaret
Lawrence, D. H., 179
Lawrence, T. E., 101, 179
Leavis, F. R., 27, 146
Lenin, V. I., 16
Levenson, Michael, 170, 176, 183
"literature of imperialism," 3, 195 n. 7, 198 n. 28
Little Shop of Horrors, 181

Livingstone, David, 110, 111
Lloyd's Bank, 168–69, 172–76, 188, 194, 219 n. 13
Lombroso, Cesare, 161
London: Baker Street, 31; Bank of England, 168; Bayswater, 166; Blackfriars Bridge, 143; Blackwall, 143; Cavendish Square, 145; Charing Cross Road, 85; Charing Cross Station, 150, 152, 161; Clerkenwell, 145, 147; Commercial Street, 123; Covent Garden, 156; Dean Street, 123, 137; Earl's Court, 74–76, 78; East and West India Docks, 143; Embankment, 133, 134, 144; Fleet Street, 135; Flower Street, 123; Greek Street, Soho, 136; Greenwich, 24, 133, 134, 153, 180; Hyde Park, 63, 64, 134; Isle of Dogs, 180; Knightsbridge, 133; Lauriston Gardens, 37; Leadenhall Street, 135; Leicester Square, 156; Lombard Street, 135, 168, 169; London Bridge, 143, 168; London Road, 128; Maidstone, 128; Malta Street, Soho, 166; Mayfair, 168; Mile End Road, 135–36, 138, 140, 141; Pall Mall, 135; Park Lane, 166; Picadilly, 122, 133; Ratcliff Highway, 135, 139–40; Regent Street, 216 n. 8; Royal Exchange, 168; Saint Katherine's Docks, 143; Scotland Yard, 145, 149; Shaftesbury Avenue, 85; Sloane Square, 133; Soho, 24, 133–67, 168; South Kensington, 74, 75, 77–78, 166, 167; Spitalfields, 123; the Strand, 122, 135, 150, 151, 152; Sydenham, 63, 64; Upper Norwood, 63; Victoria and Albert Docks, 143; Waterloo Bridge, 134; Waterloo Station, 133, 160; Westminster, 133; Westminster Bridge, 9; Whitechapel Road, 4–10; Whitehall, 133, 135, 149
London, Jack, 18, 22–23, 24, 25, 26, 96, 104–32, 133, 140, 142, 146, 149, 150, 151, 161, 168, 171, 178, 192, 210 n. 16; *The People of the Abyss*, 21–22, 104–32
Lukács, Georg, 19, 30, 40–41, 171, 202 n. 28
Lundquist, James, 130, 213 n. 9

MacKay, Inspector, 136
MacKenzie, John, 195 n. 7, 208 n. 27
Madern, Bessie, 130

Maiden Tribute of Modern Babylon (1885), 92, 209 n. 6
Malinowski, Bronislaw, 106, 212 n. 5
Manganaro, Marc, 176
Manicheanism, 142, 215 n. 14
Manifest Destiny, 33, 34
maps and mapping, 63, 139–42, 206 n. 11
Marinetti, F. T., 121
Marshall, Alfred, 198 n. 25
Marx, Karl, 15, 40, 41, 98, 137, 205 n. 7
masculinity, 3, 23, 30, 44, 56, 65, 84, 123, 199 n. 3, 202 n. 33
Masefield, John, 146
Masterman, Charles, 141
Maurras, Charles, 189
Mayhew, Henry, 6, 8, 16, 21, 80, 87, 95, 98, 175, 181, 182
McClintock, Anne, 16, 17, 74, 195 n. 7, 198 nn. 25, 27, 209 n. 5
metaphor, 1–2, 87
Methodism, 97
metoikos, 187–89, 193
Metz, Nancy, 198 n. 28
Middleton, Thomas, 183
migrants and migration, 8, 25, 169, 171, 193–94
miscegeny, 6
Moretti, Franco, 205 n. 7
Mormons, 31–36, 49, 93, 95, 200 nn. 9, 11
Morris, William, 77, 205 n. 7
Morrison, Arthur, 10, 105, 133, 135, 139–40, 215 n. 21, 217 n. 46
Mouat, Frederic, 207 n. 15
Mountain Meadows Massacre, 200 n. 13
multiculturalism, 5, 6, 137
museums, 17, 26, 151

Nash, John, 216 n. 28
nationalism, 157
natural selection, 87
Newnham-Davis, Nathaniel, 158
Nietzschean superman, 156
Nordon, Pierre, 39–40

"oceanic," notion of, 86, 112–13
Odyssey, The, 150
orientalism, 17, 21, 35, 102, 111, 196 n. 9, 208 n. 27
Orwell, George, 170
Owen, Robert, 98

Paris Commune, 137
participant-observation, 22, 104, 106, 107, 116–17, 120, 212 n. 5
Pasha, Emin, 81, 93
Pater, Walter, 155
Petronius, 183
philanthropy, 15, 87, 94, 102
photography, 17, 22, 104, 107, 119–21, 123, 127–28, 214 n. 18
place, 157, 159, 195 n. 5, 198 n. 21
Poe, Edgar Allan, 19, 29, 30, 199 n. 6
polygamy, 32–36, 93, 200 n. 13
Pondicherry, 62–65
Poradowska, Marguerite, 148
pornography, 151, 161–62
Pound, Ezra, 3, 25, 172, 173, 177, 182, 183, 192
Pratt, Mary Louise, 12, 107, 110
Punch, 46, 203 n. 41

Quinn, John, 172, 187

Raban, Jonathan, 1, 14
Reeder, David, 141
Reeves, William, 4
regeneration, 96–100
Reid, Mayne, 199 n. 7
restaurants, 23–24, 26, 139, 146, 151, 153–67
reverse colonization, 67
Richards, I. A., 174, 175
Richards, Thomas, 16, 63–64, 195 n. 7, 198 n. 27
Riis, Jacob, 22
romance, 3, 20, 28, 56, 193, 199 n. 3, 202 n. 33
Ross, Andrew, 218 n. 4
Rushdie, Salman, 6, 171, 194
Ruskin, John, 155, 205 n. 7

Said, Edward, 17, 102, 111, 195 nn. 5, 7
Saint-Simon, Henri, 98
Salvation Army, 79–103, 209 n. 6
Sandall, Robert, 81
sanitation, 9, 197 n. 15
Saunders, William, 198 n. 21
"saving illusion," 142, 145, 217 n. 45
Schoenberg, Arnold, 61
"scientific racism," 17, 74, 198 n. 25
Scott, Walter, 19, 47, 96, 97
Shakespeare, William, 184

Shaw, George Bernard, 93
Showalter, Elaine, 3, 199 n. 3
Simmel, Georg, 219–20 n. 21
Sims, George, 80, 135–36, 138, 139, 208 n. 1
Sinclair, Upton, 25, 171, 192
slumming, 147, 167
Smith, Frank, 210 n. 19
Smith, Grover, 178, 183
Smith, Joseph, 98
socialism, 87, 104, 105, 125, 126, 132
Soja, Edward, 202 n. 28
space, 152, 157, 159, 195 n. 5
Spencer, Herbert, 195 n. 4
spirituality, 88–89
Stanley, Henry, 21, 81–84, 87–92, 94, 96, 98, 102, 110, 111, 143, 160, 198 n. 28
Stead, W. T., 21, 93, 209 n. 6, 211 n. 37
Stein, Gertrude, 192
Stevenson, Robert Louis, 3, 13, 19, 28, 30, 42, 48, 195 n. 7, 200 n. 9
Stocking, George, 198 n. 25
Stoker, Bram, 13, 207 n. 17
Strand Magazine, 134–36
Strunsky, Anna, 119, 130
suburbs and suburbanization, 58, 72, 74, 205 n. 8
Summers, Judith, 137
Superman, 168
symbolic reproduction, 155–59

Tames, Richard, 146
tattooing, 10–14
Thackeray, William Makepeace, 46
Third World, 92
Thomas, Edward, 146
Thomson, James, 150
Tillet, Ben, 210 n. 19
Times (London), 95
Tolen, Rachel, 101, 211 n. 34, 212 n. 43
Tompkins, Jane, 200–201 n. 16
Torgovnick, Marianna, 112, 186
town planning, 211 n. 36
Tracy, Jack, 204–5 n. 3
Turner, Frederick Jackson, 33, 46
Tylor, Edward, 198 n. 25

urban clearance, 85, 210 n. 12
urban geography, 2, 121, 133, 145, 152, 178, 196 n. 10, 219 n. 5; "crisis in mapping," 139–42, 156

Virgil, 188

Wallace, Alfred, 181
Watts, Cedric, 145
Wayne, John, 44
Wells, H. G., 30, 124, 140, 207 n. 17
Western (genre), 19, 27, 31, 36, 39,
    200 n. 9
Wilde, Oscar, 3, 205 n. 7; *The Picture of
    Dorian Gray,* 3, 5, 13, 20, 26, 198 n. 27,
    205 n. 9
Williams, Raymond, 1, 171

Wilson, Edmund, 175
Wister, Owen, 200 n. 9
Woolf, Virginia, 86, 112–13, 152, 153, 154,
    165, 173, 174, 218–19 n. 6
Wordsworth, William, 9, 14–15
Wuthering Heights, 48

xenophobia, 8, 79

Young, Brigham, 32, 40, 98, 200 n. 13

Zangwill, Israel, 133